Sense8

Sense8
Transcending Television

Edited by
Deborah Shaw and Rob Stone

BLOOMSBURY ACADEMIC
NEW YORK • LONDON • OXFORD • NEW DELHI • SYDNEY

BLOOMSBURY ACADEMIC
Bloomsbury Publishing Inc
1385 Broadway, New York, NY 10018, USA
50 Bedford Square, London, WC1B 3DP, UK
29 Earlsfort Terrace, Dublin 2, Ireland

BLOOMSBURY, BLOOMSBURY ACADEMIC and the Diana logo are trademarks of
Bloomsbury Publishing Plc

First published in the United States of America 2021
This paperback edition published 2022

Volume Editor's Part of the Work © Deborah Shaw and Rob Stone, 2021

Each chapter © of Contributors

For legal purposes the Acknowledgments on p. viii constitute an extension
of this copyright page.

Cover design: Namkwan Cho
Cover image © Isadora Casavechia

All rights reserved. No part of this publication may be reproduced or transmitted
in any form or by any means, electronic or mechanical, including photocopying,
recording, or any information storage or retrieval system, without prior
permission in writing from the publishers.

Bloomsbury Publishing Inc does not have any control over, or responsibility for, any
third-party websites referred to or in this book. All internet addresses given in this
book were correct at the time of going to press. The author and publisher regret any
inconvenience caused if addresses have changed or sites have ceased to exist, but can
accept no responsibility for any such changes.

Library of Congress Cataloging-in-Publication Data
Names: Shaw, Deborah, editor. | Stone, Rob, 1965– editor.
Title: Sense8 : transcending television / edited by Deborah Shaw and Rob Stone.
Other titles: Sensate
Description: New York : Bloomsbury Academic, 2021. |
Includes bibliographical references and index.
Identifiers: LCCN 2021000981 (print) | LCCN 2021000982 (ebook) |
ISBN 9781501352935 (hardback) | ISBN 9781501352928 (ebook) |
ISBN 9781501352911 (pdf)
Subjects: LCSH: Sense8 (Television program)
Classification: LCC PN1992.77.S42977 S46 2021 (print) |
LCC PN1992.77.S42977 (ebook) | DDC 791.45/72–dc23
LC record available at https://lccn.loc.gov/2021000981
LC ebook record available at https://lccn.loc.gov/2021000982

ISBN: HB: 978-1-5013-5293-5
PB: 978-1-5013-7960-4
ePDF: 978-1-5013-5291-1
eBook: 978-1-5013-5292-8

Typeset by Newgen KnowledgeWorks Pvt. Ltd., Chennai, India

To find out more about our authors and books visit www.bloomsbury.com
and sign up for our newsletters.

CONTENTS

List of Illustrations vii
Acknowledgments viii

Introduction: A *Sense8* of Belonging 1
  Deborah Shaw and Rob Stone

1 What's Going On? Netflix and the Commissioning of *Sense8* 31
  Amanda D. Lotz

2 You Are No Longer Just You: Netflix, *Sense8*, and the Evolution of Television 41
  Zoë Shacklock

3 Skip Intro? *Sense8*'s Title Sequence 57
  James Walters

4 The *Sense8* Bible: The Creation of a New Creed for Our Times 71
  Deborah Shaw

5 What's Queer About a Cluster? *Sense8*'s Polycentric Imaginary 89
  Rosalind Galt

6 Between Necropower and Erotopolitics: Community and Clusterfuck as Alloerotic Distraction 105
  John Lessard

7 Sing a Song of *Sense8:* Musicality, Multiplicity, and Synchronicity 123
  Rob Stone

8 *Sense8* and the City: Frontier Cosmopolitanism 141
Luis Freijo

9 The Common Good: Birth, Death, and Self-Sacrifice in/of *Sense8* 159
Will McKeown

10 Dancing in the Streets: The Politics of *Sense8*'s Pleasure Activism 177
So Mayer

11 #WeAreTheGlobalCluster: Affectivity, Resistance, and *Sense8* Fandom 197
Rox Samer and Laura Horak

12 Revisiting the Cluster 219
Cáel M. Keegan

List of Contributors 227
Index 231

ILLUSTRATIONS

0.1 The sensate cluster 7
0.2 Will and Riley confront each other and their new selves in their mirrors 17
2.1 Lito and Nomi share a mediated form of copresence 50
2.2 Kala and Capheus's visit revolves around the television set 51
3.1 Fleeting bodies and faces offer glimpses of human life 63
3.2 A catch of breath before the episode "starts" 63
4.1 Angelica appears to Will after she has given birth to the cluster 74
4.2 Multiple images of Lito address the crowd at Pride in São Paulo 80
5.1 The cluster form enables poly attachments, as in the throuple that forms among Kala, Wolfgang, and Rajan 98
5.2 In *Sense8*'s orgies, the oval of the monogamous couple is replaced with spectacular and pretty shapes of multiple intimacy 100
6.1 Imaging ontological promiscuity and the coming community 108
7.1 Riley selects the music that will play in multiple, synchronous ways around the world 126
7.2 Riley cues, equalizes, beat-matches, and mixes her cluster 133
8.1 A split, even fragmented Sun as/and Seoul 146
8.2 Capheus's reaction constitutes a cosmopolitan expression of the moral worth of all human beings 155
9.1 Telepathic visitation as radical empathy 169
10.1 Nomi and Amanita in the still space of queer/ed femininity, remapping the world as San Francisco 182
11.1 "I am also a we" photo collage of *Sense8* tattoos 203
11.2 Map of sensies worldwide by an anonymous fan 205
12.1 Our shared moment in *Sense8*, occupied so fully together that we burst the present world's seams 225

ACKNOWLEDGMENTS

We would very much like to thank Katie Gallof and Erin Duffy at Bloomsbury for their support and guidance throughout the production of *Sense8: Transcending Television*. Thanks to them and our amazing cluster of contributors, this book also transcended the pandemic. We are especially grateful to Isadora Casavechia for her captivating cover image and to Esther Santamaría Iglesias for her superb work compiling the index.

Deborah would like to dedicate this book to her amazing academic friends and contributors to this collection who chose to merge their fandom for *Sense8* with their research. She would like to thank Rob Stone who made this a labor of love. She gives thanks to the Faculty of CCI at the University of Portsmouth for its support, and to her colleagues and students in the School of Film, Media and Communication. She would like to use this space to send her love to Lesley and Godfrey, Mitch, Theo, and the furry housemates.

Rob would like to thank Deborah for being the most brilliant and lovely clustermate throughout this venture, as well as our fellow sensates who contributed so enthusiastically to this project. He thanks Andy Henderson for his notes on world music and his colleagues in the Department of Film and Creative Writing at the University of Birmingham and the research students that make B-Film: The Birmingham Centre for Film Studies into such a wonderful cluster. He sends his love to the "woman in his head" Esther, as always.

We would like to thank the University of Illinois Press for permission to partially reprint (with significant edits and revisions) Cáel M. Keegan's "Epilogue–Event Horizon: *Sense8*" from *Lana and Lilly Wachowski: Sensing Transgender*. Copyright 2018 by the Board of Trustees of the University of Illinois. Used with permission of the University of Illinois Press.

Introduction: A *Sense8* of Belonging

Deborah Shaw and Rob Stone

Making sense of *Sense8* requires a certain sensibility. Dreamt up by Lana and Lilly Wachowski and J. Michael Straczynski for Netflix, *Sense8* dropped onto the global streaming platform on June 5, 2015, with the first episode S01:E01 "Limbic Resonance" introducing a multinational ensemble cast playing eight strangers from different parts of the world. And, as viewers discovered that these characters shared mental, physical, and emotional experiences that amounted to radical empathy, so they claimed to share them too, not only via their viewing of the series but also through an online fan base that would grow to determine the fate of the series. Ostensibly science fiction, relating how these eight sensates realize they are a separately evolved species that can communicate telepathically, body-swap in times of need, and transcend time and space to form a resistance group that fights for survival against a sinister organization called the Biological Preservation Organization (BPO), *Sense8* quickly transcended its synopsis.

Proud and loud, delirious with the possibilities of pushing aside television tropes, categories, and restrictions, *Sense8* was astonishingly queer and primed to party with big themes of religion, politics, identity, gender, and sexuality as well as to contend with addiction, corruption, racism, homophobia, transphobia, surveillance, and Big Pharma. Utopian in outlook though occurring in a recognizably dystopian world, *Sense8* used its science fiction premise to explore new forms of being and becoming that referred to and enacted social, philosophical, virtual, queer and trans potentialities. Netflix did not promote *Sense8* through traditional means but via algorithm-driven targeting to existing subscribers but, as there was little to compare it with, its science fiction label shortchanged some genre fans and its queer credentials deterred others. Nevertheless, *Sense8* garnered a devoted audience and praise for bending genre and gender, along with Emmy nominations for its music in 2016 and its cinematography in 2017, the 2016 Location Managers Guild International Award for outstanding achievement, and the 2016 GLAAD Media Award for Outstanding Drama Series in recognition of its representation of LGBTQ characters and themes.

Although never a mainstream hit that might have justified its production costs and ensured more than two awkwardly shaped seasons, *Sense8* was a wayward flagship for Netflix that still transcended television's categories of genres, regularized formats and character types, and united, inspired, and energized a global audience that discovered it had the power to similarly transcend the traditionally more passive and receptive nature of their spectatorship. Most remarkably, therefore, it is the commissioning, cult success, cancellation, and resurrection of the series that demand new frameworks for understanding the dynamics of streaming content as well as the fresh activism and resulting emancipation of an audience that is online, not just for viewing purposes but for interacting with its makers and other spectators via social media too. New viewing practices such as the single-sit series, the repetitive binge-watch, and simultaneous communal tweeting and watch parties have given rise to responsive audience-led forms of auteurism that incorporate the fan base, which duly develops its own agency to the point when it can successfully campaign for a continuation or new ending to a cherished series. Indeed, the online activity of *Sense8*'s global network of fans mirrors in a progressive and meaningful manner the interconnectivity of the series' protagonists.

As the chapters in this volume describe, explore, and analyze, *Sense8* represents and reveals numerous novel occurrences in global televisual culture in terms of its platform, content, form, and reception. Themes of queer potentiality, idealized futurity, and the transcending of national, genre, gender and sexual borders, as well as the overcoming of limiting, realist, border-obstacles to sharing, all point to a television series that transcends its own problems and limitations too.

Platform: What's Going On?

The global online distribution enabled by Netflix is an ideal fit for many of the series' themes of transnational connections, both tentative and invasive. As the eight sensates appear in each other's lives when called upon, regardless of their actual location, they also appear simultaneously on our screens. Thus, whether viewers are watching in any of the series' principal locations—Chicago, San Francisco, London, Reykjavik, Berlin,

Mumbai, Nairobi, Seoul, Mexico City, or Amsterdam—or in any other territories where the series is available, *Sense8* is its own locus for fans who subscribe not just to Netflix but to the series' inclusivity and passion as well. A single binge-friendly day or so after S02 of *Sense8* dropped onto Netflix on May 5, 2017, for example, eager fans were posting speculation about the cliffhanger ending of S02:E11 "You Want a War?" and asking when S03 would be ready for viewing. And when the news broke in June 2017 that Netflix had canceled the series on this cliffhanger ending, these same fans raged and grieved and mobilized online, creating a wave of million-signature petitions and imaginative campaigns directed at the CEO of Netflix that, in an unprecedented move, caused the network to rethink and commission a special feature-length concluding episode of the series, the aptly titled S02:E12 "Amor Vincit Omnia" (love conquers all), which dropped on June 8, 2018.

This resurrection of *Sense8* prompted show-runner Lana Wachowski to release a personal letter in which she celebrated the collaborative input of the fans, who she described as "unlike any I have ever encountered as an artist":

> By myself, there was nothing I could do. But just as the characters in our show discover that they are not alone, I too have learned that I am not just a me. I am also a we. ... In this world it is easy to believe that you cannot make a difference; that when a government or an institution or corporation makes a decision, there is something irrevocable about the decision; that love is always less important than the bottom line. But here is a gift from the fans of this show that I will carry forever in my heart: while it is often true those decisions are irreversible, it is not always true. Improbably, unforeseeably, your love has brought *Sense8* back to life. (I could kiss every single one of you!). (Miller 2017)

Fan campaigns and revivals are not unheard of in the streaming age. HBO revived *Deadwood* (2004–6) for a final, feature-length episode in 2019, *Chuck* (2007–12) squeezed three more seasons out of its fervent fan base following NBC cancelling it after two, and fans of *Veronica Mars* (2004–19), which was cancelled after its third season, raised $2 million in a day, enough to make a movie in 2014 and prompt an eight-episode S04 on Hulu in 2019. Dumps and pick-ups also happen, with *Brooklyn Nine-Nine* being cancelled by Fox (2013–18) and picked up twenty-four hours later by NBC (2019–present) after enough fans protested, while *Nashville* was scrapped by ABC (2012–16) and rescued by CMT (2016–18), and *Community* bounced from NBC (2009–14) to Yahoo (2015), prompting its star Joel McHale to say "thank you to the greatest f%$#ing fans in the history of the human race. It's the Internet. We can swear now" (Hibberd 2014). The variety of streaming platforms and pay-per-view opportunities made new territories and audiences available. Viewing practices were changing so fast that spotting opportunities became a test of reaction time. "We know we're an unlikely home, but five years ago people laughed at the idea of Netflix producing original series," wrote *Sense8* fan Alex Hawkins, CEO of Porn site xHamster, to the Wachowskis, when he offered to pick up *Sense8* after its cancellation (Brammer 2017). Netflix declined to comment or even suggest that pick-ups were possible for its original programming.

The fan-fueled revival of *Sense8* is foretold in its credit sequence, with its chaotic and kinetic catalogue of humanity. The sequence establishes a planetary context of thriving, creative, interacting humanity for the series and suggests that within this vast mass of people is found the global audience for Netflix and, more specifically, the fan base for *Sense8*. It therefore suggests how the series both challenges the limiting conventions of localized spectatorship—"I am also a we" is the repeated tagline in promotional features—and how the radical potential of global spectator-empathy might be fully realized by its rejection of conventional identificatory strategies. Most importantly, the power and beauty of *Sense8*'s concept and credit sequence lie in the fact that this utopian vision of what people can be is not reserved for its fictional characters alone. Encouraged by a visceral and intense empathetic televisual style that fosters these connections, *Sense8* frequently managed to make those watching report online to finding themselves identifying and empathizing with the characters and being entirely immersed. This was partly due to the addictive qualities of binge-watching, which pushes successive episodes to the screen and offers to erase both front and end credits, and partly because of the hypnotic rhythms occasioned by editing between eight characters and their stories that were emphasized by the insistent score and a sensitive, often bracing choice of songs on the soundtrack. But there was also a crucial role for interactive social media before, during, and after each episode, which heightened the experience of knowing oneself to be sharing the watching of *Sense8* with millions of other people worldwide.

The ability of *Sense8* to transcend television was a literal cause for celebration. Seen and thanked by the creator of the series they had rescued from cancellation, the fans rejoiced in their ability to transcend television norms by the same radical empathy and self-realization explored in the series itself. One of the foci of season two, for example, is the character Lito's coming out. Shunned by Mexico's domestic film industry, which is unable to accommodate a gay action hero, Lito is invited to be guest of honor at São Paulo's LGBT Pride event, where his heartfelt coming out speech—"I am a gay man. I am a GAY man. I AM A GAY MAN"—inspires extended scenes of revelry that invite participation irrespective of sexual and gender identities. The recording of Lito's speech goes viral and inspires millions, which helps him secure his next role playing a gay character in a prestigious project for a Hollywood director and thereby break into a film industry beyond Mexico. The message is clear: communities and, in particular, queer collective events such as Pride and progressive online groups can play their part in ending discriminatory practices, within and beyond the film and television industry. Joyful and cathartic, the scene also inspired the Wachowskis to engage with and commend the *Sense8* audience for their radical empathy and activism in self-realizing S02:E12 by diegetically including fan support for Lito in this final episode's storyline and extra-diegetically adding a closing dedication: "For Our Fans." In a case of life drawing from art, moreover, it is noteworthy that *Sense8*'s Jamie Clayton (one of the first trans actors to play a trans character) has secured a series of roles after playing Nomi. Indeed, Clayton has gained international recognition for her performances by the Human Rights campaign Time to THRIVE (Roberts 2020). She has appeared as the American president's sister-in-law in *Designated Survivor* (2016–19) and as a cis lesbian, Tess Van de Berg in the sequel to the Showtime cult series *The L Word* (2004–9) entitled *The L Word: Generation Q* (2019) (Henderson 2019).

Sense8 certainly contributed to Netflix's transcendence of television as its sixth original and, at the time, most daring series, signifying and even exemplifying the network's intended revolution of the medium. This is evident not only in the content of socially and sexually progressive shows, but also in Netflix's invitation to several well-known filmmakers to direct episodes of existing series and be show-runners of their own, creating a roster of talent that includes the Wachowskis, David Fincher (*House of Cards* (2013–18), *Mindhunter* (2017–19), Spike Lee (*She's Gotta Have It* (2017–19)), Ava DuVernay (*When They See Us* (2019)), Cary Fukunaga (*Maniac* (2018)) and Damien Chazelle (*The Eddy* (2020)) as well as, in the film section, Martin Scorsese (*The Irishman* (2019)), Alfonso Cuarón (*Roma* (2018)), Dee Rees (*Mudbound* (2017)), Haifaa al-Mansour (*Nappily Ever After* (2018)), and Noah Baumbach (*Marriage Story* (2019)). These series and films are watched on a variety of devices (smartphones, laptops, desktops, tablets) in addition to traditional television sets. Streaming platforms have also enabled many of the distinctions between television and film to be dissolved as long-form, episodic storytelling can include episodes that are the length of films. In the case of *Sense8*, for example, S02:E01 "Happy Fucking New Year" has a runtime of 124 minutes and was released five months before the further ten episodes of S02 dropped together on May 5, 2017, while S02:E12 runs 151 minutes and dropped more than a year after S02:E11. Incorporating long-form television, full-length films, stand-alone episodes, and spaced-apart seasons, *Sense8* was either a glorious love bombing or a targeted takedown of televisual norms. Or both. Either way, the fans continue to lament its absence.

Characters and Cast: Who Am I?

Lana and Lilly Wachowski cowrote S01 of *Sense8* with J. Michael Straczynski and codirected most of its episodes while Lana Wachowski took over the task for most of S02, cowriting with Straczynski and sharing out credit for directing episodes with frequent collaborators James McTeigue, Tom Tykwer, and Dan Glass. The novelists David Mitchell and Aleksandar Hemon, who enjoy cameo appearances in S02:E04 "Polyphony," joined the writing team for parts of S02 in a collaborative process overseen by principal writer Lana Wachowski (Hemon 2017). The science fiction conceit allowed for a great deal of playful, psycho-sexual drama (at least until the plot machinations of S02:E06 "Isolated Above, Connected Below" overwhelmed the delicately calibrated interrelationships), but what mattered most was that the series' makers were enjoying evident freedom to explore the fantastical ruse of eight distant strangers sharing their minds, bodies, feelings, skills, and locations. That people who have never met and who live very distinct lives in different parts of the world should discover themselves via empathy to be members of an exclusive cluster was also a perfect concept for the Netflix audience to recognize as their bonding experience of viewing *Sense8*. The underlying premise and the cause of much of the audience's devotion was the Wachowskis' recognition that in our divisive, corrupt, diseased, and burning world, a science fiction premise was necessary to recognize that empathy was a rare quality, equivalent to super strength or mind-reading, perhaps, and therefore a quality found only in superheroes, which meant that each viewer could become a superhero by simply expressing empathy.

The onscreen cluster of eight sensates shares a birth date of August 8 (the eighth month) and radical empathy is what sets them apart from stalled human evolution (8 also being the symbol of infinity). This means that they share a psychic, empathetic connection, can hear and converse with each other, and can appear in each other's lives when the occasion demands, such as when supporting Sun in her moment of grief as shown in Figure 0.1. Finding they can "visit" fellow members of their cluster, they progress to "sharing" to become an eight-strong "being." Jonas explains to Will that sharing can only occur with his "seven other selves" within the cluster; this allows them all to (in Jonas's words) access "each other's knowledge, language, skills" (S01:E04). Within the cluster each of them has equal value and all their differences are conjoined. At times of greatest emotional and physical intensity, all the sensates appear together, which turns sex into an orgy, for example, and a fight into a full-on brawl, Lito's coming out speech at São Paulo's Pride into a collective celebration of self-affirmation, a classical music concert in Iceland in S01:E10 "What Is Human?" into the occasion of group therapy, with each sensate reliving memories of his/her/their birth, and Sun's personal grief into a surge of sorrow, sympathy, and radical empathy.

FIGURE 0.1 *The sensate cluster. Standing L–R: Wolfgang (Max Riemelt) and Will (Brian J. Smith); Sitting L–R: Capheus (Toby Onwumere), Nomi (Jamie Clayton), Sun (Bae Doona), Riley (Tuppence Middleton), Lito (Miguel Ángel Silvestre); front: Kala (Tina Desai).*

One of the sensates is Bak Sun (Bae Doona), a businesswoman from Seoul with extraordinary fighting skills, who finds herself embroiled in her family's corruption and takes the fall, is incarcerated and forced to break out in search of revenge. Sun has been neglected and overlooked by her father after the early death of her mother. Since burdened with looking out for her selfish brother following her mother's dying wish, Sun expresses her frustrations via martial arts and becomes a star of underground kickboxing, a male-dominated milieu, as indicated by the title of S01:E03, "Smart Money's on the Skinny Bitch." Another is Wolfgang Bogdanow (Max Riemelt), a streetwise Berliner, expert fighter, and safe cracker, born into a gangster dynasty and pushed into a gangland culture that he rejects as much as he is able. The progeny of his abusive father's rape of his sister, Wolfgang kills his father when just a boy and still resents his cousin and kingpin uncle, who did nothing to protect him or his sister/mother from his father. Wolfgang enjoys a reciprocated passion for his Mumbai-based cluster-mate Kala Dandekar (Tina Desai). Kala is a highly competent chemist who struggles to reconcile her faith with science, her professional duties with her moral imperatives, and her chaste affection for her husband with her undeniable passion for Wolfgang, yet she has no compunction about killing people in the action scenes. Kala provides the cluster with chemical blockers to shut out their mortal enemy Whispers (Terrence Mann), a sensate working for BPO, who is committed to their destruction.

The cluster is also joined by Will Gorski (Brian J. Smith), a Chicago cop with fighting prowess and heightened detective skills, as well as a strict moral code. Although on the face of it a privileged and authoritarian white male cop, Will has been stigmatized by his psychic gifts since he was a child, when he was first "visited" by Sara Patrell, a young girl murdered by Whispers. This experience also damaged Will's relationship with his father, an alcoholic ex-cop (Joe Pantoliano), whose belief in his son's psychic gifts was ridiculed by his colleagues. Will is in love with fellow sensate Riley Gunnarsdóttir (Tuppence Middleton), an internationally renowned DJ from Reykjavik with a tragic past. Riley has experienced the death of her husband and newborn baby in a car crash and, grief-ridden, has left Iceland for London and the solace of its drug-ridden rave scene. Her increasingly maternal role and musical talents bind the cluster, attract other sensates and, to an extent, maintain their well-being throughout adventures. Then there is Capheus Onyango (Aml Ameen in S01 and Toby Onwumere in S02), a Nairobi *matatu* (pimped-up bus) driver turned political activist, known affectionately to locals as Van Damme for his love of the Belgian action star; his gifts are courage, driving skills, and honesty in the face of criminality and violence, which sees him stand as an anti-corruption political candidate in S02. Capheus is struggling to raise money to pay for his mother's AIDS medication in an honest manner, but his inter-tribal heritage renders him an outsider and his moral integrity brings conflict with local small-time and big-shot gangsters. Making up the cluster is San Francisco-based Nomi Marks (Jamie Clayton), a transgender woman and computer hacktivist, a dispenser of wry wisdom, who is on the FBI's most wanted list until she commits e-death and erases her life completely from all existing data. Nomi's mother sanctions BPO's attempts to lobotomize her in a perverse attempt to reverse Nomi's previous gender reassignment surgery. And finally, there is Lito Rodríguez (Miguel Ángel Silvestre), an initially closeted gay B-movie actor from Mexico City, who frequently shares his acting skills with his cluster members to get them out of danger. Lito keeps his true self secret from his loving mother and his fans and is ostracized when a vengeful attempt at blackmail results in his exposure and enforced coming out. But, thanks to the cathartic speech at São Paulo Pride, he becomes an internationally famous gay icon and parlays this into a breakthrough Hollywood role.

Secondary human characters inhabit a kind of hierarchy topped by those who are gradually let in on the secrets of the cluster, which includes Nomi's partner Amanita Caplan (Freema Agyeman), hacktivist buddy Bug (Michael X Sommers), Will's cop partner Diego Morales (Ness Bautista), Wolfgang's best friend Felix (Max Mauff) and, in the final episode; Sun's pursuer in romantic and law enforcement terms, Detective Mun (Sukku Son), Kala's husband Rajan (Purab Kohli), Lito's partner Hernando (Alfonso Herrera) and their companion Daniela (Eréndira Ibarra). Other close humans include Capheus's pansexual journalist girlfriend Zakia (Mumbi Maina) and his friend and business partner Jela (Paul Ogola). The plot also features other sensates in flashbacks that feature the birth of the cluster by Angelica Turing (Daryl Hannah), whose name suggests a homage to Alan Turing's advances in computing and connects the sensates with his queer history of persecution, while also suggesting a correlation between sensate powers and the connectivity of computers and cyberspace. The potential but fractious future for Homo sensorium is also considered by Jonas Maliki (Naveen Andrews), an unreliable, mystic guide for the sensates, and is projected in undeveloped storylines involving Lila Facchini (Valeria Bello), a femme fatale, and crude, predatory Puck (Christopher Gurry), whose purpose, proximity to plot-holes and peculiar pop-up in Seoul in S02:E11 "You Want a War?" are some of the least satisfactory elements of S02. Another undeveloped character is the Old Man of Hoy (Sylvester McCoy), who speaks for the Archipelago, a network of sixteen clusters, and promises a much greater context for future series of *Sense8* that due to the cancellation never transpires.

Acting styles, cultural baggage, and linguistic choices are to some extent chaotic. As several contributors to this volume point out, the common language of the sensates is English and even when characters are in their home countries or among others of their nationality this Anglocentrism is mostly maintained. Exceptions are rare but more notable toward the end of S02, which suggests the responsiveness of the series creators to criticism. Anglocentrism is disrupted to a degree in the casting. Bae Doona, who plays Sun, is Seoul-born and a Wachowski regular, having appeared in their *Cloud Atlas* (2012) and *Jupiter Ascending* (2015), and has national and international standing across mainstream and art-house cinema. She has featured in such world-renowned South Korean films as *Flandersui gae* (2000, Barking Dogs Never Bite) and *Gwoemul* (2006, The Host) for Bong Joon-Ho (director of *Gisaengchung* (2019, Parasite)), and *Boksuneun naui geot* (2002, Sympathy for Mr. Vengeance) for Chan-Wook Park, as well as in *Kûki ningyô* (2009, Air Doll) for the Japanese auteur Hirokazu Kore-eda. As the only Asian in the main cast, moreover, she does most of the heavy lifting in terms of representing the global make-up of the cluster, the ethno-cultural concept of a complex Asian protagonist to Western audiences in general, and a modern South Korean woman to East Asia more specifically. Indeed, if Sun (and so Bae Doona) could be said to represent the 1.7 billion in East Asia (followed by Kala standing for 1.3 billion from India, Capheus denoting 1.2 billion from Africa and Lito (played by a Spain actor) bridging Spanish and Latin America to represent 650 million), the disproportionate casting of Euro-American white actors renders any global analogy or correspondence incoherent. Indeed, when the cluster is completed (by Wolfgang as Central and Eastern Europe (*c.*360 million), Riley as Northern and Western Europe (*c.*300 million) and, finally, Nomi in San Francisco and Will in Chicago sharing representation of just 328 million inhabitants of the United States or 164 million each for the western-southern and eastern-northern states, respectively), the imbalance correlates more closely with Netflix markets than global population distribution. That is to say, the casting of Bae Doona partly corresponds and contributes to the aggressive expansion of Netflix in South Korea, where subscriptions in 2019 grew "from less than a million to 2.4 million. With 200,000 to 300,000 subscribers signing up every quarter [and] Netflix projected to reach nearly 4 million subscribers [in 2020] and eventually become the largest streaming platform in South Korea" (Stangarone 2019).

Sense8 is convolutedly layered in terms of cast and characters with race and gender interwoven to create myriad nexus allowing for mind-reading, body-swapping, and city-hopping. The prefix "trans" characterizes many of these interactions, and the series can be productively read through the concepts "transnational," "transgender," and "transcendence" as the cast cross the borders of space, bodies, and time. That said, the casting of the cluster can also seem conventional with mainstream standards of physical beauty certainly a common factor. Like Bae Doona, who spends much of S02 in her underwear with no clear plot rationale for this, Tina Desai used modeling as a way into acting, and was represented by Elite Model India Management prior to being cast in *The Best Exotic Marigold Hotel* (2011). Her role as Kala in *Sense8* references the performative motifs and gestures of Bollywood that are made explicit in the pastiche of her wedding but also upheld by her being the only member of the main cast never to appear nude, nudity being injurious to the erotic allure of mainstream actors of Indian cinema. Equal beauty is evident in Miguel Ángel Silvestre, who turned victory in the 2002 Mister Castelló pageant into a career as a popular Spanish television actor with both comic and dramatic range in hit series such as *Sin tetas no hay paraíso* (There's No Paradise without Tits, 2008–9) and *Velvet* (2013–16). Popular in the Spanish *prensa de corazón* (gossip mags) too for his relationships with his glamorous costars (Amaia Salamanca, María Valverde, Berta Vázquez, Blanca Suárez), Silvestre embraced the series-long arc of Lito's coming out in *Sense8* with enthusiasm and sensitivity. It is noteworthy that in the sexually fluid diegetic universe of *Sense8*, actors are not cast according to their off-camera assumed sexualities, as seen also with characters played by Freema Agyeman and Jamie Clayton.

Flipping the dynamic of Silvestre/Lito is Smith, who plays the heterosexual Will and came out publicly as gay in 2019 in an interview that warranted the cover of the December issue of *Attitude*:

> I heard all the names: pussy, faggot. I could never be who I was. ... A lot of my work is about that. The things that move me as an actor are those echoes that come up. I remember being so relaxed [filming *Sense8*]. I thought, "Finally, I can just be myself, I don't have to put on any airs for any of these people." *(Attitude* 2019)

Any tensions that might arise in the interactions between males with various sexual orientations are dissolved by the overriding fluidity of sexuality in *Sense8*, as demonstrated in one blissfully tender comedic moment shared by Lito and Will when they finally (and first) meet in S01:E12 "I Can't Leave Her" after their previous psychic coupling in S01:E06 "Demons":

WILL: "Do I know you?"
LITO: "We had sex."
WILL: (aghast) "That was ..."
LITO: "Very special."

Flourishes of nudity are frequent in *Sense8* but the only male actor in the ensemble to appear full frontal is East Berlin-born Max Riemelt, whose chemistry with Desai operates amid a similar mirroring of the male and female gaze. The shot-reverse shot is deployed when the naked Wolfgang visits the never-nude Kala during her lustless wedding to Rajan, when Wolfgang emerges, unaroused and unashamed, from the pool of a Berlin spa and finds himself naked in the midst of the Mumbai ceremony. Kala faints but the joke is flipped because in this instant Wolfgang's penis actually signifies a lack; that is, a lack of desire in Kala's relationship with Rajan, which is rapidly approaching its conclusive betrothal, prompting Kala to faint as a subconscious ruse that cancels the rest of the wedding. It is only later that the signification of Wolfgang's penis switches from a lack to a surplus, when Kala visits her favorite deity, the elephant god Ganesha, and explains her understanding of Wolfgang's appearance as Ganesha's divine message: "You sent me a man with a large ... trunk. With a *very* large trunk." The flip insists on the enduringly unsettling power of the female gaze and sets Kala on track for an erotic rite of passage from prudish virgin bride to Rajan through initiating passionate adultery with Wolfgang (*she* visits *him*), to inciting a climactic threesome with Rajan and Wolfgang, a resolution that fits perfectly within *Sense8*'s melodramatic sexually fluid universe.

At a time of increasing censure for the impersonation of race, sexuality, and disability by actors that do not themselves possess the relevant traits, it is perhaps the fluidity of the characters that has kept the series popular and relatively immune from such censure. That is to say, because it is the nature of each of the eight main sensates to absorb and act as conduit for all of the group's latent and manifest traits, abilities, and desires, the suggestion that each member of the cast should be fixed in their composition of nationality, sexuality, and language is arguably anathema to the ethos of the series. In effect, the actors and their characters, both separately and together, constitute an affectionate pastiche that goes beyond Fredric Jameson's ideas of modern pastiche as "a neutral practice of such mimicry, without any of parody's ulterior motives, amputated of the satiric impulse, devoid of laughter" (Jameson 1991: 17). Instead, the pastiche of race, sexuality, gender, nationality, language, abilities, beliefs, and skills that is rendered in the cast and the cluster it portrays resembles what Jameson defines as postmodern pastiche, that is "a field of stylistic and discursive heterogeneity without a norm [that amounts to] the cannibalization of all the styles of the past, the play of random stylistic allusion, and in general what Henri Lefebvre has called the increasing primacy of the 'neo'" (Jameson 1991: 17–18). As befits a new species of sensates, this pastiche loses its connections to history and looks forward to postmodernity, referencing the past only through styles that reference nostalgia as they attest to the waning of fixity, appearing only as simulacra such as Kala's Bollywood wedding, the rather camp machismo of Lito's action hero persona and the general abandonment of limits on gender and sexuality by participants in the series' orgies.

While *Sense8* embraces and embodies pastiche, it rarely resorts to parody. It makes clear, for example, that the problem with having a gay Mexican action film star is not the sexuality of the actor but the rigid bias of the film producers and sections of the audience as well as the journalists that whip up the mob whose homophobic graffiti ruins Lito's latest premiere. Crucially, however, the historicized "modern" audience that is second-guessed by Lito's agents, who react to his coming out by only offering him roles as gay sidekicks and villains doomed to die, is replaced by the forward-looking "postmodern" one in the San Francisco theater where Nomi, Amanita, and Bug enjoy one of his action classics in S02:E05 "Fear Never Fixed Anything." If anything, the devotion of this second audience becomes even more respectful because, understanding the basics of acting, its members appreciate both the performativity in Lito's heteronormative love scenes and the newly subversive reading of them that allows it to relish a gay action film star and read this through the film's protagonist, whose gun-kissing, flamboyant costumes and diva-like dominion over scenes of melodramatic excess only make his stardom more delightful.

Any dissonance between cast and character in *Sense8* is absorbed into the world of the series and its ethos, rather than distracting from it, thereby responding to the big question asked by the series—"Who am I?"—with the explanation that "I am also a we." Actors cast as much for the chemistry of the cluster as the character of their individual roles are charged with representation through performance, which Lito often demonstrates is the primary actor's skill and is by far the lesser of three evils, the others being impersonation and appropriation. Thus, although Tuppence Middleton is most associated with British period dramas such as the series *Dickensian* (2015–16) and the films *The Imitation Game* (2014) and *Downton Abbey* (2019), her English persona topped off with a credible Icelandic accent has not generated controversy in relation to her casting as Riley. Similarly, casting an English actor of Jamaican and Vincentian descent (Aml Ameen) as a Kenyan (Capheus) did not cause dissent; it was only when Ameen left the series at the end of S01 due to rumors of "creative differences" (Cotter

2019) and was replaced by Nigerian-born and Texas-raised Shakespearian actor Toby Onwumere in S02 that the fan base bristled, sharing allegations of Ameen's transphobia that Jamie Clayton authoritatively denounced as "an Internet rumor" (Clayton 2016). "Black" thus resembles a broad category of casting that elided the specifics of American, Caribbean, Kenyan, Nigerian, and British differences in the actors, albeit without censure.

In relation to gender, meanwhile, it was perhaps the performance and persona of Jamie Clayton as Nomi that most compensated for any potential criticism of the casting. After establishing herself in the New York milieu of fashion and make-up, the Californian Clayton used her health insurance gained from employment to seek out doctors with experience of gender correction and saved money and took hormones for five years before undergoing surgical transformation in 2003. She became cohost of the makeover reality show *TRANSform Me* on New York's cable channel Vh1 and was invited to play the recurring role of a trans woman character in S03 of *Hung* (2011). The higher profile led to numerous interviews and articles that probed her sexual history and identity; but even when her own comments in such articles are prefaced by salacious descriptions and smirks, Clayton retains an elegant, deflective responsiveness:

> I asked her if she was gay in high school. "I guess," she said. "I was gay by default. I was always just so feminine. I don't think anyone who ever met me would describe me as a man." (Morgan 2008)

The authenticity of Clayton transferred directly to that of Nomi, a transgender character created by transgender filmmakers and played by a transgender actress; but most importantly *Sense8* begins several years after Nomi has "transitioned" and finds her in the most romantic and stable, sexually fulfilling, mutually supportive and "out" of all relationships in the series. Unlike transgender Laverne Cox as transgender Sophia in *Orange Is the New Black* (2013–19), where the character's transition is a source of conflict and presages tragedy as well as fulfilment, Nomi's transition is not part of the story and no tragic ending comes close to threatening a series that ends with her spectacularly romantic wedding to Amanita in the Eiffel Tower amid a reunion of characters joined in joyful celebration of their love against a backdrop of fireworks. Even so, another slippage between cast and character that is absorbed into the cluster and gets hardly any mention in comparison with Clayton being transgender is that the actor's own declarations make clear that her sexual orientation differs from that of her character (Morgan 2008). Like Smith and Silvestre then, Clayton contributes to how *Sense8* mostly manages to move beyond any such limits of correlation between the cast, between the characters, and between the cast and characters, defying categorization. The exemplary overlap of Clayton and Nomi and that of Lito and Silvestre (which is underlined by Lito and

Nomi often visiting each other in times of need, Lito becoming inadvertently aroused in Mexico City due to Nomi having sex in San Francisco in S01:E01, their heart to heart in the Diego Rivera museum in Mexico City in S01:E09, and their igniting the orgy of S01:E06 by having same-sex sex with Amanita and Hernando, respectively) is all part of the postmodernism of its pastiche that the cast of *Sense8* artfully, playfully, and personally expose.

Themes and Techniques: You Are No Longer Just You

Beyond the machinations of the plot, what enables the empathetic connections between the principal cluster of sensates is their status as outsiders, their concomitant struggles in life, and the sensual, sexual, and emotional catharsis experienced by each of them when they find themselves part of a cluster. The vindication of equality, diversity, and interconnectedness that *Sense8* thereby promoted came out of its science fiction ruse but was quickly identified as a sensibility by which seemingly disparate characters could transcend their national and social identities and come together to form a new family that was primarily defined by its openness to queer and trans possibilities. The media of their realization were not just the fantastical telepathy and body-swapping, but an exploration of radical empathy, boosted initially by them hearing the same songs simultaneously and later by sharing in telepathic orgies. Full of utopian resolutions shot through with interpretative understandings of, first, the concept, theory, and practice of trans, and second, ideas of being and becoming that are interrogated via queer subjectivity, *Sense8* was partly received as an inspirational prologue to what its fans might go on to realize in life. Thus, when its glimpses of utopian fulfilment were snatched away by the series' cancellation, it resulted in an impassioned fan response.

In an era of visible and encroaching climate change, dysfunctional political systems that can be gamed by the highest and slyest bidders, citizen surveillance on an unprecedented and unregulated scale, and dramatically widening inequalities, *Sense8* suggested an improvement on current humanity, a better version of "us" that is a people prepared to rethink individualism, self-interest, and narrow tribalism. The eight sensates care deeply about each other with a radical empathy born of the fact that they can literally inhabit their co-sensates' spaces, walk in each other's shoes, and even become each other when the need arises. Concepts of the self and the other thereby dissolve as the boundaries between them disappear, which is an experience mirrored by immersive viewing practices. A holistic, religious aspect is even suggested by *Sense8* that is not without its own rituals of self-sacrifice and resurrection. Most innovatively, *Sense8* is shot through with interpretative understandings of, first, the concept, theory and practice of trans, and second, ideas of being and becoming that are interrogated via queer subjectivity. A commitment to testing the potential of radical empathy in relation to both trans and queer imaginaries operates under *Sense8*'s guise of science fiction but is much more about the real world of its audience.

As for corresponding innovations in the form of *Sense8*, analysis of the editing reveals as many sleights of hand as it does sequences of extravagant display. The various montage sequences that inform and are informed by the collage of music and songs deploy juxtapositions, dissolves and different film speeds in order to create a sense of reverie in which the sensates lose themselves in dance, memories, and passion. Respectively, contributors to this volume consider the construction of such bravura sequences as the birthday celebrations in S02:E01 "Happy Fucking New Year," the birth montage of S01:E10 "What Is Human?," and the orgies of S01:E06 "Demons," S02:E01 "Happy Fucking New Year," and S02:E12 "Amor Vincit Omnia." But attention is also due the editing techniques by which the sensates visit each other, body-swap, and psychically converge as a physical cluster. Footage of the filming contained in the Netflix behind-the-scenes promotional film *Sense8: Creating the World* (2015) reveals that many of the sensates' "visits" were choreographed to be achieved while cameras were running. At times the tricks are rudimentary: a sensate ducks and swerves when out of frame as their "visitor" pivots into shot, resulting in a spiral of actors around the camera. At other times, an actor tenses and is lifted out of the scene in a mannequin-like pose as the camera pans or zooms away, allowing another actor to be inserted before the camera pans or zooms back. Such low-tech ingenuity in no way detracts from the craftsmanship, however, with the lack of special effects and computer-generated imagery both evocative of and crucial to the human connections in which the series trades. Thus, the in-camera effects of *Sense8* bear conceptual weight while the editing explores patterns and motifs that play with ideas of characters becoming each other, both suddenly in match cuts and intensified continuity, and gradually in dissolves, L cuts (in which the audio from the preceding shot continues into the next), and transitions achieved by fades and sound bridges. To the extent that the makers of *Sense8* sought to communicate fluidity, connectedness, interaction, and simultaneous continuity in constructing scenes that might, for instance, start with footage filmed in Mumbai or Seoul and conclude with footage filmed several months earlier or later in Berlin or Nairobi, there is a challenge to continuity and its resolution as well as the construction of a world defined by transcendence and a conflation of time dedicated to immediacy. It all adds up to an accumulative sense of the cluster's becoming and coming together in the editing, which therefore suggests experimentation in a trans grammar of filmmaking.

One example of this is the way that characters are engaged, albeit unwittingly, in a process of becoming each other that resembles the comic mirror routine used by Groucho Marx in *Duck Soup* (1933). Yet, rather than entertain the audience with the differences between seemingly identical characters' reflections, the routine is played out in *Sense8* as a space for noting connections that dissolve individuality and create the conditions for the merging of identities between physically disparate sensates such as Will and Riley, who see each other in their bathroom mirrors in S01:E02 "I Am Also a We," as illustrated in Figure 0.2, and Lito and Sun, who touch fingers through the (inexistent) mirror in S01:E05 "Art Is Like Religion." The comic gag turns serious as the visual illusion becomes real and bears conceptual weight too because it shows the sensates recognizing themselves in each other as a prelude to visiting and sharing, while also suggesting how people can transcend their physicality by imitating or modelling an idea of themselves on the examples of others. Lacan's mirror stage ([1949] 2006), in which an external image of the body reflected in a mirror produces a psychic response that gives rise to the mental representation of an "I" (which *Sense8* insists is also a "We") is confronted by Judith Butler's concept of performativity in relation to gender construction, which includes imitation of others in the construction of a self (1990). Moreover, these sequences deconstruct Lacan's mirror stage because the sensates now negotiate and accept an initially unrecognized new self that paves the way for a freshly imagined collective identity. The routine is no longer about imitation of what already exists, therefore, but about being confronted with an unexpected other that can be incorporated into a new multiple self. And thus, Butler's concept of the learned performance of identity is also interrupted, deconstructed even, by the encounter with an "other" unrecognized self. Indeed, these early sensate visits speak to those who might come to recognize themselves in others that do not correspond to their cis- and/or heteronormative identities, thereby illustrating and even inspiring a transgender potential.

Building upon this new trans grammar of filmmaking, moreover, is the novel use of the conventional cut-reverse cut of characters conversing. Most often in *Sense8*, this basic, conventional grammar is redundant as the makers prefer to frame both speakers in a mid-shot or deploy a mobile camera to circle those speaking with additional tweaks of focus to emphasize listening too. But when the cut-reverse shot is used, it is not only a shortcut to constructing a conversation out of two characters in different parts of the world, but an extension of the mirror routine in which characters not only see themselves in each other but also the camera as audience surrogate allows spectators to play the game of becoming others too in a spatial continuum that enhances the sense of world-building. When such sequences are caught up in what David Bordwell termed "intensified continuity" (Bordwell 2007), which is used extensively in *Sense8* at times of sex and violence but also in essaying the group dynamics of the cluster, rapid editing creates a chain reaction of momentum and fragmentation that also necessarily posits glimpses of narrative resolution. Intensified continuity rejects stability and

FIGURE 0.2 *Will and Riley confront each other and their new selves in their mirrors.*

safety and suggests speeding psyches and reactive physicality. It resembles fragmentation but ultimately reveals its purpose as survival in scenes that have the cluster fighting, fleeing and body-swapping, as they do in Nomi's escape through the streets of San Francisco, for example, in S01:E07 "WWN Double D?," when she "becomes" Sun, Will, and Capheus. Thus, whereas Bordwell's focus is on "the loss of orientation" (Bordwell 2007) in the Bourne films, intensified continuity in *Sense8* expresses a maelstrom of possibilities that can be traversed by a strategy of body-swapping that transcends the self, which leads not only to survival but also to a greater sense of the self and the other that is grounded in the evidence of togetherness. While swift cuts on unstable movement sustain the condition of Jason Bourne (Matt Damon) as fragile and threatened (Stone 2021), here the technique is a strategy that evokes and enables a truly trans mode of each sensate's individual and collective becoming.

Trans: Just Turn the Wheel and the Future Changes

Recent trans theory has built on José Esteban Muñoz's concept of a queer utopia, which he develops in *Cruising Utopia: The Then and There of Queer Futurity* (2009). Muñoz's potential queer utopianism provided Lilly Wachowski with optimism during her process of coming out as transgender in order to preempt an imminent, typically antagonistic exposé by the UK's

Daily Mail. Rising far above that tabloid's intrusive hostility, she commented on what queer potentiality means for her on a very personal level:

> Gender theory and queer theory hurt my tiny brain. The combinations of words, like freeform jazz, clang disjointed and discordant in my ears. I long for understanding of queer and gender theory but it's a struggle as is the struggle for understanding of my own identity. I have a quote in my office though by José Muñoz given to me by a good friend. I stare at it in contemplation sometimes trying to decipher its meaning but the last sentence resonates: "Queerness is essentially about the rejection of a here and now and an insistence on potentiality for another world." So I will continue to be an optimist adding my shoulder to the Sisyphean struggle of progress and in my very being, be an example of the potentiality of another world. (Baim 2016)

Muñoz's ideas of queer utopia posit complex notions of inclusive potentiality and strategic modes of becoming that duly resonate throughout *Sense8*.

Following Muñoz, Jack Halberstam and Cáel M. Keegan have argued that their use of an asterisk to speak of trans* as a theoretical mode is a way into conceptualizing trans identities as an open non-category that points toward forms of becoming in opposition to fixed and enclosed minds and bodies. Halberstam writes that "the asterisk modifies the meaning of transitivity by refusing to situate transition in relation to a destination, a final form, a specific shape, or an established configuration of desire and identity" (2018: 4). The potentiality of trans* philosophy thus lies in its disruption of any clear-cut male/female binary: "We could say the term 'trans*' marks a politics based on a general instability of identity and oriented toward social transformation, not political accommodation" (Halberstam 2018: 50). This rejection of the binary was shared by Lana Wachowski in her coming out speech, given while accepting the Human Rights Campaign's Visibility Award, in which she questions the understanding of transition as a form of arrival in any fixed place and criticizes the talk show format that fulfills "the cathartic arc of rejection to acceptance without ever interrogating the pathology of a society that refuses to acknowledge the spectrum of gender in the exact same blind way they have refused to see a spectrum of race or sexuality" (THR Staff 2012). This does not mean that the Wachowskis question the validity of their identity or their transitions; rather, like trans-identified Halberstam and Keegan, they use their lived experiences and their creativity to call into question all traditional gender regimes.

Correlatively, in *Lilly and Lana Wachowski: Sensing Transgender* (2018), Keegan argues for reading the Wachowskis' entire corpus through a trans* lens and contends that their public coming out requires new critical readings of their films (2018: 5). This doubtlessly includes *Sense8* and the third sequel to *The Matrix* (due 2021), which boasts a reunion of sorts for fans of *Sense8* with its cast including Max Riemelt, Toby Onwumere, Brian J. Smith, and Eréndira Ibarra. Keegan cites Lilly Wachowski in this regard as recognizing "there's a critical eye being cast back on Lana's and my work through the lens of our transness, and this is a cool thing, because it's an excellent reminder that art is never static" (Keegan 2018: 5). Thanks in no small part to the Wachowskis, recent trans* advances in film and television have been without precedent (Halberstam 2018; Henry 2019; Steinbock 2019) as has been illustrated by the Netflix documentary *Disclosure* (Feder 2020) that features interviews with Jamie Clayton and Lilly Wachowski among many other prominent trans actors, directors, and producers. Muñoz, meanwhile, has argued that artistic practice offers these spaces to create the forms of utopian queer that he advances in his writing, holding that "often we can glimpse the worlds proposed and promised by queerness in the realm of the aesthetic. The aesthetic, especially the queer aesthetic, frequently contains blueprints and schemata of a forward-dawning futurity" (Muñoz 2009: 1). Informing *Sense8* is Muñoz's visions of a utopian artistic queer potentiality and Halberstam's understanding of trans* as a reaching beyond societal frameworks toward new ways of being. Enter Homo sensorium, *Sense8*'s separate species of human, which justifies science fiction as an artistic medium in which theoretical utopian potentialities can be realized.

Keegan finds "faith in the subjunctive quality of art to lead us elsewhere" (2018: 2) in the work of the Wachowskis, and this idea, along with much of the philosophy of *Sense8*, is echoed by Siri Hustvedt (2017) in *A Woman Looking at Men Looking at Women: Essays on Art, Sex, and the Mind*. Hustvedt has mirror-touch synesthesia, which resembles the condition and powers of a sensate because "research has shown that mirror touch synesthetes are more vulnerable to blurred self-other boundaries, identity shifts and feel more empathy for other people" (Hustvedt 2017: 378). In a chapter entitled "Becoming Others" (367–81) Hustvedt discusses the ways that authors and readers cross borders through writing and reading, entering into a "transitional space" and inhabiting other selves (376). This transitional space defines that of creatives who seek a union with their audiences/readers; in Hustvedt's words, "the making of art takes place in a borderland between self and other" (374), and it is in this context that trans* can be seen as the journey to inhabit other selves. This describes the cluster in *Sense8*, but it is also the space around *Sense8*, where audiences enter into a relationship with art, with trans* describing this journey to other realities via empathy. Approaching *Sense8* in relation to transgender phenomenology therefore requires what Keegan describes as "a ceaseless navigation between the tangible and intangible, perception and sense, the real and the imaginary" (Keegan 2018: 3).

But *Sense8* is not an exclusively queer or trans series. Its manifesto is trans, and its practice is queer, but its outcome is polyamorous. S01:E01 sets up Nomi in a romantic and fulfilling lesbian relation with Amanita, and Lito in a similarly successful gay relationship with Hernando, yet prior to their birth as a cluster the other characters are not ostensibly queer and are shown to be heteronormative in behavior. Comparatively, at the start of S01, the heteronormative sensates are all stalled or inhibited: Kala is a virgin bride, Capheus appears to be non-sexual, Riley is traumatized by the death of her child and inhabits an uncaring, self-serving group made of small-time criminals, Will is single and so stigmatized by the harm his psychic gifts have caused his father, an ex-cop, that he treats any potential moral indiscretion as a Freudian abhorrence. And Sun, it is suggested, has only ever had sex once, with a combat rival who would grow up to be the detective who pursues her. By the end of S02, however, Capheus is in love with the pansexual Zakia, and Sun is enjoying sex with Detective Mun, who shares her liking for combat as foreplay. Will is reborn by the attentions of Riley, and Lito is beginning to enjoy the sexual attentions of a woman, Daniela, in addition to those of his life partner Hernando, while Kala instigates her own thrilling threesome with her husband and Wolfgang. The only thing missing from all these representations of sex and sexuality is any notion of exclusivity, hierarchy, or limitations.

In contrast, it is vital to note that the villains in *Sense8* are those without empathy, unwilling to cross identity borders, and consequently obsessed with imposing heteronormativity. Whispers is a straight, white male, a husband and father whose anti-sensate campaign speaks of repression and self-loathing as he too is a sensate. He operates beneath a guise of science, as he dedicates himself to an extreme kind of conversion therapy, lobotomizing sensates when he captures them, erasing any divergent thoughts and gaining complete control of their minds. Other antagonists are similarly straight, fearful, and predatory. They include Joaquín Flores (Raúl Méndez), the possessive ex-boyfriend of Daniela, a brutish macho playboy who vengefully exposes the homosexuality of Lito, and Sun's weak but murderous younger brother, another corrupt playboy, who shores up his masculinity by drinking in high-class brothels. Parents are particularly subject to demonizing in this regard. Wolfgang's father, whose toxic masculinity resulted in him raping his own daughter, rails against his son's sister/mother to "stop teaching my son to sing like a queer!" and Daniela's parents are so shocked at their daughter's live-in and loving relationship with Lito and Hernando that they demand she return to live with them and effectively "reboot" her heteronormativity. Lito's agents claim to represent his audience when they refuse to entertain his career ambitions as an action star after he comes out. And Nomi's mother seeks to "correct" the corrective surgery her daughter has already undergone by facilitating the lobotomy that will also erase Nomi and reinstate her son "Michael." Heteronormativity is by no means an indication of evil in *Sense8*, but a denial of any alternative certainly is. So, is queering the world a way to save it?

Queer: If All the World's a Stage, Identity Is Nothing but a Costume

Queering the world might seem like a science fiction premise, but it is notable that *Sense8* has been released in countries with anti-LGBT policies, such as Russia, Thailand, the United Arab Emirates, Kazakhstan, India, and Pakistan, when at its heart *Sense8* suggests, even promises, and even assures us, that passion for someone and something cannot be policed. In its form and content, on its particular platform, and in its complementarity with the more progressive communities inhabiting the internet, *Sense8* also posits a supportive hive-mind as crucial to our evolving wiki-knowledge. Its fans became like the sensates in the way they have connected across space and time through streaming and social media platforms. Reading *Sense8* as a metaphor of the internet, with its networking, community-building, social interactions, sharing, telepathic orgies as allegories for cyber-sex, surveillance and stalking (by Whispers), adds further context to the grassroots online campaign for its revival. It also illuminates how its characters and concept embody a virtual community that stands against narrow populism and nationalism and for a new globalism that, as envisioned by *Sense8*, is built on solidarity, empathy, and progressive gender and sexual politics. It offers the world a queer invitation to join its party and adds a promise that progressives have more fun.

What is clear about this invitation is that when the Wachowskis apply their trans, queer, and science fiction credentials to a project there is potential for world-building of the kind that, as Rosalind Galt and Karl Schoonover describe in relation to *Queer Cinema of the World*, "promises to knock off kilter conventional epistemologies [via] a process that is active, incomplete, and contestatory and that does not presuppose a settled cartography" (Galt and Schoonover 2016: 5). To this end, *Sense8* is "a site of political ferment, a volatile public stage on which protest can be expressed and ideas disseminated. It also provides spaces in which to nourish more diffuse experiences of affinity, belonging, and intimacy, where spectatorship provokes the formation of unexpected collisions and coalitions" (Galt and Schoonover 2016: 21). This spectatorship, meanwhile, made self-aware and interactive on the parallel "volatile public stage" of the internet, sends out signals and establishes links that bring about a "community of sentiment" in response to a series that pertains to a "cinema of sentiment [that] is defined by awareness, empathy, reflection and acceptance or rejection of elements contributing to or detracting from identity" (Stone 2018: 271) in accordance with Georg Sørensen's prior definition of a community of sentiment as one offering "a dynamic picture of a contested identity always being debated" (Sørensen 2004: 85).

The sustained glimpse of a utopia provided by *Sense8*, which offers hope and also nostalgia through re-viewings, resonates among its fans all over the world and prompts transnational connections, at least online, in times of national isolationism, sexual conservatism, homophobia, and transphobia, as well as the travel restrictions and social and physical distancing occasioned by a global pandemic, if we are (re-)watching the series from 2020 onward. In locating this queer utopianism in the polyamory of its cluster, *Sense8*'s vision of collective life demands that we pay attention to its formal construction and, in so doing, draws from Muñoz's notion of queer futurity:

> Queerness is not yet here. Queerness is an ideality. Put another way, we are not yet queer. We may never touch queerness, but we can feel it as a warm illumination of a horizon imbued with potentiality. We have never been queer, yet queerness exists for us as an ideality that can be distilled from the past and used to imagine a future. The future is queerness's domain. Queerness is a structuring and educated mode of desiring that allows us to see and feel beyond the quagmire of the present. The here and now is a prison house. We must strive, in the face of the here and now's totalizing rendering of reality, to think and feel a *then and there*. Some will say that all we have are the pleasures of this moment, but we must never settle for that minimal transport; we must dream and enact new and better pleasures, other ways of being in the world, and ultimately new worlds. (Muñoz 2009: 1)

Indeed, this queerness utopia does not (yet) exist but it reveals itself in art, in connectivity and collectivity, in relational modes of being that defy negativity to point toward new modes of becoming. In one of the most celebrated scenes in *Sense8*, Hernando gives voice to this power of queer art to transform minds. In S02:E01, while he is lecturing on art theory, a student projects an image from breaking news of Hernando and Lito having sex, which has been leaked to the press, prompting alerts on social media. In response to the shock and derision of some of his students—"It looks like shit packer porn"—Hernando gives a reading of the photo that rescues the image and reclaims the sex act depicted therein as an act of love and art. Seizing the moment as an opportunity to recognize this image as revealing a queer utopia, he exhorts his students to see "two vulnerable men caught in an act of pleasure, neither aware of the camera, ... both of them connected to the moment, to each other and to love." "Art is love made public," he concludes, which is an idea that connects with Muñoz holding that queer can be harnessed to speak of potential utopian futures:

> The future is a spatial and temporal destination. ... What we need to know is that queerness is not yet here but it approaches like a crashing

wave of potentiality. And we must give in to its propulsion, its status as a destination. Willingly we let ourselves feel queerness's pull, knowing it as something else that we can feel, that we must feel. (Muñoz 2009: 185)

Sense8 certainly gives in to and actualizes a spatial and temporal queer pull and it uses the empathetic connection between the characters to transcend the "here and now" through fiction to reach a "then and there." These utopian connections include the unbounded sexual pleasure in cluster-orgies that transcend the individual and the couple. Through the combination of the two levels of experience, the sensates make quantum love, being both in the here and now with their human and sensate partners in one location, and simultaneously in a then and there with their whole cluster. Consequently, *Sense8* resolves the queer theory debates that pit LGBTQ marriage and monogamy against a resistance to hegemonic gender and sexual cultural practices (Bersani 1998; Edelman 2004; Halberstam 2018; Muñoz 2009). The sensates can simultaneously be in one place or world and another and they can bring into being the comforts, love, and security of monogamy—Nomi and Amanita, Riley and Will, Sun and Mun, Lito and Hernando (with Dani in a throuple)—while simultaneously embracing the queer polyamorous love and fulfillment of desire made possible in and by their cluster. Thus, Nomi and Amanita can be introduced in S01:E01 enjoying intimate lovemaking *and* can have the most romantic and spectacular of Parisian weddings in S02:E12, which enkindles the series' final orgy, which begins with separate couples but quickly buds bodies and blooms into a glorious revelry full of energy and love. The sequence is edited to a piece of music called "Experience" that is actually a mix of two versions, the original, lyrical piece for piano and strings by Ludovico Einaudi and its electronic remix by Starkey. The scene and its score thereby illustrate how monogamous relationship configurations (here and now) can expand with imagination to incorporate theoretical possibilities and realize startling innovation (then and there), prompting the series' final punchline from Rajan: "My God, I did not think such things were possible."

Problems and Discrepancies: Demons

For a series about utopian potential, *Sense8* is far from perfect. Problems and discrepancies include the Anglocentrism of its dialogue and songs, cultural stereotyping, and the unequal sexualization of white characters (at least in S01). Despite gestures toward polyglotism (such as in S01:E05 "Art Is Like Religion" when Lito and Sun converse in subtitled Spanish and Korean, and Kala and Wolfgang speak in unsubtitled German and Hindi, respectively), *Sense8* uses English in almost all its scenes and settings. English is Will and Nomi's mother tongue, while English is the second language in Riley's

Iceland, but many scenes require a suspension of disbelief: those of Kala, Capheus, Sun, and Daniela conversing with their close families in English, for example, instead of in Hindi, Swahili, Korean, and Spanish, as well as Sun's conversations with her fellow prisoners and guards in a Korean jail. For Capheus in Kenya and Kala in India, meanwhile, English is an official working language that is a legacy of colonial rule, which only exacerbates the problem.

A defense of English as lingua franca in *Sense8* might suggest that the sensates are not diegetically speaking English but telepathically doing so to ensure that an already complicated series is rendered more commercially viable, and that everyone hearing and speaking English is merely a way for the audience to experience what it is to communicate inside their cluster. This follows a biblical approach to the language issue, as described in the miracle of *The Epistle for the Feast of Pentecost*, in which "Jews, devout men, from every nation under heaven" were suddenly able to understand each other despite "speaking in our own tongues" (Pentecost: Acts 2:1-13, cited in Babosh 2017). Indeed, an equivalent contemporary miracle might be identified in the multitude of dubbed and subtitled versions of *Sense8* made available by Netflix, which allow for a global audience to watch *Sense8* simultaneously in their "own tongues."

Notwithstanding some defense of its unrealized ambitions, the purpose of this volume is not to absolve *Sense8* of its sins. Rather, *Sense8: Transcending Television* seeks to understand the causes and effect of the series' weaknesses and failings too. Thus, having acknowledged the fact that *Sense8* tries to foster a utopian sense of inclusivity, for example, we also consider whether the perspective it provides on utopianism leaves its short-sightedness in plain sight, such as the white saviorism attached to its self-sacrificing Chicago cop, Will. Nonetheless, we refrain from holding the series to the fire of an improbable standard that might be imposed in retrospect, because that would ignore the impact of what *Sense8* got right.

That said, in terms of inapposite inequalities and a lack of diversity in *Sense8*, there are problematic discrepancies in the early episodes of S01, with the Asian (Sun), Indian (Kala), and African (Capheus) sensates excused from any sexual activity and given to philosophizing while the white characters (Wolfgang, Riley, Will, and Nomi) and the Hispanic (Lito) get theirs. This is corrected in S02, wherein all the characters share screen time and value regardless of skin tone, gender, sexuality, or nationality, and everybody has great sex in couples, throuples, and the entire group; but juggling at least eight stories means that balls are occasionally dropped. *Sense8* has indigestible plot dumps, leaden expository dialogue, several bewildering dei ex machina and a lack of focus and balance in the latter episodes of the second series, and it tends to use violence exclusively to overcome obstacles, which leads to an absurd body-count, particularly in S02:E12 "Amor Vincit Omnia," where it ascends to Bondian levels of carnage. Perceptive criticisms have also been leveled at *Sense8* by theorists invested in queer and trans politics at the level of representation. In a roundtable discussion of the series, Moya Bailey, micha cárdenas, Laura Horak, Lokeilani Kaimana, Cáel M. Keegan, Genevieve Newman, Raffi Sarkissian, and Rox Samer (Bailey et al. 2017) were, in the main, excited by *Sense8* and positive about its attempts to create new representations of race, gender, sexuality, and national identity. Nonetheless, participants were not without censure: cárdenas is of the view that the "series relies on western colonial conceptions for its global imagination" (Bailey et al. 2017). Bailey is, in turn, critical of representations of race in the series arguing that "when race is acknowledged in the show it is done so to support the white characters' development [and that] the writing team of *Sense8* cannot imagine non-Western characters of color as instigators and occupiers of their own desires" (Bailey et al. 2017). Fans invested in the non-Western characters might contest this interpretation, however, while Western colonial critiques may be rooted in overly realist readings of a science fiction series that uses its genre to resist such readings. That is to say, while some cultural stereotyping in *Sense8* repeats generic tropes (Jonas is a mystical Indian, Sun and Mun are martial arts experts, Kala is a virginal Indian beauty, and Will is that white cop with a savior complex), others subvert them: Lito is a gay action film star, Nomi is a transgender character in the series' most loving relationship, and the entire cluster is a defensive rather than offensive coming together of individuals who are all marginalized in one way or another. *Sense8* may sometimes trip over its own plot and dialogue, but the most action-filled moments are often opportunities for subtle overthrows of conventions engineered by witty juxtapositions of characters, their skills and their personae. Characters who are not straight, white, male, or cisgendered frequently save the day and, crucially, no-one thinks to label this surprising or exceptional.

Ultimately, however, any appraisal of what *Sense8* achieves (such as that provided in this anthology) must recognize that it is part of a much larger process instead of a stand-alone product. Like the sensates learning to live in and as a cluster, *Sense8* exists alongside and among other Netflix original series that feature and explore racial and sexual diversity and equality and provide a space for evolution. These stablemates include the pre-*Sense8* prison-set *Orange Is the New Black* (2013–19), which depicts a closed world in which diverse female characters are given only as much agency and humor as is possible in a system that marginalizes, brutalizes, and criminalizes them (Shaw and Stone 2017). And the post-*Sense8* school-set *Sex Education* (2019–present), wherein a catalogue of diverse, libidinous youngsters find self-realization in friendship and explore the joy and anguish that comes with pride and sexual discoveries. As *Sense8* told its viewers at the start of its run, so its viewers can now return the thankful sentiment: you are no longer just you.

The green light that was given by Netflix to the Wachowskis was one of the streaming network's earliest moves in a strategy of commissioning original programming and, accordingly, it resulted in a series that had no need to prime its medium for the shock of its newness. Nevertheless, there were obvious predecessors too, such as *Star Trek*, which also used the science fiction genre to examine diversity, otherness, and tolerance, but it took almost fifty years to go from the first scripted inter-racial kiss in S03:E10 "Plato's Stepchildren" in 1968 to same-sex marriage in the S01:E05 "Choose Your Pain" episode of the Netflix reboot *Star Trek: Discovery* in 2017. A different ethical galaxy, perhaps, but *Sense8* started with a Black woman pleasuring her transgender, white female lover with a strap-on rainbow-colored dildo in S01:E01: "Limbic Resonance" and ended with a shot of that emblematic dildo in the series finale (S02:E12). Instead of a tentative approach to reviving atrophied hopes of what television was capable, *Sense8* was a reboot of sleeping screens. It was racially diverse without selling anything or standing for office, as queer as could be without ghettoizing its appeal, sexually startling without ever being less than swooningly romantic, and it was fast, colorful, punctuated by great music. It was fun and it was hot. It was never meant to be perfect. It was an avant-garde attack on prudery, fear, and loneliness. Indeed, the triumph of *Sense8* is that it offers an account of the way that we all, however inexactly, function, communicate, and consider ourselves alone and as participants in our own clusters, whether they be local or global, social or political, sexual or sentimental, real or virtual. It demonstrated that radical empathy, which created a novel sensibility and converted it into action, was not just a science fiction gimmick that empowered characters with superpowers, but was within reach of its audience too, not just to write a fitting end to the series but to take a fresh look at their own lives and start anew. In its celebration of interconnectedness as the means to inhabiting other selves, *Sense8* not only transcended television but did indeed suggest that it was necessary to queer the world in order to save it.

Reading *Sense8*: Amor Vincit Omnia

As already indicated, the two seasons of *Sense8* are referred to throughout this book as S01 and S02 with individual episodes identified by their designated position within either season (something which is not always logical) and the episode title is given on first mention. Cast members are given once, above, and thereafter the chapters refer only to their character's names unless, of course, the actors themselves are being discussed. Bibliographies are specific to each chapter, while the index covers the whole volume.

By way of *Sense8*, contributors consider contemporary attitudes to gender, genre, and transnational film and television. They track the phenomenon and global impact of Netflix as well as online communities, their activism and developing sense of identity. We offer close readings of the form and content of *Sense8* and examine a wide array of contemporary themes that come together in the series, including globalization, neo-liberalism and resistance to it, online activism, empathy, gender, identity, and transnationalism.

In the first chapter, **Amanda Lotz** explains the evolution of Netflix as a global platform and assesses the commissioning of *Sense8* in relation to its remit of reaching consumers on a global scale with a focus on its multi-territory strategies. Following this, **Zoë Shacklock** analyzes *Sense8* as part of Netflix's original programming strategy, which sees the company present itself as an evolution of ordinary television, and she narrativizes Netflix's own evolutionary discourse in relation to sensate evolution. In Chapter 3 **James Walters** explores the title sequence and finds its aesthetic status, which is a consequence of its skippability, functions in often uneasy relation to the program itself, despite or because of the fact that the title sequence exists as a work of independent, artistic, even abstract expression.

In the fourth chapter **Deborah Shaw** examines *Sense8*'s creation of a new mythology for the twenty-first century and argues that the series' alignment with queer and trans* radical moralities directly and self-consciously challenges the dominant belief systems of conservative iterations of organized Judeo-Christian religions. **Rosalind Galt** subsequently addresses queer relationality and how we might think of the cluster in *Sense8* not only as "trans" but also as "poly." She argues that the cluster of sensates proposes an intimate community beyond the heteronormative nuclear family, with the capacity to nourish various modes of bonding and love both within and beyond the couple form. **John Lessard** then follows Galt in analyzing *Sense8*'s queer eroticism and telepathic orgy sequences and argues that they borrow from the distractive structures of erotic daydreams and are literally clusterfucks that emphasize an aleatory eroticism.

Rob Stone explores the convergence of musicality, synchronicity, and multiplicity in *Sense8* in Chapter 7, wherein he examines how this demonstrates empathy at a practical, philosophical, and neurological level. Then, in Chapter 8, **Luis Freijo** evaluates the aesthetic representation and function of the city in *Sense8* in light of current debates about cosmopolitanism, arguing that the main cities are represented as frontier spaces demarcating unfinished political projects that reveal a problematic reliance on violence to further change. In Chapter 9 **Will McKeown** takes a close look at the cluster's ability to perceive actual and potential physical harm and psychic invasion as immediate, mutual threats that demand a constant reevaluation of the cluster and he aligns this with the cancelation of the series and its revival.

So Mayer then thinks through ideas of assembly and choreography as activist techniques in relation to *Sense8* in Chapter 10. Reading the coming together of bodies in dance, sex, and violence, they consider the extent to which this embodied ecstasy becomes an effective resistance. And, following

Mayer, in Chapter 11, **Rox Samer** and **Laura Horak** consider the campaign that resulted in Netflix agreeing to commission a feature-length finale. Recognizing that the feelings and practices of fandom are written into the very fiber of *Sense8*, they frame the campaign to renew *Sense8* as a fight for justice in the same imaginative universe as the series. And finally, **Cáel M. Keegan**, author of *Lana and Lilly Wachowski: Sensing Transgender* (2018), re-views and reviews the entire series, examining how its narrative and characters, its plot and aesthetics, its resolution and meaning, posit a radically open state of becoming.

Individually, but more importantly together, our contributors seek to provide a range and level of expertise that allows for collaboration on a dialogue that invites debate about the very limits of what television—and people—are capable.

Works Cited

Attitude (2019), "*Sense8* Star Brian J. Smith Recalls Growing Up Gay and 'Terrified' in Suburban Texas," November 7. Available online: https://attitude.co.uk/article/sense8-star-brian-j-smith-recalls-growing-up-gay-and-terrified-in-suburban-texas-1/22207/.

Babosh, F. T. (2017), "On Pentecost: What Language Was Heard?," *Orthodox Christianity*, June 5. Available online: https://orthochristian.com/104031.html.

Bailey, M., m. cárdenas, L. Horak, L. Kaimana, C. M. Keegan, G. Newman, R. Samer, and R. Sarkissian (2017), "*Sense8* Roundtable," *Spectator*, 37 (2): 77–88.

Baim, T. (2016), "Second Wachowski Filmmaker Sibling Comes Out as Trans," *Windy City Times*, March 8. Available online: http://www.windycitymediagroup.com/lgbt/Second-Wachowski-filmmaker-sibling-comes-out-as-trans-/54509.html.

Bersani, L. (1998), "Against Monogamy," *Oxford Literary Review*, 20 (1–2): 3–21.

Bordwell, D. (2007), "Unsteadicam Chronicles' Observations on Film Art," August 17. Available online: https://www.davidbordwell.net/blog/2007/08/17/unsteadicam-chronicles/.

Brammer, J. P. (2017), "Porn Site Offers to Save LGBTQ-Inclusive Netflix Show *Sense8*," *NBC News*, August 18. Available online: https://www.nbcnews.com/feature/nbc-out/porn-site-offers-save-lgbtq-inclusive-netflix-show-sense8-n793871.

Butler, J. (1990), *Gender Trouble: Feminism and the Subversion of Identity*, New York and London: Routledge.

Clayton, J. (2016), "No. That Is an Internet Rumour," @MsJamieClayton, Twitter, 4:51 p.m., April 27, 2016.

Cotter, P. (2019), "Why Aml Ameen Left *Sense8*," *ScreenRant*, March 6. Available online: https://screenrant.com/aml-ameen-leave-sense8-reason/.

Edelman, L. (2004), *No Future: Queer Theory and the Death Drive*, Durham, NC: Duke University Press.

Galt, R., and K. Schoonover (2016), *Queer Cinema in the World*, Durham, NC: Duke University Press.
Halberstam, J. (2018), *Trans*: A Quick and Quirky Account of Gender Variability*, Berkeley: University of California Press.
Hemon, A. (2017), "The Transformative Experience of Writing for *Sense8*," *The New Yorker*, September 27. Available online: https://www.newyorker.com/culture/personal-history/the-transformative-experience-of-writing-for-sense8.
Henderson, T. (2019), "*The L Word* Reboot Casts *Sense8* Star Jamie Clayton," *Pride*, August 1. Available online: https://www.pride.com/tv/2019/8/01/l-word-reboot-casts-sense8-star-jamie-clayton.
Henry, C. (2019), "The Swash of the Trans New Wave," *Senses of Cinema*, 92. Available online: http://sensesofcinema.com/2019/cinema-in-the-2010s/the-swash-of-the-trans-new-wave/.
Hibberd, J. (2014), "*Community* Saved! Yahoo Orders Sixth Season," *Entertainment Weekly*, June 30. Available online: https://ew.com/article/2014/06/30/community-sixth-season/.
Hustvedt, S. (2017), *A Woman Looking at Men Looking at Women: Essays on Art, Sex, and the Mind*, London: Scepter.
Jameson, F. (1991), *Postmodernism: Or, the Cultural Logic of Late Capitalism*, London and New York: Verso.
Keegan, C. M. (2018), *Lana and Lilly Wachowski: Sensing Transgender*, Urbana: University of Illinois Press.
Lacan, J. ([1949] 2006), "The Mirror Stage as Formative of the I Function as Revealed in Psychoanalytic Experience," in B. Fink (trans.), *Écrits*, 75–81, New York and London: W. W. Norton.
Licari, G. (2011), "Anthropology of Urban Space: Identities and Places in the Postmodern City," *World Futures*, 67 (1): 47–57.
Miller, J. (2017), "Netflix Revives *Sense8*: Read Lana Wachowski's Heartwarming Letter," *Vanity Fair*, June 29. Available online: https://www.vanityfair.com/hollywood/2017/06/netflix-sense8-lana-wachowski.
Morgan, S. (2008), "The Second Most Beautiful Girl in New York," *The Observer*, August 26. Available online: https://observer.com/2008/08/the-second-most-beautiful-girl-in-new-york/.
Muñoz, J. E. (2009), *Cruising Utopia: The Then and There of Queer Futurity*. New York: New York University Press.
Roberts, M. (2020), "HRC to Honor Actress Jamie Clayton, Teacher Sam Long at Time to THRIVE Conference," *Human Rights Campaign*, January 31. Available online: https://www.hrc.org/blog/hrc-to-honor-actress-jamie-clayton-teacher-sam-long-at-time-to-thrive-confe.
Shaw, D., and R. Stone (2017), "How *Orange Is the New Black* Raised the Bar behind Bars," *The Conversation*. Available online: https://theconversation.com/how-orange-is-the-new-black-raised-the-bar-behind-bars-78702.
Sørensen, G. (2004), *The Transformation of the State: Beyond the Myth of Retreat*, Basingstoke: Palgrave Macmillan.
Stangarone, T. (2019), "How Netflix Is Reshaping South Korean Entertainment," *The Diplomat*, April 29. Available online: https://thediplomat.com/2019/04/how-netflix-is-reshaping-south-korean-entertainment/.

Steinbock E. (2019), *Shimmering Images: Trans Cinema, Embodiment, and the Aesthetics of Change*, Durham, NC: Duke University Press.

Stone, R. (2018), "Cinemas of Citizens, Cinemas of Sentiment: World Cinema in Flux," in R. Stone, P. Cooke, S. Dennison and A. Marlow-Mann (eds.), *The Routledge Companion to World Cinema*, 267–89, Oxford and New York: Routledge.

Stone, R. (2021), "The Bourne Multiplicity: Quantum Europeanness in the Bourne Films (2002–16)," in S. Hayward and G. Gegely (eds.) *The Routledge Companion to European Cinema*, forthcoming, Oxford and New York: Routledge.

THR Staff (2012), "Lana Wachowski's HRC Visibility Award Acceptance Speech (Transcript)," *Hollywood Reporter*, October 24. Available online: https://www.hollywoodreporter.com/news/lana-wachowskis-hrc-visibility-award-382177.

1

What's Going On? Netflix and the Commissioning of *Sense8*

Amanda D. Lotz

Were it not for Netflix, there would likely not be *Sense8*. So, an apt place to begin is with exploring what Netflix is and how its peculiarity allowed for *Sense8*'s creation. As many will know, Netflix is a video distribution service that delivers video using the internet instead of technologies such as broadcast signal, cable or satellite transmission, or DVD. As a distribution technology, the internet has different capabilities than broadcast or multichannel services that are only able to transmit a single signal per channel to their audience. This limited capacity necessitates an organization of programs into a schedule. In contrast, internet-distributed services allow on-demand access to a library of programs. This allows internet-distributed services much more capacity—adding a show does not require taking another away—but they also are not limitless. Internet-distributed services are constrained by the budget available for programming.

Netflix also relies on a business model relatively unprecedented for the forms of video distribution that preceded it. Netflix is subscriber-funded, thus is not reliant on advertisers or public funds. Its precise model, in which subscribers pay a monthly fee for unlimited access to a library of programming, is thus more like the economics of paying to see a film or rent a video than the way most video to the home is funded, but the fact that payment allows access to a bundle of content also makes it quite different (Lotz 2017, 2018, 2019). Although many other companies such as Amazon, Apple, and Disney also distribute video using the internet, it is important to recognize that each of these companies conglomerate many businesses, and video distribution is just one piece of the overall enterprise—in some cases, a very small one. Netflix, in contrast, is purely a subscriber-funded video service.

These features derived from distributing by internet are very important in driving the programming strategy of the service. Netflix's primary goal is to expand the number of people who subscribe to its service and maintain those that already do so. To attract subscribers, Netflix must offer them something of such value that they are willing to pay for it. Consequently, the content most valuable to Netflix is that which is not available anywhere else. This is very different to the strategy behind advertiser-funded programming, in which the goal is to attract the most attention—typically the most viewers—so that they and their attention can be sold to advertisers.

Beyond these core features of distribution technology and business model that differentiate Netflix from most twentieth-century video, it is necessary to account for the company's constant evolution. Netflix was born in the United States as a DVD rental-by-mail service that is credited with the destruction of the video rental store business (Keating 2012). In this first Netflix era, which spanned roughly from 1997 through 2010, Netflix was primarily associated with film rather than television. Throughout the latter half of the first decade of the 2000s Netflix pivoted its business toward using the internet to distribute video in the United States. A component of that transition from mail to internet distribution involved the service emphasizing television over film titles as it increasingly became recognized as a service that offered past seasons of well-known American television series. Netflix also offered a healthy film library for streaming access, but the film library was far less robust than the DVD rental-by-mail service because of the difference in rights regimes for these different formats.

Netflix began the pivot to its third identity—multinational video distributor—in 2010 when it became available in Canada. Its reach expanded yearly, launching a year later in Latin America and the Caribbean in 2011; the UK, Ireland, and Scandinavia in 2012; the Netherlands in 2013; Austria, Belgium, France, Germany, Luxembourg, Switzerland, and India in 2014; and then Australia, New Zealand, and Japan in 2015, before CEO Reed Hastings's announcement in January 2016 of its "global" roll out and availability in 130 countries, which has since climbed to 190, or all but Iran, Syria, and China.

At the same time as the service expanded its multinational reach, it began to diminish its reliance on licensing titles that had been produced for other networks and channels to instead begin financing the production of series commissioned by Netflix. Some of the earliest of these series were only "Netflix shows" in the US market—the non-US rights for *House of Cards* and *Orange Is the New Black* were sold to other distributors, frustrating new Netflix subscribers in those markets. But as Netflix's strategy as a multinational video distributor solidified, it began purchasing global rights for the series it developed, and often for much longertime horizons than the norm—ten to fifteen years instead of two or three.

Though this practice deviated from the conventions of television trade, this strategy corresponded to the difference of Netflix's distribution technology and business model. What incentive would people have to subscribe if the service was not the exclusive rights holder? Moreover, the on-demand ability of the distribution technology and the scale of its multinational subscriber base enabled considerable capacity. Where networks had to stop airing a show to make room for a new one, Netflix had no such capacity issues. The service derived value from its library reliability—from maintaining access to series. Also, the fact that Netflix does not sell attention to advertisers means that it is not driven to try to gather as many people viewing at a particular time.

Sense8

Sense8 was the sixth series Netflix commissioned. In its marketing, Netflix uses the terms "original" and "exclusive" somewhat liberally to include a series that it had no hand in making, but to describe the purchase of exclusive rights in foreign markets from whatever production company holds the rights. *Sense8* meets a more rigorous and standard designation of "original" because Netflix funded the cost of the series' creation. Although contract details are not disclosed publicly, it is likely the case that Netflix retains global rights to the series for a decade or longer in exchange for funding its production. Netflix did not yet have its own studio when *Sense8* began development; it contracted Lana and Lily Wachowski's Anarchos Productions to make the series.

Netflix released all twelve episodes of the first series of *Sense8* simultaneously—as is the norm for the service—in June 2015. It had announced the deal for the series more than two years earlier, in March 2013 (O'Connell 2013). These dates are important because of the fluidity in Netflix's aims and identity over this period. Appreciating when Netflix began *Sense8* crucially informs arguments about what was attractive about the series for the service and the service's approach to the series.

Netflix agreed to produce *Sense8* a month after the debut of its first, and much hyped, original series, *House of Cards*. Because of its simultaneous full-season release, Netflix would have already had an indication of the response to *House of Cards*. In addition to data such as how many subscribers streamed the series, how many episodes they watched, and how quickly they watched all the episodes, Netflix would have monitored new subscribers and whether *House of Cards* was among the first series watched by new subscribers in order to assess the performance of the series and the viability of its commissioned series strategy (Sarandos 2019).

Even before the first episodes dropped, the commissioning of *House of Cards* had provided the service with an extraordinary amount of free publicity as the top-level talent attached to the project and its jaw-dropping budget generated buzz and expectation from the first announcement in March 2011. The buzz only continued as *House of Cards* launched and stories of viewers "binge watching" the season over the course of day mixed with accounts debating the foolishness of Netflix's simultaneous release strategy and extended the unpaid publicity of the series and service further.

When *Sense8* was greenlit, Netflix reached roughly thirty-three million US subscribers and nearly eleven million in countries including Canada, Central America, and Northwest Europe. A month later Netflix released its second series, *Hemlock Grove*, which Hastings claimed was viewed by more subscribers in its first days on the service than *House of Cards*, but *Hemlock Grove* never received the critical acclaim or general attention of other Netflix series (Ludwig 2013). Thus, Netflix had a basic sense of the viability of its strategy shift toward commissioning series at the time it began developing *Sense8*.

Sense8 was similar to other early Netflix commissions in that the announcement of the series alone made news. Just as the idea of acclaimed film director David Fincher and actor Kevin Spacey had attracted attention to the *House of Cards* order, the news of a series from the Wachowskis drew notice—as was likely intended. Such announcements of forthcoming work from well-known talent were not only helpful in providing unpaid publicity for the service but also valuable motivation to encourage potential subscribers who were curious about the service to take the step of subscribing, or at least starting a free trial of the service that represented a different type of video experience than was common.

The series' budget was part of the initial deal, which has been anecdotally reported as nine million dollars per episode, a sum that lands it on lists of the most expensive television series made as of 2020 (Kurland 2019). This high budget was not particular to *Sense8*, but characteristic of the early shock and awe campaign Netflix embraced in moving into commissions and a result of the uncommon terms of Netflix deals. Nearly all of the early Netflix commissions had comparable budgets and are included among lists of the most expensive television series produced. A significant part of the high price results from the different terms Netflix demands. Where traditionally the rights of US television shows have reverted back to the company that produced them after a first airing on the commissioning network—so that the rights can be sold again and again in other markets and countries either immediately or within a few years—Netflix seeks global and perpetual rights. The financing of most television shows allowed for additional earnings by talent and producers if the show earned significant revenue after its first license window—and it is from these sales that the series that amassed perceived great riches achieved this revenue. There is likely no additional revenue to come for the producers or talent making shows for Netflix. One of the reasons the service spends such high sums is in order to build a stable, multiyear library of series. This is very different from the existing norms of television.

The high budgets of Netflix shows often covered long-term rights, but they also typically bought top-shelf talent. The budgets also made clear to a skeptical Hollywood talent pool that the service was serious about creating programming and could be the destination for those with stories that might not match the narrow confines of ad-supported television. Netflix followed HBO's business model and likewise sought to create a reputation as a favored partner for creative talent.

Netflix's goal in commissioning series was to have shows that people would watch, but early on, compelling subscriber growth was crucial. In the case of *Sense8*, the premium budget bought high-profile creators. The series spent minimally on acting talent, with few established actors, but, to put it in industry parlance, put the rest of the budget "on the screen." *Sense8* relied upon on-location shooting in multiple countries on multiple continents, all of which is very expensive and unusual. Moreover, episodes featuring climaxes in the storyline about BPO's pursuit of the cluster featured expensive chase scenes and special effects. The cinematographic richness of the series' sweeping landscapes and special effects also benefited Netflix. Of its other early commissions, only *Marco Polo* featured the visual excess that allowed Netflix to claim its offerings surpassed the visual conventions associated with nontheatrical audiovisual entertainment to be visually distinctive.

As this account suggests, it is not difficult to see why Netflix developed *Sense8*. It capitalized on several of the strategic features of the shows it commissioned during its first phase of series. Of course, most of those passionate about the show likely care little about these strategic components and prefer instead to discuss features of the story and their favorite characters. In truth, story likely had little to do with bringing the series to life. Stories are difficult to promote—unless they are based on real events or established intellectual property. Science fiction tends to struggle even more with this issue because of the idiosyncratic worlds in which its stories and characters exist and the common play with allegory. For example, the IMDb description of *Sense8* is: "A group of people around the world are suddenly linked mentally, and must find a way to survive being hunted by those who see them as a threat to the world's order." While yes, the series is this, it was also much more, as the chapters in this book suggest. But Netflix was unable to rely on those features in paid promotion and would have to rely on word-of-mouth about the complex characters and relationships to drive viewership.

Notably, there was little formal similarity across Netflix's first shows. *House of Cards* is a political thriller based on a book and previous British series, *Hemlock Grove*, a horror series, *Orange Is the New Black* is a women's prison dramedy based on a true story, *Marco Polo*, a historical epic, and *Bloodline*, a comparatively mundane dysfunctional family thriller. Enter *Sense8*, unlike any of these other series. With the advantage of time, Netflix's programming strategy during these early years has grown clearer. The service does not aim to make series that are likely to attract all, or even a significant portion of its subscribers. Instead, it achieves mass scale by "conglomerating niches" (Lotz 2017). Netflix executives have talked of creating series for different "taste communities," basically pockets of interests and their overlap (Adalian 2018). Rather than trying to appeal to the preferences of many different audiences in a single show, Netflix makes a variety of series distinctly targeting specific taste cultures. Because it is distributed on demand, it does not have to pick and choose among which taste culture it serves at a particular time to find the show most attractive to the most viewers in the manner broadcast schedulers must. Moreover, its ability to gather data about what viewers have watched enables it to target specific programs to the viewers most likely to watch them.

This is not to say the story of *Sense8* is not important. Two features of *Sense8* stand out as components that may have been strategic or perhaps mere coincidence. First, the explicitly global nature of the series fits well with the service's aspirations to evolve from a US to a multinational service. By the time the series was greenlit in 2013, Netflix was clearly on a road toward becoming a global service. Notably, this is an aspiration that has no precedent. Though international television trade has long been important to the business, the norm has been to develop series for a particular market with the hope of then selling it in other places. There was no precedent for how to run a multinational internet-distributed video business, and certainly no known plan for a service that aimed to make a significant portion of its library simultaneously available in all the countries it reached.

Sense8 features an organic cosmopolitanism that is not without reason for critique, but also suits a service aiming to attract subscribers in countries around the world. With the exception of *Marco Polo* (which was a notable disaster for the service), all of the other early commissions were very American. Netflix launched *Narcos* a month after *Sense8*, and that series was an important success and set in Colombia but filmed in Brazil by a French production company with extensive use of spoken Spanish and English subtitles. *Club de Cuervos*, Netflix's first Mexican-set Spanish-language (and first non-English) series followed a month later in August. Accounts suggest *Narcos* was widely viewed and a surprise success for the service, both around the world and in the United States, where conventional wisdom believed that Americans would not watch subtitled content (Shaw 2017). Netflix still had mostly US subscribers at this point, so the series was a decent gamble, or aimed at a long-term strategy.

Although Netflix notoriously refuses to divulge consistent information about series' performance, the pattern of commentary suggests *Narcos* attracted more viewers than *Sense8*. Its performance may have encouraged Netflix to embrace a more place-specific approach to storytelling than *Sense8*'s multinational cosmopolitanism. (Though it must be noted that *Sense8*'s stories were well grounded in the cultural particularities of its multiple locations and evidence much less an exploitative tourist view or thin national specificity than other stories aspiring to be perceived as global. It is also notable that *Sense8* rarely used subtitles, but relied nearly exclusively on spoken English.)

The other significant formal feature is genre: science fiction. In the years since Netflix committed to the production of *Sense8*, science fiction has proven a priority genre. Netflix's first commissioned film, *Bright* (2017), starring Will Smith, was science fiction, as were series *The OA* (2016–19), *Black Mirror* (2011–), and *Altered Carbon* (2018–). Netflix also struck high-profile distribution deals licensing series such as *Star Trek: Discovery* (2017–) outside the United States and Canada, and films such as *The Cloverfield Paradox* (2018), *Annihilation* (2018), *Extinction* (2018), and *Spectral* (2016), among many others. It is clear that science fiction is one of the "taste communities" Netflix caters to across its many markets. For a multinational distributor, the appeal of science fiction is clear—the genre is often not geographically bound to real locations, which reduces a sense of national specificity, and has a long history of strong fan communities. Yet, even in a large and wealthy media market such as the United States, the science fiction audience was too niche to enable expensive production within a single national market. Notably, the US SciFi (now SyFy) cable channel was among the first to commission scripted series in the early 1990s, but these series remained bound to limited budgets and few became larger cultural phenomena in the manner of shows such as AMC's *Mad Men*.

While these narrative features may make for a compelling argument for the series, it is unclear how they informed the decision to commission *Sense8*, if they did at all. *Sense8* emerges so early in Netflix's strategy of commissioning series that it is plausible none of these factors were considered, though retrospectively, the series maps well onto its growing multinational aspirations. In 2013, it is unlikely that the service had accumulated significant data illustrating the viability of science fiction programming across a multinational audience, although its experience with DVD rental-by-mail service would have offered a longer history among US viewers.

Just as the peculiar features of Netflix explain why it funded and distributed *Sense8*, these peculiar features may explain *Sense8*'s fate. The series was canceled shortly after the second-season debut. Such patterns were fairly new in 2017 but have become common.

Though Netflix continues to derive value from series months and years past their debut, the size of the audience that turns up immediately after new episodes are available is an indication of the audience interest. Netflix likely calculated that *Sense8* had done all it would in driving subscribers to the service. By 2017, Netflix also had more insight on the return on investment for series. Although extraordinary budgets persisted in some cases, the service also began spreading those budgets across more shows, but there was no satisfactory way to make *Sense8* cheaper to produce.

Netflix's reputation in the creative community was also established by 2017. Where initially creative talent had to be convinced to bring projects to Netflix and not view it as a lesser distributor than broadcast or cable, the shock and awe campaign quickly established it as a desirable buyer. Netflix shows—particularly *House of Cards*—were seen as buzzy, well-promoted, and awards contenders. Moreover, creators recounted a hands-off creative environment. Canceling *Sense8* after one season would have risked establishing a reputation that the service did not give its series an adequate opportunity; this risk was much less significant after the second season.

Fans rallied behind the series and circulated petitions in response to the cancelation—all known techniques for protesting decisions of linear television. But the calculus for a service such as Netflix is different. Linear services must cancel a show to add a new one. When they make that decision, it is because a show has become too expensive for the audience it attracts, or they believe a new show is likely to attract a bigger audience. That is a tricky proposition—a known show has more name recognition than a new show—so it is a trade-off not made lightly. But a nonlinear service can have as many titles in its library as it can afford to license or produce. Being a known property does not confer as much additional value.

Also, because subscribers buy access to a bundle of shows and movies, Netflix's value to the subscriber rarely rides on a single title. While fans were certainly—and reasonably—disappointed, it is unlikely that many were subscribing just for access to this one series. The marginal benefit of each series is just much less when paid for in a bundle.

Less than a month after cancelation, Lana Wachowski announced an agreement for a two-hour finale episode. Such things are not unheard of in series created for linear networks, but they are uncommon. Once actors and other talent are released from contracts, it is often difficult to reunite them. But *Sense8*'s writing team was quite small, there were no sets to recreate because it was shot on location, and Netflix did not need to find room on its schedule—it just needed to commit the funds for production. Given the fan outcry and the fact that the series had concluded at such an unsatisfying point, committing the funds for a proper conclusion seems a relatively obvious decision. But this would have been much more difficult had the show originated somewhere other than Netflix.

It is important to understand that in the same way internet-distributed, subscriber-funded services such as Netflix make possible series that would struggle or be impossible in other industrial contexts, these services have their own constraints. The norm of long-running series that produced more than twenty episodes per season developed because of the industrial structure of US television. It was not that most of those series had that many good stories to tell, but once a series becomes a hit the riches grow exponentially with more episodes that can be sold again and again around the world. Because there is no second market for Netflix shows—producers are paid so that shows remain exclusively in the Netflix library for a long time—there is not that similar commercial drive to keep making episodes.

The fact that there were only two seasons of *Sense8* should not be viewed as an indication of failure. The profit structure of ad-supported, linear television created the perception that hundreds of episodes were normal and a sign of success, but this is not the case. The different industrial norms that allowed *Sense8* to be created and to have a production budget of $9 million also required that the duration of the story needed to match the scale of the audience.

Long after the added two-hour finale dropped, the affordances of Netflix then allowed *Sense8* to exist as a twenty-six-hour story available to subscribers across the globe for the foreseeable future. The show is not particularly marked by the passage of time, but remains meaningful and effective for viewers who find it years later and can access it in its entirety.

Moreover, the algorithmic recommendation functions enable Netflix to suggest it to new subscribers whose viewing record matches those who viewed *Sense8*, or those interested can easily search and find it. This increases the likelihood that the series has a more significant long tail of viewership than many of the "reruns" of the past.

As this analysis suggests, situating *Sense8* within the strategic development of Netflix creates deeper understanding of much of the show's distinction. Although the series produced for Netflix and other streaming services seem very much "like television," it is crucial to also account for the specific attributes of these services that distinguish them. Netflix commissions are designed with different goals, are measured by different metrics, and, consequently, often tell different stories in different ways. This is not because Netflix is more or less artistic, but because it uses a particular distribution technology and business model. A decade from now, Netflix will know much more about what kinds of shows to buy, how much to pay for them, and how to know they have reached their maximum value. Scholars too will have more complicated frameworks and theories for understanding the strategies of these services and the pressures creators face making series for them and the types of series or series features that align well with industrial factors. Given the rapid and pronounced change that has characterized Netflix's existence to this point, it is a fool's errand to speculate on what that future might look like, but *Sense8* provides a rich case to consider the recent past.

Works Cited

Adalian, J. (2018), "Inside the Binge Factory," *New York Magazine*, June 11. Available online: https://www.vulture.com/2018/06/how-netflix-swallowed-tv-industry.html.

Keating, G. (2012), *Netflixed: The Epic Battle for America's Eyeballs*, New York: Penguin.

Kurland, D. (2019), "The 30 Most Expensive TV Shows Ever Made (and How Much They Cost)," *SCREENRANT*, March 24. Available online: https://screenrant.com/tv-shows-most-expensive-cost/.

Lotz, A. D. (2017), *Portals: A Treatise on Internet-Distributed Television* Ann Arbor, MI: Maize Books.

Lotz, A. D. (2018), *We Now Disrupt This Broadcast: How Cable Transformed Television and the Internet Revolutionized It All*, Cambridge: MIT Press.

Lotz, A. D. (2019), "Teasing Apart Television Industry Disruption: Consequences of Meso-Level Financing Practices before and after the US Multiplatform Era," *Media, Culture and Society*, 41 (7): 923–38.

Ludwig, S. (2013), "Netflix Says More People Watched *Hemlock Grove* on First Weekend than *House of Cards*," *VentureBeat*, April 22. Available online: https://venturebeat.com/2013/04/22/netflix-hemlock-grove-first-weekend/.

O'Connell, M. (2013), "Netflix Gives 10-Episode Order to Wachowskis' 'Sense8,'" *Hollywood Reporter*, March 27. Available online: https://www.hollywoodreporter.com/live-feed/netflix-gives-10-episode-order-431307.

Sarandos, T. (2019), "Netflix's Ted Sarandos on Streaming, Competition, and What's Next," *Aspen Institute Podcasts*, January 23. Available online: https://www.aspeninstitute.org/podcasts/netflixs-ted-sarandos-on-streaming-competition-and-whats-next/.

Shaw, L. (2017), "Netflix Wants the World to Binge-Watch," *Bloomberg*, January 12. Available online: https://www.bloomberg.com/news/features/2017-01-12/netflix-wants-the-world-to-binge-watch.

2

You Are No Longer Just You: Netflix, *Sense8*, and the Evolution of Television

Zoë Shacklock

In January 2016, in a keynote address at the annual Consumer Electronics Show in Las Vegas, Netflix CEO Reed Hastings announced that the service had at that moment gone live in 190 countries around the world—130 more than at the beginning of his speech. "Today, right now," Hastings dramatically announced, "you are witnessing the birth of a global TV network—and I do mean the birth" (CES 2016). Emphasizing the global "simultane[ity]" of the platform, he declared that "whether you are in Sydney or St Petersburg, Singapore or Seoul, Santiago or Saskatoon, you can now be part of the internet TV revolution." Hastings's language here reflects the standard promotional rhetoric of the company—that Netflix creates something new, something innovative, something groundbreaking that takes one giant leap forward in the history of television.

Yet there is something of an oscillation between revolution and evolution in the discourses surrounding the platform, an uncertainty as to whether to frame its position in the television landscape through incremental change or dramatic upheaval. Two years later in 2018, Hastings moderated his language slightly, stating that Netflix was "more evolutionary than revolutionary" (Turek and Moynihan 2018). Where YouTube can be understood as revolutionizing media production, he argued, in terms of user-generated content and open platforms, Netflix remains an evolution of television. Hastings is correct, of course—to argue that Netflix is a break with modes of television that came before is at best naïve and at worst willfully ignorant.

However, Hastings still believes that Netflix is an *improvement* on previous modes of television, stating that "I would say we've very much improved television" (Turek and Moynihan 2018). Here, he evokes the popular way in which evolution is deployed—as a natural pathway of progression toward some ideal fit, in which every step advances what came before. Indeed, in his keynote, Hastings began by setting up a historical trajectory from broadcast to cable to internet television, suggesting that "each of these bring[s] a better experience." Here, Hastings presents Netflix as the pinnacle of televisual development, and, consequently, as taking broad steps into the future.

The elements that Hastings pulls out to discursively frame Netflix's global rollout—a magical moment of birth, a sense of simultaneity, and a connection between disparate cities across the world—all describe the flagship original program *Sense8* as equally well as they do the platform, in which members of a cluster become attuned to one another in a "birthing," and connections happen across eight different cities. The program is invested in the exact same ideas of globality, simultaneity, connection, and moments of change as the platform itself. Interestingly, it also articulates an identical concept of "evolution" as superior development. The sensates have a genetic mutation that facilitates their connection with one another. While Homo sensorium may ostensibly be a parallel branch of humanity, the narrative very much presents them as a *superior* form of humanity, in which they feel more intensely and form stronger connections than their Homo sapiens counterparts. Yet *Sense8* also strongly resists teleological narratives of progress: it presents a mode of life that exists outside of linear connections and linear temporality, and it is interested in questions of empathy and connection, rather than simply the survival of the fittest. In this sense, *Sense8* seems to work through the conditions of its own platform, negotiating Netflix's features and promotional discourses in ways that act as a simultaneous reiteration and resistance.

Sense8 offers a lesson on how to approach Netflix in the age of streaming media, particularly in terms of its relationship to broadcast television. In this chapter I do want to position Netflix as something of an 'evolution' of television—but not as simply a step toward the future. In its original, Darwinian sense, evolution does not tell us anything about the future at all: the traces of evolution we see reveal the successful adaptations of the past, rather than pointing toward future change. In this sense, if *Sense8* negotiates the terrain between evolutionary and nonlinear temporality, Netflix can and must be understood through how it negotiates foundational features of television, such as serial narration and serial consumption, temporality, liveness, and a sense of place. Graeme Turner and Anna Pertierra (2013), in their work on the local meanings and circulation of television, argue that too much of television studies is blinded by the newness of internet television. There is "limited interest in examining the similarities, to the same extent as the differences," they argue, "between the viewers' experience of consuming television via the box and via the computer" (2013: 10). Following Turner and Pertierra, I want to trace the continuities between these two evolutionary stages, rather than simply attending to the differences, and to argue that Netflix is as much in dialogue with televisual pasts as it is with televisual futures.

Sense8 also offers a way to interrogate Netflix's original programs: to explore the extent to which they might reflect, or embody, or promote the features and conditions of the platform itself. All media texts bear the traces of the industrial conditions in which they are produced. Texts can also act as allegories, or narratives, of those very conditions—whether in direct support or in contradiction. In his work on the television landscape in the 2000s, Shawn Shimpach (2010) identifies an allegorical trend in serial television, in which programs deliberately dramatize their own industrial conditions in order to normalize changes in the medium. Writing on mid-2000s programs that emphasize the temporal and spatial agency of the white male hero, he suggests that these texts offer "fantasies of transcendence, of temporal and spatial mobility that serve, almost allegorically, to underscore their very conditions of production and circulation" (2010: 9). Following Shimpach, I believe that Netflix programming, which also seeks to carve out a stable position in a rapidly changing television landscape, demonstrates a similar allegorical trend (albeit one with different identity politics). From *Black Mirror: Bandersnatch*'s emphasis on interactivity and personalization to *Russian Doll*'s anxiety about temporal consumption, to *Sex Education*'s infamous (and very deliberate) geographical confusion, Netflix's original programs work through their own industrial conditions. They explore questions of time, of place, of agency, and of identity, narrativizing the very elements that structure debates and experiences of the platform itself.

Sense8 is a particularly crucial example here. The program is one of the earliest of Netflix's original dramas and was promoted as an incentive to gather more subscriptions. Much was made of the high budget of the program, with each episode costing approximately $9 million. Similarly, the presence of acclaimed auteurist (previously film) directors Lana and Lilly Wachowski, along with screenwriter J. Michael Straczynski, was positioned as a significant draw for new subscribers. Finally, the international scope of the program was very attractive in both promoting the platform in new territories around the world, and in appealing to new subscribers in the West. Finance, authorship, and globality are all elements that Netflix presents as a source of distinction from broadcast television. They are also all things that arguably led to the series being canceled after two seasons: its costly international scope, its appeal to international viewers who may have been pirating the program (Spangler 2015), and the difficulties of realizing the Wachowskis' ambitious artistic vision. In this sense, *Sense8* may also point to the limitations of focusing entirely on the new at the expense of continuities with televisual pasts. Helen Piper astutely notes that despite the enthusiastic, at times hyperbolic, language of both the industry and academics, she remains "not convinced that the transformation [from broadcast to online television] is as absolute and complete" as the promotional rhetoric may tell us (2016: 173). It is my intention to similarly resist the transformative siren of streaming television, and to trace instead how streaming originals might continue to point to modes of television they seek to outpace. *Sense8*, I argue, narratively works through the tension between new and old industrial structures, narrative modes, and consumption practices, offering an exploration of what we mean when we talk about both Netflix and television.

Serial Stories

One of the most apparent ways in which Netflix distinguishes itself from broadcast television is through the control and choice it offers the viewer. Rather than the fixed temporality and choices of the broadcast schedule, Netflix provides an on-demand service that can be consumed according to the pace and preference of the viewer. In Reed Hasting's CES keynote, he argues that Netflix fulfills a long-standing desire for agency on the part of the audience, emphatically declaring that while the DVD and VCR were "early efforts to give the people what they wanted," with Netflix, "you don't have to sit through commercials, or be at the mercy of an 8pm tune-in. You just click and watch: a simple yet revolutionary shift from corporate to consumer control" (CES 2016). Again, we see clearly the ways in which Netflix's promotional rhetoric evokes ideas of revolutionary improvements on broadcast television; and again, we see the evolutionary discourse that positions the platform as the pinnacle of televisual progress. This dream of agency manifests clearly in Netflix's release strategy, in which whole seasons of programs are "dropped" at once (as opposed to the weekly release of broadcast television), so that a program can be consumed according to the viewer's pace. Similarly, programs are offered to viewers in horizontally organized categories, with thumbnails placed alongside one another within algorithmic categories such as "Because You Watched," or taste groupings such as "Gritty TV Dramas." Here, the horizontal organization of the interface stands in contrast to the vertical construction of a TV schedule, emphasizing that all of these choices exist simultaneously at this moment of time. By offering a buffet of consumption to its viewers, rather than the staggered meals of broadcast television, Netflix presents itself as a progressive development of broadcast television.

Sense8 shares the same emphasis on plenty and the present as the platform itself, the same feeling of, to quote Marshall McLuhan, *all-at-once-ness* (McLuhan and Fiore 1967: 63). The program is known for the recurring sequences in which all eight of the sensates share experiences, such as sex, dance, music, and celebrations: for example, the sex scenes in S01:E06 "Demons" and S02:E01 "Happy Fucking New Year," the karaoke scene in S01:E04, and the birthday celebration in S02:E01. Each of these sequences operate as a musical montage, and the impact of the sequences emerge from the choreographic spectacle of bodies moving with the music. In their focus on multiple bodies in different spaces and times united through kinetic movement, the sequences emphasize exuberance and simultaneity of experience. In S02:E01, the sensates celebrate their birthday in a sequence that begins with all eight of the sensates blowing out Lito's candles together. Accompanied by Steve Aoki and Walk Off The Earth's "Home We Go," we see a fast-paced montage of the sensates' birthday celebrations, in a kaleidoscope of color and movement. The speed of the montage flattens out the temporality of the sequence, presenting everything as happening *now, at once*. The content of the sequence mirrors its formal excess: the sensates revel in excessive consumption of cake and whipped cream. In foregrounding the effects of simultaneous consumption, the sequence, and by extension, the program itself, models the preferred consumption model of the interface—a splurge of *all-at-once-ness*.

Such an emphasis on abundant consumption is often framed (and, indeed, promoted) through the lens of dangerous excess, or the "binge." Mareike Jenner argues that while binge-viewing is not specific to Netflix, the platform has "employed it more centrally" than others, and it remains a crucial part of its distribution strategy (2018: 110). It is also a key part of the Netflix interface: the "autocue" function, which immediately starts playing the next episode during the credits of the previous one, encourages continuous viewing on the part of the audience. It is important to remember that continuous viewing has been part of the television landscape for decades—Raymond Williams's (1974) work on what he calls televisual flow shows how the broadcast schedule is arranged to maintain audience interest across an evening, or afternoon, of programming. Yet Netflix undoubtedly encourages marathon consumption: through the affordances of its interface, through its promotional tactics (its categories include "Binge-worthy TV"), and also through the narrative structure of its original programs, which are made to fit the affordances of the platform. Most episodes of *Sense8* end rather abruptly, and often on "cliffhanger" moments, such as Kala fainting in S01:E05 "Art Is Like Religion," the apparent suicide of Whispers in S01:E07 "W.W.N. Double D.," and Jonas's lobotomy in S02:E04 "Polyphony." There are relatively few episodes that end in ways that aim to give the episode closure—S01:E04 "What's Going On," which ends with the triumphant conclusion of Nomi's hospital admission, is one of the few. In this, the episodes depart from the narrative structure that has dominated broadcast drama in the last three decades: what Jason Mittell terms narrative complexity, in which episodes both have some degree of closure and point onward to the next episode (Mittell 2006: 32). *Sense8*'s narrative structure thus fits the specific conditions of Netflix and reflects the platform's aim to distinguish itself from broadcast television.

Endings that resist closure are by no means new: the cliffhanger has been a staple of serial storytelling since its inception. However, I would argue that the cliffhanger functions somewhat differently in Netflix programming to broadcast television—and as such, continues to function as a form of distinction, or evolutionary marker. In broadcast television, an effective cliffhanger ends on a question, on a moment that leaves the narrative stakes precariously suspended. Jeremy Butler suggests that the soap opera cliffhanger leaves characters "interrupted just as they are about to commit murder, discover their true paternity, or consummate a romance" (2012: 12). Here, the cliffhanger sets up "will they/won't they" questions, leaving lives, loves, and identities hanging in the balance. Broadcast television cliffhangers must sustain interest and debate over a period of time between instalments (whether a week, months, or simply a commercial break), and so need to pose questions that inspire debate and imagination. Netflix cliffhangers, in contrast, simply need to prevent us from exiting the stream.

Sense8's cliffhangers tend to occur just *after* a pivotal action has occurred. Two key examples here are the suicide of Nigel Bolgers in S01:E07, and Lito's attempted suicide in S01:E09 "Death Doesn't Let You Say Goodbye." Both of these episodes end after the gunshot, leaving no doubt as to whether a life remains at risk. After Lito narrowly avoids shooting himself, what prompts us to cue up the next episode is not the question of his life, but our affective entanglement with his emotions. Similarly, after Bolgers dies, the episode ends abruptly with a close up of Nomi and Amanita's weeping faces: here, we are drawn along in the undercurrent of Nomi and Amanita's shock and relief, rather than an unfinished plot point. Michael Newman suggests that in broadcast television, cliffhangers employ "highly focused questions" that direct the main plot of a particular episode (2006: 20). In Netflix programming, I would argue, these questions tend to be generalized questions about emotion and reaction, constructing an affective undertow that carries viewers into the next episode. Netflix's stream, then, is an affective one.

These questions of affective entanglement are also *narrative* concerns for many of Netflix's original programs. Casey McCormick, in her work on *House of Cards*, suggests that the program places a "thematic emphasis on addiction, power and bodily exhaustion" in order to reflect the physical and mental experience of marathon viewing (2016: 105). Following McCormick, we can see how *Sense8* might similarly place a thematic emphasis on the experience of its marathon viewing—in this case, intense emotional connection. The connection between the sensates is an open affective bond, in which emotions and experiences are shared freely and smoothly throughout the cluster. There are no boundaries between the sensates, much in the same way that Netflix aims to lower the boundaries between episodes themselves, instead constructing a smooth affective flow. The structure of feeling between the sensates models the same structure of feeling the Netflix interface encourages between audience and cliffhanger: one of emotional, affective entanglement. Such emotional sharing is, of course, the key feature that distinguishes Homo sensorium from Homo sapiens. Yet within the program, this difference between the two evolutionary strands is presented in terms of value and quality. In S02:E02 "Who Am I?," Nomi and Amanita attend a university lecture by Professor Kolovi, an academic who had previous posited the existence of the Homo sensorium species. In his lecture, Kolovi suggests that early human ancestors such as the Neanderthals and Denisovans were killed in a "genocide" by Homo sapiens. Here, he echoes an earlier comment from villain Whispers, who describes Homo sapiens as "more violent, intolerant and possessive than any species in the history of the planet." The implication is that sensates, who possess a greater capacity for empathy, might be an *improvement* on the violent, intolerant Homo sapiens. In a direct echo of Netflix's own promotional rhetoric, evolution is not just a random matter of chance, but a search for a pinnacle, superior form of existence. *Sense8*, in working through these questions of consumption and affect and experience, cannot entirely divorce itself from the discourses of quality that the platform itself promotes.

It is important to remember that "binge viewing" is not an invention of either Netflix or streaming platforms: fan communities have engaged in marathon viewing practices for decades (Stevens 2021), and the packaging of television into DVD box sets in the 2000s also encouraged marathon consumption (Brunsdon 2010). It is also important to remember that television has always been understood as a medium of the present moment—namely, through its focus on live transmission (which I will discuss later in this chapter), and its ability to conflate different temporal modalities together (Caldwell 1995). And television has always promised emotional connection, aiming to foster what Karen Lury terms a "common culture of empathy" (2011: 201). In this sense, *Sense8* (and Netflix more generally) continues to point back to the things that television has always promised us, even while negotiating the demands and rhetoric of the digital platform. *Sense8* works through the implications of contemporary media consumption, narratively exploring issues of time, pace, and affect in ways that emphasize both foundational features of television and their reconfiguration in the Netflix interface.

Liveness and Simultaneity

Sense8 effectively presents a vision of community, a global network of people connected by shared empathy and emotional experience. This dream of a global, empathic community can be read as a direct response to the seeming fragmentation of community in the post-broadcast era. For much of the history of broadcast television, programs were broadcast as they were recorded, meaning that television became understood as a "live" medium. While scholars such as Jane Feuer (1983) have rightly argued that television's "liveness" is an ideological construction more than an essential component of the medium, liveness continues to function as a signifier of the televisual—of what television is and what it, uniquely, can do. This largely operates through what we can call copresence, or the way in which liveness allows members of an audience to feel connected: across a country or a region, all members of the audience watch a program at the exact same time. As John Ellis says, broadcasting facilitates a feeling of community, "a sense that others, anonymous though they may be, are sharing the same moment" (2000: 75). Post-broadcast television, in contrast, seemingly shatters this sense of "copresence." When an entire season of a program is released all at once (as per the Netflix model), it can be watched according to an individual viewer's preferred pace and time. The Netflix audience, then, may lack a sense of being part of a simultaneous, copresent viewing community.

However, Nick Couldry (2004) argues that "liveness" is a concept with broader cultural significance, which needs to be detached from its tight connection with broadcast media. He suggests that "liveness" shifts to adapt to new cultural forms: with the rise of the internet and mobile forms of media, we see multiple nodes of simultaneous communication and connection rather than a single, central, mode of transmission (2004: 356). Couldry identifies two key modes: first, "online liveness," in which online spaces create clusters of liveness across multiple sites and platforms, which exist in parallel with one another but do not necessarily intersect. Second, he identifies "group liveness," in which a social group can remain in constant contact with one another through digital technology. With a smartphone in your pocket you can take your social circle with you no matter where you travel, hence maintaining a constant sense of copresence. Both of these forms of liveness lack a single "institutional 'centre' of transmission," as Couldry suggests, but they still act as means of "coordinating communications and bodies across time and space which, like 'liveness' proper, involve (more or less) simultaneity" (2004: 356). In this sense, we can see that while it may take different forms, the cultural currency of liveness persists into the digital age and is extended geographically.

There are clear similarities with streaming audiences. As I suggested earlier, streaming platforms do not offer the same kind of copresence as broadcast television—the sheer number of offerings and the temporal flexibility of the platform mean that audiences lack a central structure of copresence. However, streaming audiences may still possess feelings of simultaneity, or of belonging to a viewing audience of a particular program, albeit one that is slightly more fragmented across both time and space. Such structures of feeling are encouraged by the Netflix interface itself. Categories of "Popular on Netflix," "Trending Now," and "Top 10 in [country] Today" all allude to the presence of a larger community of viewers.

These categories deliberately emphasize simultaneity through their focus on the present temporal moment—these programs are being watched "now" and "today," fostering some semblance of copresence. However, it is important to remember that these categories are tailored to individual viewers—my "Trending Now" category is not what is trending on Netflix overall, but among people with similar viewing histories to me. In this sense, the copresence facilitated by Netflix is more akin to the multiple clusters of "online liveness" that Couldry proposes, in which there are multiple, parallel bubbles of somewhat copresent viewers. Of course, this is not to suggest that liveness is the only means through which Netflix texts become meaningful to audiences—many Netflix originals have active and invested fan audiences that value repeated viewings. Yet it is clear that liveness retains some form of cultural cachet, as it remains a valuable experience that Netflix continues to embed within its interface, even if it takes a slightly different form to the more traditional understanding of the term.

These new ideas of liveness—as multiple, parallel, and transportable—are also akin to the structure of relation between the sensates. When Couldry suggests that digital technologies allow individuals to remain "continuously co present to each other even as they move independently across space" (2004: 357), he could equally be describing the connections between the sensates themselves. In the mythology of *Sense8*, there are three main abilities: visiting, sharing, and psychic connection. All of these abilities offer a sense of copresence, in which the sensates experience time, space, language, and physicality in a simultaneous fashion. Yet all of these experiences remain mediated, in that the sensates do not physically travel to other places and remain aware of their own bodies and of their own locations. The connections between the sensates thus act as a form of mediated copresence, in which the sensates are geographically isolated from one another but possess a feeling of simultaneous existence. And importantly, these experiences operate in parallel, smaller configurations as much as singular ones: the sensates share and visit in parallel configurations of pairs and threes, not just as the whole cluster. These mediated, fragmented, and granular forms of copresence directly model the "liveness" experienced by the Netflix audience, who experience overlapping connections with others while remaining within their own spatiotemporal sites.

As I suggested earlier in this chapter, the program foregrounds its spectacular group sharing/visiting scenes. However, throughout the two seasons, the most common connection scenes happen between pairs of sensates in moments of quiet conversation, not the group as a whole. In a particularly moving example from S01:E09 "Death Doesn't Let You Say Goodbye," Nomi and Lito "visit" one another as the latter sits in the Diego Rivera museum in Mexico City, in front of sketches of Rivera's *Man at the*

FIGURE 2.1 *Lito and Nomi share a mediated form of copresence.*

Crossroads mural, as illustrated in Figure 2.1. The two discuss their shared experiences of queerness, desire, fear, and shame. Throughout the scene, the location swaps between the museum and Nomi's living room in San Francisco, and the camera helps construct a spatial differentiation between the two locations, placed in front of the pair in the museum and behind them in the living room. By depicting two individuals in individual spaces, brought together in a shared experience, the scene depicts the mediated copresence that defines liveness.

In the following episode, we see a similar sequence between Kala and Capheus, who watch Van Damme's *Lionheart* (Lettich 1990) together, as we see in Figure 2.2. Again, the sequence focuses on two characters sitting side by side, connecting through their shared desire to move beyond the limitations of their own lives. While this sequence does not interweave the two locations—it begins with Kala on a park bench in Mumbai, and then shifts smoothly to Capheus's couch in Nairobi—it again emphasizes the way in which they remain both within their own spaces and times, and also that of their companion.

While there are many similar scenes throughout *Sense8*, I have drawn attention to these two specifically for what they have to offer our understanding of the program's industrial allegory. Both sequences deliberately present their characters connecting while seated in front of a form of art—Rivera's *Man at the Crossroads*, and Van Damme's *Lionheart* (1990). Both sequences pair domestic space with public space, and both organize the "visit" specifically around the media object—we spend more time with Rivera and *Lionheart* than we do in Nomi and Kala's locations. As

FIGURE 2.2 *Kala and Capheus's visit revolves around the television set.*

such, the sequences offer a direct presentation of the copresence promoted by Netflix: individuals in individual spaces and on individual couches, across public and private spaces, brought together in shared experiences that cohere around a particular media text. Once again *Sense8* narrativizes the conditions and experiences of its own platform through an emphasis on copresent communities that intersect in mediated, yet connected, ways. The message seems to be that, no matter where (or when) an individual might be, there is always a connection to be found in front of the screen. The program thus presents a new model of community, and in particular, *viewing communities*, in the Netflix era.

I have also focused on these two sequences for what they tell us about Netflix's relationship to broadcast television. It is important not to lose track of these ordinary scenes of companionship, particularly in a program that places a large emphasis on corporeal spectacle. And it is important to remember what they say about foundational televisual pleasures of community and belonging. As I suggested earlier, it is well-established within television studies that liveness is more an ideological structure of television than a purely technological or ontological one. Yet it is one that Netflix may have inherited, through the platform's focus on promoting structures of copresence and mediated community. Netflix is not a complete break with models of broadcast television but continues to draw from its foundational features: as Ramon Lobato reminds us, "Netflix may still feel like TV to viewers, and it relies on this familiar pleasure for its success" (2019: 34). To return to the evolution of narrative at the heart of both the platform and the program, *Sense8* presents an *evolution* of community and human connection, one that is both more fragmented yet all the more connected because of it. By working through the parameters of televisual liveness and copresent communities, the program interrogates how both liveness and the "televisual" continue to function in the age of streaming media.

Reaching for the World

Of course, the copresent community in *Sense8* is not a local group, or even a national community, but precisely a global one. The eight sensates are located in eight different cities across Europe, Asia, Africa, and North America. The program was filmed in these different cities as a measure of authenticity, and while the majority of the dialogue is in English, there are moments of multilingualism. *Sense8* is very clearly about global connection, and in particular, about the universal experiences that we share no matter where we live—emotion, desire, sex, and love. And in this way the program is very clearly, once again, a narrative of its own industrial conditions—it is not hard to see why Netflix may have chosen a program with such a global imagination for one of its first originals, a program that is so obviously about transnational connection and global connection. As a so-called "global" platform, Netflix promises both universality and diversity: transforming global distribution flows so that texts are accessible at the same time in every place, and widening access to a broader range of world media. Ramon Lobato notes that "global simultaneity" is a distinctive feature of Netflix, particularly in contrast to historical (and more sequential) patterns of global distribution (2019: 69). Similarly, Mareike Jenner argues that the Netflix audience is "not simply an accumulation of 'fragments' of different national audiences," but a transnational collective that operates across multiple zones of consumption (2018: 251). Once again, *Sense8* narrativizes the particular aims and affordances of Netflix—in this case, its presentation as a global platform.

Sense8's opening credits offer a visual depiction of this global ambition. Jonathan Gray describes title sequences as "offering 'proper interpretations' of genre and character," suggesting that their repetition works to "reaffirm what a show is about, how its characters are related, and how we 'should' make sense of them" (2010: 74–6). *Sense8*'s opening credits work on a double level, affirming not just the concerns of the program but also those of its platform itself. The credits consist of a rapid montage of people and places around the world, beginning with slower-paced wide shots of the eight cities featured in the program, then gradually transitioning to rapid close-ups that depict people and scenes of everyday life. Designed by Karin Winslow Wachowski, the sequence can be read as an exhilarating kaleidoscope of people and places, and a multicultural, queer vision of the world. The credits clearly reiterate the program's message of universality in diversity, or the celebration of both difference and commonality. Yet the sequence is also overwhelmingly an experience of *movement*: almost every shot contains movement, whether of the camera, the natural world and weather, transportation, or the movement of people. It is here, I would argue, that we can identify another parallel between the program and the platform: the credits mirror the experience of the Netflix interface itself. In her work on media interfaces, Lisa Parks conceptualizes the interface as a "kinetic screen," arguing that the predominant experience of an interface is one of movement: scrolling, surfing, browsing, and so on (2004: 54). We see this clearly in the Netflix interface, which consists of content moving at different scales, from thumbnails we scroll through to the trailers that begin to play when we hover over them. In terms of the qualities of the kinetic experience, this flurry of movement at different speeds and scales mirrors what we see in the *Sense8* credits. These credits can be read as a rapid scan through a catalogue of experiences and places, almost a browsing, perhaps, of the world. Both Netflix and *Sense8* thus promise a feeling of travel through a cornucopia of image and stories across the world, and the structure of feeling embedded in the Netflix interface—of the multiplicity and kineticism of the world presented for our consumption—parallels that of the *Sense8* opening credits.

This vision of global universality is, of course, a somewhat utopian dream. Both *Sense8* and Netflix aim for global reach yet continue to struggle to truly transcend the national. Ramon Lobato presents a very thorough analysis of the ways in which Netflix remains locally specific, from its catalog to its regulatory functions. As he says, Netflix may be global but it "does not envelop the world evenly," remaining caught by local content regulations and national distribution agreements, which control what the platform can host (2019: 71). The content that can be distributed globally is, of course, the platform's originals, which are dominated by American productions. *Sense8*'s global scope can be understood as similarly uneven. In a widely circulated blog post for *Nerds of Color*, Claire Light suggests that the programs' "depiction of life in non-western countries is built out of stereotypes, and ... suffused with tourist-board clichés" (2015). Both platform and program may promise to give us access to the world, but this continues to operate through Hollywood-tinted glasses.

Indeed, both *Sense8* and Netflix have specifically been criticized over the question of monolingualism. Despite sharing an outward looking dream of a global community (and a global catalog), the English language remains by far the automatic and dominant presentation. Cáel M. Keegan notes that the program's utopian image of global connectivity is "softened by the prosthetic use of English," thus catering overwhelmingly to the comfort zones of Anglophone viewers (2016: 609). For while the sensates converse with one another in different languages, and occasionally show moments of self-reflexive knowledge of their multilingualism, the narrative always presents their psychic link in English. There are pragmatic reasons for this—namely the costs of dialect coaches and translation services in an already expensive program—but the message is clear: if the sensates draw attention to the universality of experience and emotion, then they also imply that English is the universal language. An identical kind of linguistic dominance happens at the level of the interface itself. In a *Variety* exposé on the "secrets" of Netflix, it emerged that Netflix deliberately presents non-English programs (such as the German drama *Dark* and the Brazilian science fiction *3%*) in their dubbed format to Western audiences, rather than their original language with subtitles (Roettgers 2018). Despite audiences stating during consumer testing that they preferred subtitles, Netflix's own data suggested that viewers were more likely to finish dubbed series. Just like *Sense8*, then, Netflix itself continues to suggest that moments of transcultural encounter require English translation. The fact that the very same critique is leveled at both the narrative program and the platform to which it belongs furthers my argument: the two can be read as invested in similar values, properties, and aims.

Of course, it is too simple to suggest that with the rise of Netflix, television suddenly becomes "global." As the quintessential "window on the world," television has always been a source for popular knowledge about the world, and as the archetypal "global village," television has always promised to bring the whole world together within the intimate ties of community and belonging. Netflix's aim toward the global, while ostensibly a means of distinguishing itself from ordinary, "national" television, is thus simultaneously an extension of television's promise to act as a window on the world. Yet television's global reach has always been something of an imperfect one. The history of global television is one in which international exports are localized and distribution flows are uneven, suggesting that the medium continues to be particularly meaningful at a national and local level. Lobato astutely points out that Netflix follows the same pattern as earlier "revolutionary" television services such as cable: a push toward global universality, and a pull back toward the value of local specificity (2019: 63). *Sense8*'s uneven reach toward globality again demonstrates how the program negotiates its position between the industrial models of streaming television and the legacy of broadcast television.

To return to Hastings's CES keynote, the event marked the debut of a promotional trailer celebrating Netflix's global rollout. The trailer consists of a montage of clips from its various programs, including *Sense8*, edited together into an uplifting message of community and togetherness. Here, Netflix turns to its own storytelling in order to communicate its own values and qualities, suggesting that its storytelling is, in effect, a story of the platform itself. Yet too often, the stories that Netflix tells of itself remain one-directional stories, focused on emphasizing its difference and its novelty, and a linear evolutionary narrative of progress. It is important to tell a different story: to continue to read Netflix as part of the history of television, and to continue to understand it through the foundational features of the medium.

Sense8 offers a key lesson here. It does gesture toward the future of audiovisual media, through its emphasis on different configurations of serial storytelling, its reconfiguration of liveness, and its reach for global address. And it simultaneously shows us what television has always done and what it has always offered its audience, whether the promise of emotion, of the present, of liveness, of community, or of access to the world. These properties may look somewhat different in the age of streaming television, yet they remain part of a continuity of television history, rather than a mode of experience to be entirely left behind in leaps and bounds. And this is what *Sense8* ultimately tells us, in the program's reminder that difference is less important than the threads of commonality that bind the world together.

Works Cited

Brunsdon, C. (2010), "Bingeing on Box-Sets: The National and the Digital in Television Crime Drama," in J. Gripsrud (ed.), *Relocating Television: Television in the Digital Context*, 63–75, Abingdon: Routledge.

Butler, J. G. (2012), *Television: Critical Methods and Applications*, New York: Routledge.

Caldwell, J. T. (1995), *Televisuality: Style, Crisis and Authority in American Television*, New Brunswick, NJ: Rutgers University Press.

CES (2016), "Reed Hastings, Netflix – Keynote 2016," YouTube, January 7. Available online: https://www.youtube.com/watch?v=l5R3E6jsICA&t=196s.

Couldry, N. (2004), "Liveness, 'Reality', and the Mediated Habitus from Television to the Mobile Phone," *Communication Review*, 7 (1): 353–61.

Ellis, J. (2000), *Seeing Things: Television in the Age of Uncertainty*, London: I.B. Tauris.

Feuer, J. (1983), "The Concept of Live Television: Ontology as Ideology," in E. A. Kaplan (ed.), *Regarding Television: Critical Approaches—An Anthology*, 12–22, Frederick, MD: University Publications of America.

Gray, J. (2010), *Show Sold Separately: Promos, Spoilers, and Other Media Paratexts*, New York: New York University Press.

Jenner, M. (2018), *Netflix and the Reinvention of Television*, Cham, Switzerland: Palgrave MacMillan.

Keegan, C. M. (2016), "Tongues without Bodies: The Wachowskis' *Sense8*," *Transgender Studies Quarterly*, 3 (3–4): 605–10.

Light, C. (2015), "*Sense8* and the Failure of the Global Imagination," *Nerds of Color*, June 10. Available online: https://thenerdsofcolor.org/2015/06/10/sense8-and-the-failure-of-global-imagination/.

Lobato, R. (2019), *Netflix Nations: The Geography of Digital Distribution*, New York: New York University Press.

Lury, K. (2011), "The Loss of the Contingent in Digital Television," in J. Bennett and N. Strange (eds.), *Television as Digital Media*, 181–203, Durham, NC: Duke University Press.

McCormick, C. (2016), "'Forward Is the Battle Cry': Binge-Viewing Netflix's *House of Cards*," in K. McDonald and D. Smith-Rowsey (eds.), *The Netflix Effect: Technology and Entertainment in the 21st Century*, 101–16, New York: Bloomsbury.

McLuhan, M., and Fiore, Q. (1967), *The Medium Is the Massage: An Inventory of Effects*, London: Penguin.

Mittell, J. (2006), "Narrative Complexity in Contemporary American Television," *Velvet Light Trap*, 58, 29–40.

Newman, M. Z. (2006), "From Beats to Arcs: Toward a Poetics of Television Narrative," *Velvet Light Trap*, 58, 16–28.

Parks, L. (2004), "Kinetic Screens: Epistemologies of Movement at the Interface," in N. Couldry and A. McCarthy (eds.), *Mediaspace: Place, Scale and Culture in a Media Age*, 37–57, Abingdon: Routledge.

Piper, H. (2016), "Broadcast Drama and the Problem of Television Aesthetics: Home, Nation, Universe," *Screen*, 57 (2): 163–83.

Roettgers, J. (2018), "Netflix's Secrets to Success: Six Cell Towers, Dubbing and More," *Variety*, March 8. Available online: https://variety.com/2018/digital/news/netflix-success-secrets-1202721847/.

Shimpach, S. (2010), *Television in Transition*, Malden: Wiley-Blackwell.

Spangler, T. (2015), "Netflix '*Sense8*' Thriller from Wachowskis Pirated More Than 500,000 Times Since Debut," *Variety*, 8 June. Available online: https://variety.com/2015/digital/news/netflix-sense8-piracy-wachowskis-1201514526/.

Stevens, C. (2021), "Historical Binge-Watching: Marathon Viewing on Videotape," in M. Jenner (ed.), *Binge-Watching and Contemporary Television Research*. Edinburgh: Edinburgh University Press.

Turek, A., and R. Moynihan (2018), "Netflix's Reed Hastings Tells Business Insider Why He Doesn't Care about the Cannes Film Festival," *Business Insider*, April 27. Available online: https://www.businessinsider.com/head-of-netflix-we-have-improved-television-2018-4?IR=T.

Turner, G., and A. C.Pertierra (2013), *Locating Television: Zones of Consumption*, Abingdon: Routledge.

Williams, R. (1974), *Television: Technology and Cultural Form*, London: Fontana.

3

Skip Intro? *Sense8*'s Title Sequence

James Walters

While location shooting was taking place for the first season of *Sense8*, Karin Winslow (who is married to cocreator Lana Wachowski) journeyed with a camera assistant in a rental car to gather footage for the show's title sequence. As Winslow explains: "My directive from Lana was to go out and describe each country by what you see; find the nuances, find the food, find what people are doing, get a feel for the place. ... It was one of the funnest [*sic*] things I've ever done in my life" (Rackl 2015). We might find cause to commend Winslow's enjoyment of her task, given the challenging parameters that she was working within as she sought to present cultures in authentic detail but, at the same time, deliver only brief, snapshot portraits of those places and people. Furthermore, Winslow's work on the *Sense8* title sequence might be seen to provide a particularly potent encapsulation of the complex relationships that title sequences can have with their programs. They are fundamentally bound to the thematic concerns of the main text (with Winslow presumably possessing a strong appreciation of *Sense8*'s central interests) and, at the same time, they have often been created away from that main text to greater and lesser extents (in many cases, handed over to an entirely independent production team). As a consequence, the nature of the relationship between television programs and their title sequences becomes a matter of critical interest as they are both unified and distinct aesthetic elements. If we take that critical investment further still, we can consider the extent to which *Sense8* and its title sequence correspond with or diverge from each other in terms of any claims for value and achievement that we might seek to articulate. Can the title sequence be incorporated straightforwardly into an overall evaluation of the show as a consistent and complementary element or are there useful tensions to be explored?

Valuing Title Sequences

Before focusing specifically on *Sense8*, it is worth considering the status of title sequence analysis in television criticism more generally. Jason Jacobs provides an extended comparative analysis of title sequences from a collection of medical dramas—*ER* (NBC, 1994–2009), *Casualty* (BBC, 1986–), *Cardiac Arrest* (BBC, 1994–6), and *Chicago Hope* (CBS, 1994–2000) —and sets out a feature of his concerns in the following way:

> They are something like the covers of books or magazines. Title sequences have communicative and expressive functions; our judgement of them will not need to spend much time on the former since a basic competent rendering of the show's title and a repetition of its music is likely to be successful in this respect. But in terms of expressive content, judgement is likely to go beyond the acknowledgement of mere functionality. (Jacobs 2001: 438)

For Jacobs, title sequences have the potential to bring focus to some key tensions between, on the one hand, a traditional emphasis on television's functionality and, on the other, an appreciation of the medium's rich capacity for creative expression. He builds his analyses of the respective title sequences upon questions of value and, as a consequence, gets to the central question of whether they are any good or not. This concern, it should be noted, was not voiced with excessive frequency in television studies in 2001 and yet, within the industry, title sequences did receive appraisal and judgment. Indeed, the Primetime Emmy Awards have honored Outstanding Main Title Design since the 1970s (albeit under various award categories over those years). Elsewhere, Jacobs's line of inquiry has been followed by scholars who make title sequences a sole focus. David Johansson, for example, devotes himself to a sustained and detailed analysis of *The Sopranos*' (HBO, 1999–2007) famous title sequence, which he regards as "a 'road movie' in miniature" that merits a thorough thematic deconstruction (Johansson 2006: 31). As a means of moving toward a consideration of the *Sense8* sequence, it is useful to note the ways in which Johansson sets out the terms for his approach, the kinds of references he draws upon in building his case, and the relationships he establishes between this title sequence and the television viewer:

> In opera the overture introduces conflicts, sets up issues and foreshadows themes, establishing patterns and motifs which will run through the work until they collide, crash and climax, ending in resolution. Similarly, the title

sequence of *The Sopranos* sets the mood and tone of the show, functions as prologue, and becomes epilogue, the tag by which the viewer remembers the whole series. Specifically, the word "overture" derives from the Latin *apertura*, source of the English word "aperture," suggesting an engagement of the audience as deep or deeper than in the operatic sense. That is, in order to see through an aperture the audience must actively participate, as if leaning forward to spy through a peephole which, although small, provides a wide-angle view of a world outside the familiar door, a world as alien as it is hostile. Impelled by curiosity, the audience pays attention to the opening credits so as to get a glimpse through this *apertura*, this peephole, to see something forbidden, illegal, criminal. (Johansson 2006: 27–8)

The allusion to operatic overture at the beginning of this account serves an effective critical purpose as a means of establishing a framing device for the themes that Johansson seeks to pursue in his evaluation of the title sequence from *The Sopranos*: that it performs an equivalent structural role and function (as well as, perhaps, acknowledging the relationship of the show's title to the musical form). It is inevitably the case, however, that the mention of opera in relation to television also serves a purpose of implicitly elevating (or attempting to elevate) the cultural status of the latter to somewhere near that enjoyed by the former, with opera susceptible to a range of connotations associated with notions of refinement, connoisseurship, and elitism. And yet, it is not the case that Johansson seeks to persuade us that *all* television title sequences reach and maintain these high standards of artistic expression. Rather, it is clear that he identifies and holds up *The Sopranos* as a singular case that rewards special attention and, indeed, he finishes his article by extolling "the brilliance of *The Sopranos* title sequence" (2006: 36). Given that *The Sopranos*' reputation as a work of considerable ambition and achievement was already firmly entrenched by the mid-2000s (with Johansson's chapter even appearing in an edited collection dedicated entirely to the program), the discussion seeks to explore the extent to which the title sequence measures up to the already-acknowledged accomplishments of the program. With this in mind, Johansson sets out his position early: "By examining this title sequence, this overture and frame, we may come to an appreciation of the art at the very heart of *The Sopranos*" (2006: 28). From this perspective, it could be said that those few minutes or even seconds before a program "starts" once again have the potential to become pivotal in our critical understanding and appreciation of television.

Streaming Sequences

Reflecting on the status that title sequences might be afforded in relation to programming in general, and series such as *Sense8* specifically, it is inevitable that we should also acknowledge the ways in which the standing of title sequences has changed as the medium (and, more specifically, the ways in which the medium is accessed) has evolved fairly rapidly. Thus far, our discussion has made assumptions about title sequences that rely upon the more traditional model of viewer engagement outlined by Annette Davison:

> Title sequences also enable viewers to ready themselves for the move to a period of focus and engagement with a show. Given that many serials are originally broadcast in a weekly pattern (same day/time each week), such preparations may also become ritualized, born of anticipation and excitement for a planned period of escapism and/or engagement. Indeed, anecdotal evidence suggests that for many viewers a title sequence is part of this ritualized experience. (Davison 2013: 148)

Davison follows this description with an acknowledgment of the layers of choice that have gradually been built into television viewing experiences, mentioning on-demand services, PVRs, DVDs, and the range of screens on which television can be watched such as computers, tablets, and phones (2013: 148–9). In doing so, she demonstrates a clear awareness that the place of title sequences within the scheduled or ritualized experiences of audiences was becoming fragmented and dispersed as those audiences enjoyed the freedom to develop new schedules and rituals due to consumer choice continuing to expand. As a result, Davison's account anticipates the next phase of this diversification as corporations and streaming services such as Netflix, Amazon, Hulu, and Apple began to exert ever-greater influence over the production and distribution of television content, leading to the simultaneous release of episodes that disrupted the "weekly patterns" that were previously in place. Kathleen Williams notes that the widening out of viewing opportunities has not led to the demise of the title sequence but, instead, may result in more complex configurations of viewer experience and engagement:

> Netflix's brand imprint is dominant in the title sequences for shows such as *Narcos* (2015–) and *Orange is the New Black* (2013–). However, and defying the streaming services' promotional use of title sequences for their shows, the technological and social features of streaming may lead to different patterns of consumption. In the course of a binge-watching marathon, the viewer, whether on streaming services or on DVD, can of course skip title sequences, but these are still something they might happen to encounter several times in one day. (Williams 2016: 63)

It is not difficult to recognize the relative disparity between Davison's description of title sequences enabling viewers to "ready themselves for the move to a period of focus and engagement with a show" and Williams's acknowledgment that they may be skipped or that any encounter with them might be happenchance. In terms of Netflix, these latter scenarios have certainly increased in likelihood since the "skip intro" button was introduced in 2017. Intended to further ease the binge-watching experience, this feature effectively reframed title sequences as superfluous elements that can be dismissed in an instant. It is perhaps unsurprising that a Netflix show like *Ozark* (2017–) should opt for a brief, cryptic, title card format, given the reshaping of the television landscape and the diminishment of traditional title sequences within certain viewing contexts. Programs appearing on Netflix do still possess discernible title sequences, of course, whether they are newly made or exist within the archive of past shows that are available to stream. *Orange Is the New Black* (2013–19), for example, features a sequence that runs to over one minute and achieves a striking tonal complexity. It is dominated by a rapid succession of extreme close-up shots of female former prison inmates' faces, focusing on their mouths and their eyes as they look into the camera.

This series of portraits creates an intensified connection between viewer and individual as they simulate reciprocity: each looks into each other's eyes. This intimacy involves both empathy and resistance as the viewer's gaze is returned and the object of our gaze is given agency within the constructed relationship. The sequence invites engagement with the faces on-screen, but at the same time challenges us to consider what we are looking at, what we think we see, by returning our gaze. As a consequence, the titles emphasize the impossibility of understanding another human through their outward appearance alone, and this theme is encapsulated through the rapid transitioning from one face to the next (and in the accompanying Regina Spektor song "You've Got Time" whose tone and structure balances vulnerability and defiance, aggression and introspection). In this way, the title sequence for *Orange Is the New Black* can be seen to express certain themes that will be taken up and expanded upon within the show. However, the skippability of such title sequences means that anyone selecting them via Netflix has the opportunity to either watch them in their entirety or click forward and past them. Within this context, we are therefore entitled to ask what critical merit can exist in staying with *Sense8*'s title sequence, reinstating it as part of an overall viewing experience, and revisiting it in detail. Unlike the examples mentioned thus far, I want to explore some of the tensions that exist between the title sequence of *Sense8* and aspects of the program itself and, as a result, consider their relationship to one another within broader critical appraisals of the show.

Sense8's Title Sequence

The sequence begins with a sustained, electronic, major chord as the title cards "A Netflix Original Series" and "Sense8" slowly fade in and out of the darkness. We cut to a gentle traveling aerial shot of the Golden Gate bridge at sunrise. The pace of the camera movement and the tone of the soundtrack create a sense of a world gradually emerging and, given our high angle as we survey an iconic landmark, we might initially take this to be a conventional establishing shot. That sense is disrupted, however, as the scene changes abruptly to frame a new skyline, a Chicago cityscape; the cut timed almost precisely with the introduction of a piano chord on the soundtrack. The idea that those two locations were linked dualistically in the montage is almost immediately discarded as we cut again to a faster-traveling camera skimming across a natural ravine outside Reykjavik and then to another shot of a city, this time the banks of the River Thames in central London. The piano continues under these transitions, becoming a five-chord phrase that aligns rhythmically with some of the cuts—a further five chords taking us through yet more city locations: Berlin, Nairobi, Mexico City, and Seoul. From here, the momentum that the ascending piano chords and the sharp shifts in geography have created increases as sound and image begin to deepen and intensify. More instruments, both electronic and acoustic, are added to the orchestration, combining in a new minor key arrangement that gradually works in a relentless background pulse, as well as introducing a series of melodies and countermelodies that intertwine, running into, over and away from each other. On-screen, the balanced visual repetition of sweeping aerial shots is broken apart as briefly held images of neon signs, elephants, afternoon tea, a giraffe, religious trinkets, sculptures, horses, cricket, sheep, a volcano, zebras, and streetcars become interwoven with more skylines, bridges, and landmarks.

There is of course, a narrative rationale that links these images to *Sense8*'s plot: they are taken from the nine cities where the series was mainly shot: Mumbai, San Francisco, Chicago, London, Seoul, Berlin, Nairobi, Mexico City, and Reykjavik. The sequence itself, however, works against any formality inherent in that structure, creating a frantic and sometimes chaotic set of associations between images and repeatedly pulling back from imposing an interpretative logic on those relationships as each scene is rapidly replaced by the next in a widely varying assortment of scales, styles, and tones. The music, likewise, resists settling upon a particular mood as different instruments and melodies combine and compete to invite a whole range including danger, fear, excitement, contemplation, joy, and hope. As the sequence progresses, individual people and groups become more prominent, intercut with structures and landmarks, sometimes aware of the camera, sometimes oblivious as they are caught up in the activity of their own lives. Again, the images of faces and bodies are sustained only briefly as we gain fleeting access to these glimpses of human life, as shown in Figure 3.1, and, indeed, queer identities that are rarely integrated into equivalent overviews of people and cultures in mainstream popular television.

FIGURE 3.1 *Fleeting bodies and faces offer glimpses of human life.*

FIGURE 3.2 *A catch of breath before the episode "starts."*

Finally, with the combination of shots and sound reaching a cacophonous crescendo, the pace drains from the sequence and we are left with a single, low note on the soundtrack and a slow-traveling aerial shot of San Francisco, moving with the mist as it rolls in off the hills, as seen in Figure 3.2. The flow of the water vapor is reminiscent of a gentle expulsion of breath and we are released from the frenetic, claustrophobic and, indeed, breathless aesthetics of the opening sequence. This new opportunity to "catch our breath" in a moment of calm tranquility might reinforce the disorientating onslaught of audiovisual detail that we have been drawn into up to that point. It may be a moment to ask what we just saw and heard.

One of the title sequence's achievements could lie in its resistance to providing any definitive answer to such a question. The credits are inherently ambiguous, involving the viewer to a great extent in the processes of developing associations and resonances. With such an array of images on offer, delivered at speed, we are bound to create relationships between them that are particular to each of us, as some register more prominently and some are lost in the fast-flowing montage. Similarly, tonal aspects of the densely layered soundtrack have the capacity to suggest sets of connotations that differ from viewer to viewer, depending on what we each pick out. And, of course, it is also the case that our individual interpretations of the title sequence might reshape and recalibrate through repeat viewings, as previously unnoticed aspects suddenly come into focus while others diminish. In these respects, the sequence offers an experience that is especially interactive as it leaves open the possibilities for finding meaning and significance. Central tensions and contradictions are balanced within its construction, as the sequence highlights the seemingly boundless access that television can provide to people and locations across the globe and, at the same time, emphasizes the fundamental limits that are always intrinsic to televisual representation: that the reality of people and places will always be inaccessible as they are presented in fragments and fitted into overarching aesthetic patterns. Even as television makes the world visually available to an increasing degree—we can ride above the clouds, make our way through market stalls, or stand on the edge of volcanoes—it is restricted to a particular view of that world. As the title sequence pushes into societies from around the world, it quickly and repeatedly snatches the experience of them away from us, reinforcing again and again that we can never fully know these people, these places. We can only make a set of contrived connections which are, themselves, susceptible to changes and fluctuations as we watch the titles anew. It is not difficult to expand this theme to incorporate a broader critique of Western tourism, which is often built upon transient encounters with exactly the kinds of landmarks and cultures that appear in the title sequence, and which frequently offers restricted engagements amid apparently limitless travel opportunities. In this sense, the structure of the *Sense8* title sequence mimics and, perhaps, mocks the cascade of snapshots a wealthy Westerner might generate in their lifetime, and the experiences we might claim for ourselves. Such activities and attitudes possess underlying political implications, as Deborah Shaw makes clear: "There is a power dynamic in the tourist gaze which often rests upon an assumed viewer of the developed world observing a 'third world other' or objects of that culture which are often deemed to be more desirable than the people themselves" (Shaw 2011: 18).

The *Sense8* title sequence might therefore be seen to invest in the notion that global communities will always remain profoundly unknowable and inaccessible despite the efforts of television to know and access them. As a result, it exposes the limits of the medium and equally, perhaps, the limits of our ambitions as viewers. Do we care whether a fictional drama represents cultures sensitively, or are we happy to accept the snapshots? The frenetic rhythm of the editing and the discordant complexity of the soundtrack emphasizes the impossibility of forcing coherent relationships between cultures through audiovisual technique, reminding us emphatically that any meaning is, to a significant degree, constructed through our interpretation of those rapid flashes of faces and places. The sequence is bold: confronting our expectations and challenging them as it refuses to settle into an easy or straightforward pattern, yet possessing a flow and movement that maintains its status as an engaging aesthetic event. If, as Davison suggests, title sequences prepare us for "a period of focus and engagement with a show," we might feel entitled to question whether *Sense8* will meet and expand upon these provocative concerns within a similarly ambiguous aesthetic style.

Sense8 and Its World

There is no great novelty in pointing out that *Sense8* runs into significant difficulties as it attempts to portray multiple identities, cultures, and nationalities. As several contributors to this volume examine, the decision to make English the default language of communication in the program self-evidently places restrictions on representation, not only in terms of inadvertent cultural imperialism but also by imposing an additional challenge on those actors whose first language is not English when they are tasked with creating nuance and subtlety in their verbal expression. This at least curtails efforts to afford diverse nationalities a voice within *Sense8*, given that some cast members are not free to communicate in their native language, and a potential imbalance is thus introduced between actors, characters, and nationalities.

Such issues become more acute when taken alongside the program's set of broad racial stereotypes, which again creates a series of careless divisions between characters that *Sense8* ostensibly seeks to unite. Andrea Merodeadora attends to the relatively complex narratives white characters are afforded in the show, noting that

> the characters of color don't get these luxuries. When you boil down their stories to the basics you get that the Indian woman's plot is reduced to loveless marriage and struggles with sex; the Korean woman gets patriarchal oppression and martial arts; for the Black Kenyan man we have poverty, AIDS and gang wars; and Lito's (and the other Mexican

characters') story revolves around the machismo and homophobia of Mexican culture. (Merodeadora 2017)

While we may find legitimate reasons to query such a "boiled down" appraisal of television narratives, Merodeadora's account nevertheless outlines some of the fundamental errors in judgment that *Sense8* commits as it embarks on a project to draw together its international storylines. It is also the case, however, that the program struggles more broadly in its attempts to represent human behaviors and interactions convincingly. Given our focus on *Sense8*'s title sequence, it seems appropriate to look toward moments in the program that occur immediately after the titles. S01:E08 "We Will All Be Judged by the Courage of Our Hearts," for example, follows its title sequence with a shot of Nomi and Amanita sitting on a hillside as they gaze across the glimmering lights of the San Francisco skyline at dawn. The scene is held for a few moments in three still, sustained shots, with only birdsong forming a gentle soundtrack. Nomi's voice breaks in: "Do you know that feeling when you're sitting in a movie theater and everyone's laughing at something and you just don't get it?" Mid-way through this sentence, we cut to a two-shot from behind the couple, capturing Nomi's turn to Amanita as she finishes speaking. Amanita replies: "Like, all the time," and Nomi continues: "This is where I'm at right now. I'm sitting looking at the sunrise, the city, and I'm wondering: how can something still look so beautiful after we saw what we saw? It just doesn't seem right." Amanita shakes her head gently and concludes: "No, it doesn't." They lean into each and watch the sunlight reach across the city.

This short scene encapsulates *Sense8*'s preference for overt delivery of information over ambiguous portrayals that might require the show's audience to interpret character behavior to a substantial degree. In this way, it departs from the stylistic approach of the title sequence (whose brevity makes ambiguous portrayals not only a creative choice but also a practical necessity). Nomi's speech moves from the relatively opaque—the line about the movie theater—to a straightforward declaration of how she feels: how can the world still be beautiful when she has experienced brutality? (The pair witnessed a series of murders in the climactic finale of the previous episode.) The conversation follows a repeating pattern in *Sense8*, whereby characters frequently sit or stand together and feed each other unequivocal information about themselves: their lives, their thoughts, their feelings. It reverses the standard wisdom of "show don't tell" in storytelling, which was an underlying facet of the title sequence's form, and instead crams the dialogue with information relay, leaving little room for conjecture or speculation. We almost always know why characters act as they do, because they will often tell us directly. In this scene, however, we might take time to reflect upon what exactly we are being told. The experience of sitting in a movie theater and genuinely not understanding why everyone is laughing seems highly particular—different to, say, understanding why something is comical but not finding it funny—and would possibly indicate that someone simply lacks a sense of humor. Perhaps it is an indication of Nomi and Amanita's intense affinity that they both experience this "all the time." But even this moment of empathy registers as implausible: do they both keep going to see funny movies and sit in stony silence while all around them *everyone* is laughing, because they just don't *understand* comedy? A wider point is clearly being reached for in this interaction, as we are surely meant to understand Nomi and Amanita's specific sense of otherness (being out of place in a cinema audience) as an allusion to their lived experience as a transgender lesbian and Black lesbian, respectively, in heteronormative society. The exploration of these important themes in *Sense8* is crucial (not least because of their sparse representation in mainstream television). And yet, any symbolism that can be drawn from the characters' dialogue relies upon those words fundamentally making sense as coherent interactions within the fictional world of the television drama, whereas the significance of Nomi and Amanita's profound sense of otherness is built upon the flimsy foundation of a dubious conversation about mismatched responses to comedy in cinema. Moreover, we might find further cause to question the link that is being made with divergent responses to comedy and the disparity Nomi experiences between the beauty of the city and the violence that she witnessed earlier. There is a kind of broad relationship in terms of binary dissonance (humor/non-humor, beauty/brutality), but the sensation of being unable to understand a joke does not connect naturally with a struggle to comprehend the world's capacity for both grace and cruelty. Indeed, the connection seems forced and contrived, as though two separate points have been joined together inelegantly in the writing, which has obvious implications for any sense of a character's status as a living, thinking person within a fictional world. Ultimately, the scene appears to be reaching for significance at the expense of coherence, whereas coherence is the prerequisite of meaning and, in turn, significance. If the words that the characters speak only make sense because they symbolize a wider or more profound experience, then the internal credibility of the scene is compromised. At a basic level, the conversation has to make sense within the fictional world's moment, as well as alluding to crucial issues of belonging and identity.

As the opening to a new episode, this scene might be seen to fall short in terms of setting up new concerns, advancing the narrative or challenging an audience's perception of events. Moreover, in attempting to declare something about the characters' perspectives and emotions, the program equips them with dialogue that lacks credibility within a fictional reality, compromising the plausibility of these individuals as intricate, complex human beings. We might therefore question why the scene exists at all, were it not for the fact that the reason becomes apparent as we transition to the next scene. The sound of extra-diegetic laughter breaks into the shot of Nomi and Amanita and then we cut to a traveling dolly shot of cinema audience members laughing enthusiastically, some almost uncontrollably, as they watch a film (whose soundtrack can be heard under their laughter). As the camera scans the audience, we find Kala sitting among her family. She is visibly upset and her emotional disquiet is amplified as we cut to a close-up of her face that captures the tears blurring her vision and running down her cheeks (following a reverse shot to the cinema screen that reveals a comic Bollywood movie to be the source of everyone else's enjoyment). As a result, Nomi's peculiar expressive choices in her earlier scene (and Amanita's responses) only really make proper sense in the context of Kala's experience in the following scene: that there is connection between these characters that derives from *Sense8*'s central narrative premise of extraordinary empathy existing between eight characters (which, of course, include Nomi and Kala). That is to say, Nomi's dialogue has clearly been written with Kala's following scene in mind. This kind of reverse-coherence undermines the authenticity of Nomi and Amanita's thoughts and feelings, however, exposing the extent to which they have been contrived only to fit an overarching rhyming pattern. On their own terms, Nomi's words possess sparse coherent meaning and, indeed, constitute a somewhat misplaced reflection on her situation. As a result, we may lose confidence in the notion that Nomi is a complex, idiosyncratic person inhabiting this fictional world precisely because the two scenes have so overtly and awkwardly equipped the character with words that are revealed to be a somewhat trite linking device.

It is hard to imagine any equivalent multicharacter television drama risking the exposure of its plotting in such obvious fashion, and yet the characters in *Sense8* frequently behave in ways that compromise the inner consistency of their fictional world precisely because their actions are contorted to fit a broader, restrictive narrative structure. The Nomi/Kala connection exemplifies this tendency, but it hardly seems worth diluting character authenticity in the pursuit of such a superficial connecting of scenes. Indeed, Nomi's emotional reflections are arguably weakened by the insertion of the foreshadowing device, and Kala's desolation is undermined as it is revealed to be part of a fairly banal causal link. Crucially, in moving from the fleeting ambiguity of the title sequence to more sustained, intimate portrayals of individuals on-screen, *Sense8* often fails to imbue its characters with nuance, subtlety, and complexity as it reduces their dialogue to the straightforward relaying of thoughts and emotions, forgoes their internal coherence in the pursuit of wider allusions, or exposes their contrivance by making them functional links within a linear causal chain. We might suggest, therefore, that the title sequence's lightness of touch has been replaced by a more heavy-handed approach.

Conclusion

As mentioned previously, I have chosen these scenes because they occur immediately after *Sense8*'s title sequence in the episode and it is my contention that this proximity provides an illustration of the ways in which the themes and concerns of the title sequence—its commitment to ambiguity and its rejection of rigid causal structures—are not taken up consistently in the show. Indeed, *Sense8*'s episodes generally take a different route by opting for the explicit relay of information and by reducing character behavior to functional plot points. My tentative suggestion would be that this is representative of certain shortcomings in the program's overall design—that it actually struggles to match the ambition and achievement demonstrated in the title sequence. A pronounced tension exists, therefore, between *Sense8*'s title sequence and its main narrative, given their disparate approaches to the challenges of representing individuals and communities in television. Unlike the examples described earlier in this chapter, *Sense8* offers the prospect of a dissonant relationship across title sequence and program, revealing a set of divergent aims and accomplishments. This disparity is brought into focus and reinforced only if the two are viewed together; if, in fact, we decline the invitation to skip the intro. The title sequence therefore has the capacity to become a pivotal element in assessing *Sense8*'s wider aesthetic and thematic composition.

A title sequence is not only a way into a program, an "aperture" into its world, but a crucial aspect against which the merits of its main narrative might be appraised. Although *Sense8* represents a particular example, and perhaps not all title sequences would attract equivalent interest, it is nevertheless the case that the increasing tendency for title sequences to be skipped over or even to be absent from programs entirely risks losing potentially important expressive elements in television. Indeed, the experience of beginning new episodes of *Sense8* with the title sequence helps to bring into focus some of the difficulties the program encounters in its attempts to fit its characters within storylines and to transition from the fragmented ambiguity of the titles to the specificity and detail of individual lives. Whatever weight we place upon *Sense8*'s fallibilities, they have the potential to become points of interest because the title sequence expresses so emphatically the scale of its framing ambition: to move across and between cultures and nationalities. It perhaps should not be surprising if the coherence of the program's fictional world becomes strained within such broad parameters and, as a consequence, the credibility of character behavior is compromised. There was undoubtedly an economic rationale behind Netflix's decision to cancel *Sense8* after two seasons, but it is telling that its longer-running titles such as *House of Cards* and *Orange Is the New Black* (which ran for six and seven seasons, respectively) placed very firm, narrow boundaries around their central narratives, effectively trapping their characters within specific locales to varying degrees. Both programs possess title sequences that embed that sense of claustrophobic entrapment, either through the tight focus on real-life former inmates' faces (*Orange Is the New Black*) or through a succession of shots that are bound to a desolate representation of Washington, DC, streets and landmarks (*House of Cards*). *Sense8*'s title sequence, in contrast, might be seen to contain ambition that was never quite realized, promise that was never properly fulfilled. As a consequence, any sense of its accomplishments becomes ever more complex when compared to the failings of the show, making this skippable element actually essential to our critical understanding of *Sense8* as a whole.

Works Cited

Davison, A. (2013), "Title Sequences for Contemporary Television Serials," in J. Richardson, C. Gorbman and C. Vernallis (eds.), *Oxford Handbook of New Audiovisual Aesthetics*, 146–67, New York: Oxford University Press.

Jacobs, J. (2001), "Issues of Judgement and Value in Television Studies," *International Journal of Cultural Studies*, 4 (4): 427–47.

Johansson, D. (2006), "Homeward Bound: Those *Sopranos* Titles Come Heavy," in D. Lavery (ed.), *Reading the Sopranos*, 27–36, London: I.B. Tauris.

Merodeadora, A. (2017), "The Problem with *Sense8*: Or How *Sense8*'s Faux-Progressive Worldbuilding Falls Apart," *Medium*, August 12. Available online: https://medium.com/@puentera/the-problem-with-sense8-90964685c62f.

Rackl, L. (2015), "Where in the World: Pinning Down the 108 Scenes in *Sense8* Intro," *tv trippin*, June 23. Available online: https://web.archive.org/web/20160507195318/http://tvtrippin.com/travel/where-in-the-world-pinning-down-sense8-openers-108-scenes/.

Shaw, D. (2011), "*Babel* and the Global Hollywood Gaze," *Situations: Project of the Radical Imagination*, 4 (1): 11–31.

Williams, K. (2016), "The Wonder Years: Nostalgia, Memory and Pastness in Television Credits," *Alphaville: Journal of Film and Screen Media*, 12: 59–77.

4

The *Sense8* Bible: The Creation of a New Creed for Our Times

Deborah Shaw

In many ways *Sense8*'s alignment with queer and trans* radical moralities opposes the dominant belief systems of conservative iterations of organized Judeo-Christian religions. The focus of this chapter is on the ways in which the series appropriates and subverts tropes and imagery from both the Old and New Testament in order to critique many of its beliefs and values particularly relating to a rejection of LGBTQ identities, and of non-procreative forms of sexuality. That is not to say that other expressions of religious practice are not present in *Sense8* or are all seen as negative. Indeed, Kala's devotion to the Hindu elephant-headed deity Ganesha is a source of strength, comfort, and guidance for her, despite the tensions that it creates with her husband and his modern secular family. Nonetheless, this chapter argues that the series develops a *Sense8* creed that is forged by creating a new mythology that explicitly overthrows beliefs associated principally with right-wing evangelical Christianity. Indeed, it is the contention of this chapter that *Sense8* transcends television through the creation of a new mythology that promotes new beliefs designed for the twenty-first century.

To begin I will consider the ways in which three women in *Sense8* take key roles in the creation, spread, and understanding of a *Sense8* creed: Angelica is the female, anti-patriarchal, creator-goddess who brings forth new sensate lives, and Riley and Nomi are the high priestesses of the series' moral universe. Riley has an evangelical function in the way that she connects with others through music in the Archipelago (the network of sensates and clusters) and draws strength from union as she brings them together. Meanwhile, Nomi provides the moral framework to understand the importance of the series' trans* and LGBTQ politics and its opposition to a conservative Christian ethos. Furthermore, because Pride is a "holy day" in *Sense8*, denoting its importance in advancing LGBTQ rights, attention must be paid to the significance of Lito's appearance in São Paulo as "high priest" of this festival.

Following the study of the way in which Pride is raised to the status of a religious celebration in *Sense8*, I produce a reading of S02:E01 "Happy Fucking New Year" and consider the ways in which the series reimagines this Christian holiday period of Christmas and New Year and has it work with *Sense8* values and beliefs and its queer families. Finally, I draw together what I propose as the *Sense8* Eight Commendments, wherein that "e" is not a typo but a recognition that these are not laws or orders, not commandments, but rather a guide by which to live a free life.

Sense8 is evangelical in its approach and utilizes ingredients from popular culture to preach its core tenets. It functions as a superhero wish fulfilment narrative with music video aesthetics and martial arts flourishes; it serves to make a marginalized community powerful and desirable. Its platform, to use a religious analogy, is the broad church of Netflix with its enormous global congregation. And yet, despite preaching a message of diversity and queer inclusion, Netflix almost martyred its creation in 2017 on the altar of commercial imperatives before the mythology was complete, as the viewing figures were not felt to justify its budget. The threatened cancelation of the series also fed into an anti-Trump, anti-austerity, anti-Brexit, that is, an anti-nationalist zeitgeist in the year after the election of Trump, and of Brexit, providing fans with something to fight for and against. This has all helped in the establishment of a *Sense8* creed with a value system, heroes and villains, and faithful followers, complete with a resurrection narrative. *Sense8* establishes a queer congregation that everyone is invited to join.

Creation Myths and *Sense8*

All Abrahamic religions have creation myths at their center—whether that be the all-powerful Allah (Islam Creation Story), or the Judeo-Christian God's creation of the world in six days, and the Adam and Eve (or Hawwa in Islam) story shared by Jews, Muslims and Christians, in which the first moral restrictions are laid down. These faiths also share birth myths with babies who are to grow up to be saviors to their people. We are familiar with the story of baby Moses—for example, whose identity was hidden as he was brought up by the Egyptian persecutors of his people and, once an adult, was to lead the Jewish people out of slavery—and the birth of Jesus who will become the Christian messiah, the Muslim prophet, or Jewish false prophet. These patriarchal, monotheistic faiths have one creator who commands total submission from His adherents. Christian mother Mary gives birth to

Jesus, but she is a vessel for this deity, and her supposed virginal status has been used for centuries to equate moral virtue with a negation of sexuality outside of procreational duties. As Rita Segato, the Argentinian decolonial feminist, has observed, monotheistic religious regimes have combined with patriarchal social regimes to justify colonization and marginalization of nonconforming "others": "For the patriarchy, capital, and fundamentalist monotheisms there is only one truth, only one way of living well, one god, one form of the future, one form of justice. They are in this way monopolies, governed by an exclusive and exclusionary logic" (Segato 2019). Segato's solution (speaking of the need for Latin America to replace patriarchal monotheistic regimes) is to embrace a "vital intensity of disobedience [and a] logic that is consistently for something: for conserving life and guaranteeing the continued and improved well-being of more people, for keeping the horizon of history open without a predetermined destiny, for keeping time moving" (Segato 2019).

I begin with this overly simplistic overview of Abrahamic creation myths, and an eloquent feminist critique of harm done in the name of the single creator and exclusionary truths, as an oppositional starting point to read *Sense8*. The series begins with miraculous births that, like Mary's virginal conception of Jesus, defies biology: those of the eight characters who form the sensate cluster and whose lives we will follow through the series. As Angelica births the cluster, the visual codes of biological births are followed through Angelica's suffering body as she writhes, perspires, and cries out in agony. And yet, her eight "children" already exist as fully formed adults with their own disparate lives in distinct geographical spaces. This newly formed family share a first birth date of August 8, 1988, with 8 a sacred number within this mythology because it also resembles the mathematical symbol for infinity. This second birth is a binding together, a re-creation of new selves into a new cluster-self; they are, to use a Christian evangelical analogy, born again. It is the second cluster that Angelica births; the sensates of her first brood were hunted down and destroyed by the series demon, Milton Brandt, also known as Whispers. The fact that *Sense8* begins with a creation miracle forewarns viewers that we are to be invited to join a new congregation with a fully formed belief system that in many ways counters Judeo-Christian models and in others echoes them.

Significantly, the birth itself takes place in a church, yet there is an inversion of Christian iconography to indicate to viewers that this will be a very different religious order. The church is derelict, and this mother is ailing and surrounded by objects of her abjection—a dirty mattress, and the paraphernalia of heroin use, which viewers do not yet know is used by Angelica's cluster to block unwelcome visits by hostile sensates. And, this mother will kill herself with a single gunshot through the roof of her mouth as soon as she births her new family. Yet, this suicide is an act of love, a sacrifice to keep Whispers from entering her mind and finding and destroying her birth-cluster, as he has traced her despite the heroin. More subversion of religious iconography can be seen as she is visited by Jonas, her former lover and clustermate. He holds her hand and cradles her in a visual reworking of Michelangelo's *Pietà* in which Mary cradles the body of a dead Jesus; here it is the mother who sacrifices herself for her children in order that they may survive. Following the agony of the cluster-birth, Angelica sees each one of her brood and appears to them simultaneously in a vision, transcending the reality of her immediate surroundings. In a subversion of a virginal birth she is dressed in a dirty white dress that appears clean in the visions in which she is serene and illuminated by key lighting, even in night time scenes such as in Will's vision shown in Figure 4.1 in S01:E01 "Limbic Resonance," with the lighting enhancing the miraculous nature of the apparition.

For each member of the cluster the image of Angelica is presented as a moment out of time and space, a vision seen only by them, and of course the viewers, who see the same image in different times, time zones, and spaces. *Sense8* uses the birth scene to show us that, like religious visions and prayer and screen images in film and television, presence transcends materiality. The opening credits follow, and the sacrificial suicide scene is then replayed in Will's dream, with a new heightened fantastical reality that draws from the subconscious, replacing realism as the dominant storytelling mode. It is from this point in S01:E01 that the cluster experiences the connections that begin with music as Will hears the DJ set played by a fellow sensate Riley, the woman who he will discover is his cluster-mate and true love. Popular music, acid house, and rave and rap will subsequently take the role played

FIGURE 4.1 *Angelica appears to Will after she has given birth to the cluster.*

by hymns in Christian rituals, with the profane acquiring the status of the sacred in the *Sense8* creed.

Like all origin myths, the birth scene is pivotal, and the birth and suicide sequence is replayed throughout the series, signifying hope and fear. Angelica continues to be revealed to the cluster in visions, as she transcends her physical death and appears to them in times of greatest need. These are in the tradition of visions experienced by biblical prophets of the Old Testament (Niditch 2020), and of the Marian apparitions experienced by faithful devotees in the Christian tradition, an example being the visions of Our Virgin of Guadalupe who appears to Juan Diego in colonial Mexico in 1531 (Our Lady of Guadalupe). Yet Angelica, unlike the various incarnations of the Virgin Mary throughout the Catholic world, believes in and practices a love that is carnal as well as spiritual; and, as a creative force in her own right and an ecologist with a history of multiple lovers, she is closer to the Greek goddesses Gaia or Athena than to the biblical patriarchal progenitor.

The principal creative forces in the *Sense8* diegetic universe are then feminine, and this mirrors the production of the series with both Lana and Lilly Wachowski as the principal showrunners, writers, and directors for S01, and Lana for S02. *Sense8* is a matriarchy with Angelica and the Wachowskis as the principal generative forces in a collaborative project with cocreators. Collectively, these creative forces harness the radical empathy that accompanies motherhood, creative writing, and image making. Creators of imaginary universes have the empathy that comes with inhabiting other selves as discussed in the work of Siri Hustvedt (2017). But what is new in *Sense8*, and what makes this radical empathy (feeling and action combined) is the way that the creators share their gifts of empathy with the created, and how the members of the cluster in turn share their individual gifts and talents between themselves. This is in clear opposition to the biblical stories of the Garden of Eden or the Tower of Babel in which an all-powerful and demanding deity punishes his human creations when they seek knowledge or aspire to greatness in a way that appears to challenge their creator.

Music as Prayer

It is significant that in S02:E05 "Fear Never Fixed Anything" Riley uses a repurposed church for her DJ set, which is planned to summon a selection of members of what we discover to be a network of sixteen clusters known as the Archipelago, with music performing the evangelical function of the hymn in connecting global congregations. Riley is the closest character to Angelica, and she performs the function of cluster-mother following Angelica's death; while Angelica has given them a sensate life, Riley in her role as high priestess DJ will bring the sensates together. The set begins with "What's Up?," the 4 Non Blondes' hymn-anthem of the series, a song that also connects to the fans who have reclaimed the song to express their love of the series. Riley then delivers a speech-sermon which is a declaration of love to Will, but also to her audience, to her cluster, and to the fan-viewers. She tells the ravers (and viewers): "Tonight I want everyone in this room to know that I see you, and I believe in you, and as long as we're together I know there is nothing that we can't do." These words are followed by a reprise of "What's Up?" and the first lyrics heard are "I pray" to emphasize that in the *Sense8* universe the rave is the church, and music and dance act as collective prayer. The dance remix of "What's Up?" ramps up the pace and features a repeated loop of the following lyrics:

And I pray,
Oh my God, do I pray.
I pray every single day,
For a revolution. (Linda Perry 1992)

Here the sacred and the secular and the personal and the political merge with the power of faith, harnessed to create a moment of hope and a call for a radical change in human relationships (a Revolution). This hope is followed in the narrative plotting, as despite Whispers' agents surrounding the rave-Church, the cluster manage to escape. Most significantly, sensates from other clusters appear for the first time drawn by Riley through the hope and the energy of the rave and Riley's speech-sermon. The Old Man of Hoy (Sylvester McCoy) utters the profane "Holy Shit" as he appears on the dance floor and simultaneously to Riley at her decks, presented in its raised positioning like an altar at this church. As prefigured through Riley's choice of clothing (a top with patterns resembling a planetary constellation), The Old Man of Hoy, drawn out of hiding by Riley, will connect their cluster to the Archipelago.

Sense8 and Conservative Christianity

And yet, despite the way the series creates a syncretic new faith that co-opts elements of Christianity (sacred spaces, miracles, spiritual leaders and high priestesses/priests, prophets, community, love, song), a particular narrow right-wing form of this faith is singled out for direct criticism in a selection of specific moments. In S02:E3 "Obligate Mutualisms" we learn of Todd W. McCarver, a member of Angelica's own cluster who is unable to accept his sensate identity as a result of his Christian faith, in a metaphor for LGBTQ self-repression among certain Christian denominations. It is significantly Todd, now in the hands of the Biological Preservation Organization (BPO), who murders Mitchell Taylor, a British politician giving a speech in a mosque at an event that is a celebration of multicultural, interfaith, and atheist coexistence. Taylor, in the speech recorded before his murder and replayed on Amanita's smartphone, says, "free societies are stronger societies—open multicultural societies are where the world's best and brightest have wanted to go to, while monocultural repressive societies are places they've wanted to escape from." It is then that a man revealed to be Todd shoots dead everyone in the audience, including the speaker, who Nomi and Amanita discover is connected to Ruth El Saadawi, the founder of (the original and pro-sensate) BPO. *Sense8* delivers a direct message through sequences such as these: right-wing repressive Christianity is lacking in the empathy required to ensure that a multicultural intersectional society can function. Those who try to destroy this vision are the demons within the *Sense8* faith, and they are the enemy throughout the series as embodied in the transformed BPO and in Whispers. Their lobotomized sensate victims, such as Todd, perhaps reference congregants who unthinkingly follow right-wing evangelical religious leaders and are taught self-loathing if they depart from prescribed heteronormative models.

This direct attack on this strand of Christianity continues through the series in the form of Janet, Nomi's mother, while the celebration of the new *Sense8* creed is embodied in Nomi and through her, the privileged space of LGBTQ Pride. Nomi's mother is unable to accept her daughter as she is trapped within the fixed, heteronormative gender binary stipulated by her Christian faith. Her insistence on calling Nomi by her first assigned birth name, "Michael," is rendered sinister within the plot. While she is unaware of the BPO zombie project that turns sentient sensates into assassins whose minds can be controlled, her desire to "fix" her daughter, to turn her back into her version of her son, is aligned with BPO's project to lobotomize Nomi, and she collaborates with BPO employees to imprison Nomi in the hospital against her will in S01:E02 "I Am Also a We." At Nomi's time of need in hospital, her mother berates and negates her: "You were Michael when you came out of me and you will be Michael until they put me in my grave." In a desire for a happy ending in the season finale *Amor Vincit Omnia* (S02:E12), Janet, rather implausibly, lovingly accepts her daughter at her wedding and is helped toward her road to redemption where love does indeed conquer all by unwittingly eating a weed brownie.

Pride, the Holiest of Holy Days

Audiences are prompted to see the reasons for Nomi's rejection by her mother as rooted in Christianity, as suggested by Nomi's vlog recorded prior to her hospitalization. Nomi is recording her thoughts on the importance of the Pride celebrations that she is about to attend with Amanita:

> I was taught by my parents that there's something wrong with someone like me. Something offensive, something you would avoid, maybe even

pity. Something that you could never love. My mom, she's a fan of St. Thomas Aquinas. She calls pride a sin. And of all the venal and mortal sins, St. Thomas saw pride as the queen of the seven deadlies. He saw it as the ultimate gateway sin that would turn you quickly into a sinaholic. But hating isn't a sin on that list. Neither is shame. I was afraid of this parade because I wanted it so badly to be a part of it. So today, I'm marching for that part of me that was once afraid to march and for all the people who can't march—the people living lives like I did. Today, I march to remember that I'm not just a me but I'm also a we. And we march with pride. So, go fuck yourself Aquinas!

This speech is intercut with images of the cluster engaged in activities that for conservative Christianity are considered sinful: Wolfgang and Felix celebrate as they get drunk together in a bar, countering religious opprobrium with fraternal love; Will gathers up his drunken father from the floor of a bar, countering shame with filial love; Capheus is transported to the green spaces of San Francisco's Pride as post-march attendees gather in a park, an image that indirectly counters Kenyan homophobia by showing peaceful loving expressions of Pride to a man, who, although not homophobic and open to the polyamorous pleasures of his cluster, comes from a majority Christian country in which 90 percent of the population were recorded as being against homosexuality in 2013, according to the Pew Research Centre (2013). *Sense8*'s moral universe overturns that of conservative Christianity and inverts what this faith considers to be sinful. Nomi's vlog is immediately followed by high-energy dance music and joyous celebrations of the San Francisco Pride Parade that features aerial shots to highlight the scale of numbers of the people who form this collective "we" as the queers and queer allies take over the city. Nomi and Amanita join the actual Dykes on Bikes parade in a sequence that was shot during Pride (*Sense8: Creating the World*, 2015), and that manages to capture the energy, color, and joy of the event.

Through Nomi's vlog *Sense8* roots Pride in the resistance of its political history and turns oppression into defiance, celebration, and a party. Pride commemorates the Stonewall riots of June 28, 1969, that were sparked by the police raid of the Stonewall Inn bar in New York's Greenwich City—riots that have been seen as a significant date in the gay and later LGBTQ rights movement (Gay Pride 2019). *Sense8*'s Pride scenes also serve the purpose of positioning trans identity at the heart of Pride and redress some of the criticisms leveled at screen narratives that have erased transgender struggles that were central to LGBTQ resistance. The film *Stonewall* (Emmerich, 2015), for instance, was critiqued by many in the LGBTQ community for its whitewashing and cis-washing, and significantly underplaying the roles of Marsha P. Johnson, a Black trans woman, and Sylvia Rivera, a Latina trans woman in the riots (Mayer 2015; Smith 2015).

As with religious High Holy days, Pride is made up of global celebrations that are repeated annually wherever communities are free to practice their traditions. As Segade (2017) notes: "Yes, Pride is contested: In some contexts it's too radical, in others, too normative, but the ethical position of *Sense8* begins with the self-determination it symbolically enacts." The global significance of Pride acquires additional significance in its next representation in S02:E06 "Isolated above, Connected Below." The high point of the episode is São Paulo's Pride event for which Lito has been invited to be the Grand Marshall. This honor is granted to Lito as he has achieved a global queer following as a result of the way he responded to his outing in Mexico by the tabloid press (S02:E02 "Who Am I?"). Brazil's is among the best-known Pride celebrations in the world. As in S01, this episode is filmed at the actual event, and once again aerial shots introduce the parade to capture its scale and spectacular and colorful nature. A mass of bodies shot from above flows through a single street surrounded by the buildings in this cityscape, with the individual subsumed in the crowd. Then, on a platform stage above all the other revelers, Lito delivers his speech:

All of my life, I've had to pretend to be something I wasn't … I couldn't be what I am. I am a gay man. I've never said those words in public before. I am a GAY man! I AM A GAY MAN! Why did I have to be so afraid to say that? Because I know that people are afraid of people that are different than them.

He goes on to speak of the layers of dishonesty involved in keeping up a pretense, in forging an image for his career in the pretend world of the movies, before declaring his love for Hernando. There are echoes here of Riley's speech during her DJ set. This is Lito's version of the sermon that begins with love for his partner and merges with a love for all present; and this stage serves as his altar for this secular mass, as he ascends to his priestly status by becoming a role model to others fearful of their sexuality, through this public coming out to a queer congregation. This speech-sermon also serves an evangelical function as it goes viral through digital media, which has parallels with the ability of sensates to connect with strangers. This is noted by friends and partners of the sensates when trying to understand their abilities; for instance, Amanita notes to Nomi that her visits to other cluster members are like "Facetime without a phone" (S01:E08).

As Lito is speaking he is reflected back to the crowd (and to diegetic viewers who will watch recordings, and to Netflix viewers) on giant multiple screens set up behind him, with each image projected in a display of millisecond lags (Figure 4.2). This creates an intriguing and dramatic effect as other images of Litos appear behind the speaking Lito, thereby suggesting how his speech will reach digital viewers in different times and places, while an embodied Lito reaches the sanctified Pride gathering while he is speaking. The screens

FIGURE 4.2 *Multiple images of Lito address the crowd at Pride in São Paulo.*

also serve the function of having his multiple selves on show to all, and through publicly coming out in such a loving environment, these selves are able to finally come together and heal the damage he has done to himself by adhering to societal codes of Mexican masculinity through the repression and false unitary heterosexual self he has offered to the public. Like his cluster he is multiple but no longer fragmented. Through these images Lito embodies the "I am a we" of Nomi's speech in S01:E02, and like her he also embodies and transcends the seven other selves that Jonas has spoken of in relation to the cluster.

This collective self is that of the LGBTQ community and the *Sense8* fans. Lito's final words—"Let's party!"—are followed by the dance anthem "Back Where I Belong," which initiates scenes of revelry and pure joy for the crowd and for the cluster who are all present. The lyrics of the song's chorus highlight *Sense8*'s key belief that so resonates with global fans—that home and family are states of feeling and transcend geography and biology:

> Now I'm back where I belong
> No matter where I'm from
> It's been here all along.
> I finally made it home. (Otto Knows, feat. Avicii, 2016)

The speech and lyrics in English, apparently understood by all, root a Brazilian event in the global but linguistically Anglo-centric *Sense8* culture; yet the rhythm unites all present, and the Brazilian crowd are multiethnic, and this is an inclusive LGBTQ event with men, and women, both cis and trans, all united in their celebration of Pride. In a case of life merging with art, a number of cast members along with Lana Wachowski were guests of honor at Vancouver Pride in 2017, in which she and the cast engaged in a meet and greet with fans onstage at Vancouver's Sunset Beach Party (Takeuchi 2017).

Dreaming of a Queer Christmas

Despite its invention of its own holy days, the series also co-opts Christian high holy days and rituals and fills them with its queer families. This notion of the chosen family is common within queer and trans culture (Demory and Pullen 2013; Halberstam 2018), as non-biological family units have been central to providing support to people who have been cast out of their biological families and friendship groups. In his discussion of *Paris Is Burning* (Livingstone 1990), the documentary on New York's queer ballroom scene of the 1980s, Jack Halberstam notes the importance of the film in putting on-screen these chosen family formations:

> This remade understanding of family, kinship, and cross-generational care in the context of drag houses was one of the most important legacies of the film and offers still an enduring reminder that mainstream notions of family have little to do with many of the ways in which queer and trans* people of color have created life under harsh conditions, one expressive of their "mutual bond." (Halberstam 2018: 65)

The television series *Pose* (2018–) by showrunner Ryan Murphy and a team of queer and trans writers and directors, also a legacy of *Paris Is Burning*, has the chosen family as its central theme as trans and queer house mothers and fathers create homes and families from the community of performers at the balls, many of whom were previously homeless and driven through circumstances into sex work to survive. The final credits always end with an inspirational quote from a leading figure of the ballroom scene and S02:E02 of *Pose* ends with the words of Hector Crespo, known as Hector Xtravaganza, house father and also a consultant on the series (Bernstein 2019): "Blood does not family make. Those are relatives. Family are those with whom you share your good, bad, and ugly, and still love one another in the end. Those are the ones you select."

Sense8 is then part of queer culture that celebrates queer family formations. Where *Sense8* is unique is in the sacred vision it presents of this family. This is depicted in the Christmas and New Year special episode, S02:E01 "Happy Fucking New Year." This 124-minute special (more like a standalone film than a television episode) makes Christmas a celebration of diverse families—biological and non-biological. The episode's family focus is on Lito's mother's full acceptance of her son and her pride in his refusal to deny his sexuality following his outing by the tabloid press; it also focuses on idealistic queer family celebrations with Amanita, Nomi, and Bug, celebrating Christmas with Amanita's white mother and her three African American fathers. Nomi expresses her admiration that none of them knows who Amanita's biological father is and, most importantly, that it does not matter. Although Amanita's three fathers could be coded as gay, the fact that they look back fondly on their relationship with Amanita's mother places them within the polyamorous *Sense8* family. In scenes such as these, concepts of heterosexual and homosexual exclusivity and monogamy are swept away and replaced with inclusive queer polyamory, and this is naturalized through the happy banality and everyday pleasures of Christmas family gatherings, and their shared love for their daughter.

The snowy picture postcard images of Western Christian Christmases are also featured in this episode in the scenes where Will and Riley momentarily come out of hiding to enjoy the wintery scenes of their surroundings in Amsterdam, and as the backdrop to Kala and Wolfgang's flirtations when she "visits" him. Wolfgang has already indicated that his belief system is very different from a religious one as he decorates Felix's shop with an image that he calls Evil Santa. A Judeo-Christian worldview would represent his relationship with Kala as an adulterous sinful affair, and adultery is also considered a moral sin within Hinduism (Hinduism and Adultery 2020), but within *Sense8*, their relationship is presented as joyful and an inevitable expression of desire and love. Kala, despite her feelings of guilt for her desire for Wolfgang, is awestruck by her first sighting of snow and the two engage in playful snowball fights, prompting Felix, who cannot see Kala, to exclaim to a lone Wolfgang apparently throwing snow at "nothing": "What the fuck are you on, and where can I get some?" Kala's dilemma of fearing she has to choose between Wolfgang and her husband Rajan is also reconciled in a *Sense8* way when the three of them come to form a queer throuple, with Rajan joining Kala and Wolfgang in their lovemaking as his understanding of the possible and the desirable expands (S02:E12). The figure of Ganesha features prominently in Kala's story as she is a devotee of the elephant-headed deity, and here again a syncretic religious world view is presented as Ganesha is a god of new beginnings and a remover of obstacles (Doniger 2015).

Nonetheless Christianity is the principal reference point for S02:E01 "Happy Fucking New Year." *Sense8* provides a lesson on how to incorporate Christmas references and signs in a series that challenges the beliefs and practices of conservative churches. A musical montage follows Capheus's admission to his mother that he loves watching *It's a Wonderful Life* (Capra 1946) as it believes in people. Watching this film at Christmas is another Western Christian tradition that has transnational reach through global Hollywood (although Capheus lives in a slum and is unlikely to be watching it on Netflix due to the prohibitive cost), and it is significant that

Capheus celebrates the human not the divine spirit in this Christmas drama. There follows a musical montage that brings together each of the eight sensates: alone (Sun in jail) or coupled (Kala and Rajan, Riley and Will) or with friends (Wolfgang and Felix) or celebrating Christmas with community and family (Lito, Hernando, and Dani; Nomi, Amanita, and Bug). The song chosen to connect the cluster is significantly Leonard Cohen's "Hallelujah" covered by Daniel Moore and the Apollo Choir of Chicago. "Hallelujah" is a secular hymn (Thomsen et al. 2016), a celebration of the transcendence that comes through passion and love. Cohen has said that he wanted to "push the Hallelujah deep into the secular world, into the ordinary world. … I wanted to indicate that Hallelujah can come out of things that have nothing to do with religion" (Light 2019). Lisa Dalton, a Religious Studies academic, highlights the Old Testament Samson and Delilah and David and Bathsheba references in the song, and speaking of David and Samson, she notes, "both are heroes that are undone by misbegotten relationships with women. Both are adulterers. Both are poets—Samson breaks into verse right after smiting the Philistines. Both repent and seek divine favor after their transgressions" (Light 2019). And yet, in Cohen's song no repentance is required for passion which is not a transgression, regardless of the fact that love may leave the lover in a vulnerable state:

> She tied you to a kitchen chair,
> She broke your throne, she cut your hair
> And from your lips she drew the Hallelujah. (Cohen 1984)

Old Testament commandments evaporate in 'Hallelujah', with the song containing the paradox of taking God's name in vain, while simultaneously praising God (the meaning of Hallelujah), and questioning his existence. Whether or not you are a believer, for Cohen and the Wachowskis, secular love is the state of grace attained in the song and in *Sense8*:

> You say I took the Name in vain.
> I don't even know the name.
> But if I did—well, really—what's it to ya?
> There's a blaze of light in every word.
> It doesn't matter which you heard,
> The holy, or the broken Hallelujah. (Cohen 1984)

In *Sense8* the song is played in full and the lyrics are matched to the images of the cluster and all the forms of love that they are experiencing: "Your faith was strong but you needed proof" is synched to an image of imprisoned Sun receiving a chocolate from Min-Jung (Yuh-Jung Youn), who becomes a prison mother to her. Other images illustrate new family units and community; among these we see Lito, Hernando, and Dani joining the

Mexican candle-lit procession to the local Church, and Felix receiving a Christmas gift of condoms from Wolfgang, in reference to his multiple lovers, an example of the fusion of the sacred and the profane.

This fusion is most clearly illustrated in this Christmas and New Year special episode when the montage ends, and the scene settles on Amanita and Nomi's queer family unit shown listening to the San Francisco Gay Men's Choir's performance of "Hallelujah." All the sensates visit through their connection with Nomi, and this is where we see the queer family sanctified in a form of syncretism in which Christian Christmas rites and rituals are adapted and the holy Christian family is replaced with polyamorous queer, multicultural, and multifaith families. The faith of the cluster members is not explored beyond Kala's as she is the only cluster member with any stated religious faith, yet here their individual faith backgrounds are rendered irrelevant, as they are folded into a communal queer US-centric Christmas with its secular hymn composed by the Jewish-born songwriter Leonard Cohen.

The choir scene is analyzed elsewhere in this collection, but a reading of its religious and traditional iconography and its appropriation for the *Sense8* creed is also vital. The singers of the Gay Men's Choir are all wearing Santa Claus costumes, and all the sensates light candles as they share in the wonder of the moment. As the choir begins to sing, Angelica, still in her white dress, appears to the cluster as a vision floating above the choir; in one shot Angelica is looking toward the screen and the cluster, and the cluster members (Lito, Sun, and Kala) are looking at her, with the choir facing forward, looking toward their audience in an anti-realist image. This moment of transcendence and miracle is interrupted by Whispers appearing to Will with an ironic "Merry Christmas, Will" as Angel (Angelica) and Demon (Whispers) fight their battles through the cluster. As well as the transcendent, peaceful, angelic visions, *Sense8* also preaches a bellicose message more in line with Old Testament stories of the destruction that will be unleashed on enemies of the "chosen people," with the series' writers as the creation goddesses and gods who will ensure that the enemies of the cluster will be eliminated. Despite all of the nuance in *Sense8*, with many sensates of other clusters morally flawed (Whispers, Lila Facchini, Puck), there is a clear-cut vision of good (Angelica's second birth cluster and its allies) and evil (their enemies) with none of the radical empathy on offer for the series' enemies. The *Sense8* ethos is certainly not pacifist, and here we see the limits to its radical empathy in contrast with that proposed by Judith Butler in her book *The Force of Nonviolence* (2020). Explaining the key ideas to Masha Gessen (2020), Butler argues that every life is connected to the self and thus violence inflicted on an apparent enemy is violence inflicted on a self:

> If the self I'm trying to defend is also in some sense related to the person I'm tempted to kill, I have to make sure not to do violence to that relation, because that's also me. One could go further: I'm also attacking myself

by attacking that person, since I am breaking a social bond that we have between us. The problem of nonviolence looks different if you see it that way. (Butler in Gessen 2020)

As mainstream entertainment, albeit with a radical ethos, *Sense8* has a traditional action genre approach to violence as the solution to dispatching its enemies and their beliefs. The episode ends with an instrumental version of the traditional New Year's tune Auld Lang Syne as the cluster come together, but not before Song, Will, and Wolfgang combine in Wolfgang's body to violently defeat a Berlin gang seeking to kill him. The cluster survive as their enemies are felled, and the loss of life leaves no impact on the audience beyond relief. Wolfgang closes the episode with the words "Happy fucking New Year" in this profane conclusion to the Christmas story.

The Eight Commendments

Cultural texts have used their privileged platforms to present new belief systems to their audiences often in opposition to biblical commandments. A prime example of this is the documentary *Hail Satan?* (Lane 2019), which follows key figures of the Satanic Temple and documents how "across the US, civic-minded millennial satanists combine activism with pranks calculated to wind up the Christian right" (Clarke 2019). The film's sympathetic take on this pseudo religion demonstrates how, in the words of its director Penny Lane, the "temple represents a radical and much-needed reinvention of the very idea of religion in a way that makes sense in the 21st century" (Morrison 2019). It does this by revealing the hypocrisy and evil in conservative Christian morality and proposing an alternative belief system rooted in a form of outsider humanism (Morrison 2019). Their moral code is clear from their Seven Tenets (The Satanic Temple):

1. One should strive to act with compassion and empathy toward all creatures in accordance with reason.
2. The struggle for justice is an ongoing and necessary pursuit that should prevail over laws and institutions.
3. One's body is inviolable, subject to one's own will alone.
4. The freedoms of others should be respected, including the freedom to offend. To willfully and unjustly encroach upon the freedoms of another is to forgo one's own.
5. Beliefs should conform to one's best scientific understanding of the world. One should take care never to distort scientific facts to fit one's beliefs.
6. People are fallible. If one makes a mistake, one should do one's best to rectify it and resolve any harm that might have been caused.

7. Every tenet is a guiding principle designed to inspire nobility in action and thought. The spirit of compassion, wisdom, and justice should always prevail over the written or spoken word.

I have included this as an interesting counterpoint to *Sense8* as it also seeks to redefine a value system through an emphasis on empathy and sexual freedoms, although *Hail Satan?* places more value on the right to offend and scientific truths. *Hail Satan?* is a provocation while *Sense8* is an invitation: an invitation to join a fan community and be accepted through the series and its fans, particularly if audiences identify with a group that is classified as evil by right-wing conservative Christians, hence the popularity of the series with LGBTQ fans.

Sense8 does not explicitly lay out its tenets in the way that *Hail Satan?* does, yet the series has its own belief system that stands against conservative Christianity and for an intersectional queer community. The *Sense8* creed can be found in what I have termed the "Eight Commendments" and these can act as both a guide to the moral code of the series and a conclusion. I have chosen the term "commendments" rather than "commandments" to indicate the difference between the *Sense8* creed and the Judeo-Christian laws laid out in the Ten Commandments.

The *Sense8* Eight Commendments:

1. You shall transcend all restrictive boundaries placed on your gender, your nationality, and your sense of reality.
2. You shall create your own family.
3. You shall remember the sacred day of Pride and celebrate it.
4. You shall not restrict love for "love like art must always be free" (S01:E09).
5. You shall be empathetic, for blessed are the empaths.
6. You shall fight using any means necessary to protect yourself, your cluster, and your values.
7. You shall use the power of music to connect with others.
8. You shall seek pleasure with those you love.

Works Cited

Bernstein, J. (2019), "The Extravagant Life of Hector Xtravaganza," *The New York Times*, January 5. Available online: https://www.nytimes.com/2019/01/05/style/hector-xtravaganza-memorial.html.

Butler, J. (2020), *The Force of Nonviolence*, London: Verso.

Clarke, C. (2019), "Hail Satan? Review—Sympathy for the Devil, Socks for the Homeless," *The Guardian*, August 21. Available online: https://www.theguardian.com/film/2019/aug/21/hail-satan-review-penny-lane-documentary-satanic-temple-florida.

Demory, P., and C. Pullen (2013), *Queer Love in Film and Television: Critical Essays*, New York: Palgrave Macmillan.

Doniger, W. (2015), "Ganesha." Available online: https://www.britannica.com/topic/Ganesha.

"Gay Pride" (2019), *Encyclopaedia Britannica*. Available online: https://www.britannica.com/topic/Gay-Pride.

Gessen, M. (2020), "Judith Butler Wants Us to Reshape Our Rage," *The New Yorker*, February 8. Available online: https://www.newyorker.com/culture/the-new-yorker-interview/judith-butler-wants-us-to-reshape-our-rage?fbclid=IwAR28gi3ZnzG5wQY_lzUCNd36HfE4rfai8Jf3XBJ1usz5Kc6YAH8e8 gWEVdI.

Halberstam, J. (2018), *Trans*: A Quick and Quirky Account of Gender Variability*, Oakland: University of California Press.

"Hinduism and Adultery." Available online: https://www.advocatekhoj.com/library/lawareas/divadultery/1.php?Title=Adultery%20Divor ce&STitle=Hinduism%20and%20adultery.

Hustvedt, S. (2017), *A Woman Looking at Men Looking at Women: Essays on Art, Sex, and the Mind*, London: Scepter.

"Islam Creation Story." Available online: http://www2.nau.edu/~gaud/bio301/content/iscrst.htm.

Light, A. (2019), "How Leonard Cohen's 'Hallelujah' Brilliantly Mingled Sex, Religion." *Rolling Stone*, December 12. Available online: https://www.rollingstone.com/feature/how-leonard-cohens-hallelujah-brilliantly-mingled-sex-religion-194516/.

Mayer, S. (2015), "Beyond Stonewall: Screening Trans* Lives, Seeing Trans* Histories," *Verso Books*, September 10. Available online: https://www.versobooks.com/blogs/2232-beyond-stonewall-screening-trans-lives-seeing-trans-histories.

Morrison, D. (2019) "Hail Satan? Director Penny Lane: 'This Is What Religion Would Be if We Were Starting from Scratch,'" *BFI*, August 23. Available online: https://www.bfi.org.uk/news-opinion/news-bfi/interviews/hail-satan-director-penny-lane-what-religion-would-be-if-we-were.

Muñoz, J. E. (2009), *Cruising Utopia: The Then and There of Queer Futurity*, New York: New York University Press.

Niditch, S. (2020), "Prophetic Dreams and Visions in the Hebrew Bible," *Bible Odyssey*. Available online: https://www.bibleodyssey.org:443/en/passages/related-articles/prophetic-dreams-and-visions-in-the-hebrew-bible.

"Our Lady of Guadalupe: Patron Saint of Mexico," (2018), *Encyclopaedia Britannica*. Available online: https://www.britannica.com/topic/Our-Lady-of-Guadalupe-patron-saint-of-Mexico.

Pew Research Centre (2013), "The Global Divide on Homosexuality: Greater Acceptance in More Secular and Affluent Countries," *Global Attitudes and Trends*, June 4. Available online: https://www.pewresearch.org/global/2013/06/04/the-global-divide-on-homosexuality/.

The Satanic Temple (n.d.), "About Us." Available online: https://thesatanictemple.com/pages/about-us?fbclid=IwAR0LJPNndH_4Xp9RMa6JXW9ZsNxa3SurZ74KkTvu30BRiolXbYbEC6kleHg (accessed March 13, 2021).

Segade, A. (2017), "We Belong: Alexandro Segade on *Sense8*," *Artforum*, August 24. Available online: https://www.artforum.com/slant/alexandro-segade-on-sense8-70597.

Segato, R. (2019), "The Virtues of Disobedience," *Rosa Luxemburg Stiftung*, July. Available online: https://www.rosalux.de/en/publication/id/40778/the-virtues-of-disobedience/.

Smith, N. (2015), "Gay Rights Activists Give Their Verdict on Stonewall: 'This Film Is No Credit to the History It Purports to Portray,'" *The Guardian*, September 25. Available online: https://www.theguardian.com/film/2015/sep/25/stonewall-film-gay-rights-activists-give-their-verdict.

Takeuchi, C. (2017), "'*Sense8*'s Lana Wachowski and Cast Thank Fans in Video, with Clips from Vancouver Pride," *Georgia Straight*, August 11. Available online: https://www.straight.com/blogra/947346/sense8s-lana-wachowski-and-cast-thank-fans-video-clips-vancouver-pride.

Thomsen, S. R., Q. Randle, and M. Lewis (2016), "Pop Music and the Search for the Numinous: Exploring the Emergence of the 'Secular Hymn' in Post-Modern Culture," *Journal of Media and Religion*, 15 (3): 146–55.

5

What's Queer About a Cluster? *Sense8*'s Polycentric Imaginary

Rosalind Galt

The central social form in *Sense8* is the cluster—eight people who are connected at the level of the sensorium—and the show figures this concept of the cluster as both culturally and biologically polycentric. In S01:E01 "Limbic Resonance," Nomi and Amanita attend a Pride event in San Francisco, at which a gay playwright tells them how "my life and all of this is made possible by those lives and all of those deaths." We cut to a performance about AIDS in which four men dance together, their bodies closely choreographed. Even before Nomi sees a vision of their sensate mother Angelica appear onstage, this performance prefigures the concept of the cluster. The unity of gesture that transforms the dancers' bodies into a single entity will be repeated throughout the series as a formal mechanism through which the sensates' experiences and embodiment are shown as aligned and in emotional sync. The way the semi-naked bodies of the dancers intertwine imbues their performance with an erotic intimacy that we will see repeated most clearly in the orgy scenes in which the sensates and their various partners share group sexual encounters. Moreover, in this Pride performance, both the mode of intimacy and the history of social solidarity are specifically located as queer. All this is made possible, the writer says, by those lives and all of those deaths: in other words, all that we are about to watch is an inheritance of the AIDS crisis and the forms of collective living made possible by the queer artists and activists of the past. If this key scene in the first episode proposes the cluster in terms of queer history, a scene in S01:E10 "What Is Human?" offers an ecological metaphor. More experienced sensate Jonas insists to Will that sensates are not quite human. When Will demurs, saying that he feels the same as other people, Jonas replies: "When you're not sharing your most intimate thoughts with someone on the other side of the world?" Jonas conjures this experience in terms of nonhuman nature, saying: "Watch a flock of birds or a school of fish move as one and you glimpse where we came from. Ask how aspen trees feel trauma hundreds of miles apart." Here, he sets up sensate ecology as a polycentric form of connection and affection, another mode of collective life to be set beside that of queer activism. These figurations—as queer community and as network of natural affinity and care—imagine the sensate cluster in terms of the radical potentiality of group attachment. The cluster form is at once a kind of family, a mode of group sex, a collective subjectivity, and a queer polycule. Across these imperfect analogies, it is posed within the show as an alternative model to humanity's isolation and violence, and as a form of relationality resistant to dominant practices of capitalist life. *Sense8* has been widely theorized in terms of its queerness, and as a trans* text, but in this chapter, I outline the specificity of its poly imaginary.

I propose "poly" as a productive concept with which to analyze the cluster form in *Sense8* as a specific mechanism of queer textuality. Poly primarily refers to polyamory, meaning a relationship model based on nonmonogamy in which varied groups of partners and partners-of-partners form what in the real world are referred to as polycules, and which might easily be called clusters. The "poly" in polyamory also operates as a prefix that renders *Sense8*'s more capacious polycentricity: it features a multitude of characters and international locations and draws on multiple genres. The nature of sensate subjectivity is also multiple, so that each individual's experience is polycentric; as Nomi says in S01:E02, "I Am Also a We." *Sense8* does represent polyamory directly—in the intersecting relationships of Wolfgang, Kala, and Rajan—and in those of Lito, Hernando, and Daniela. But just as Cáel Keegan (2016: 605–10) persuasively claims that the show is formally and aesthetically trans* in ways that far exceed the representation of Nomi as a trans character, I will argue that *Sense8*'s poly imaginary is much more substantially found in the cluster form itself than in these specific relationships. It is in the shaping of the cluster as an affective and effective structure of queer relationality that *Sense8* constructs poly as a televisual form.

Before we consider the value of "poly" as an organizing principle, it is instructive to note how existing criticism of *Sense8* has struggled with the show's politics. Despite its overt appeal to queer audiences, *Sense8* has generally disappointed those media scholars who have been most invested in ideological approaches. Cáel Keegan critiques the show's "flawed racial politics" (2016: 606), and Alexis Lothian similarly argues that the show's "seemingly liberatory globalised vision fails to confront the contradictions of racism, sexism, and class exploitation that shape the sensates' lives"

(2016: 94). In a roundtable discussion, all of the participants articulated problems with the show's representation of race, gender, and power. Lokeilani Kaimana and Rafi Sarkissian, for example, speak of "*Sense8*'s failed global imagination" (Bailey et al. 2017: 81), which they see as a centering of white characters and a lack of concern for how race works as an issue of global power. micha cárdenas finds that "the series relies on western colonial conceptions for its global imagination ... [and] is based on a western liberal colonial concept of multiculturalism, centered in white American culture, whose empathy relies on the universality of western values" (Bailey et al. 2017: 80). These critiques focus on *Sense8*'s globality, considering its attempts at a transnational or polycentric narrative to flatten out the realities of class and geopolitical difference, and thus to fail at the difficult work of forging meaningful connections across the world. Other critics have found the show's pathbreaking representation of a trans protagonist to be problematic. Rye Gentleman claims that "this futuristic framing of transness reinvigorates cultural tropes that imagine transgender people as unreal, impossible, and unknowable, contributing to the social othering of trans people" (2019: 150). In this reading, the way in which *Sense8* translates transness into aesthetic form actively contributes to transphobia, because speculative fictional form does not contribute to positive representation in the here and now. Without rejecting the value of a suspicious hermeneutic, I want to read both *Sense8*'s queerness and its science-fictional imaginary in a way that does not inevitably end in such disappointment.

Genevieve Newman points to the Wachowskis' "intersecting positions of privilege and marginality" (Bailey et al. 2017: 4) as wealthy white American trans women, and this multiple location within the landscape of contemporary queer politics speaks to the trouble that scholarship has had with the textual politics of *Sense8*. On the one hand, the show is obviously a progressive work: it is the first major television show created by trans showrunners and starring a trans actor. Moreover, it features a racially and sexually diverse group of characters and makes this diversity its central affective intervention. On the other hand, it is clearly not radical in the way that contemporary queer theory aspires to be radical. *Sense8* supports marriage—lesbian, trans marriage but marriage nonetheless—and its message that "Amor Vincit Omnia" (love conquers all) falls significantly short of demanding revolutionary change. Moreover, although its casting is more diverse than most American television, white characters are predominant and the smooth way in which love crosses national, ethnic, and religious lines might be viewed as obscuring the violence of real-world borders. Both the representational parameters of *Sense8* and the ambivalence of its critics index a particular moment in queer cultural politics in which the mainstreaming of Pride and popular support for same-sex marriage coexists with violent threats to the lives of queer people, and in particular minoritized groups such as trans women of color. Radical critique remains as crucial as ever, and yet the terrain of popular cultural contestation has shifted significantly. What is valuable in *Sense8* might partly be its ability to stage this moment in queer cultural history, in all its progress and its limitations. As much as it is symptomatic of the difficulties of politically engaged queer media, though, *Sense8*'s science-fictional form resists a straightforward realist account. The cluster form is not, or not only, a reflection of real-world identities, and its vision of collective life demands that we pay attention to its formal construction of utopian queer futures.

Nonmonogamous Theory

How does thinking of *Sense8* as a poly text elucidate these critical issues? Polyamory has only relatively recently been studied within queer theory, but those scholars who have addressed it are clearly thinking within this same critical moment. Mimi Schippers points out that most queer theory understands monogamy as central to both hetero- and homonormativities. The monogamous couple is a foundation for definitions of normativity, yet there are "few theoretical interrogations of how monogamy is implicated in and productive of gender, race, and sexual hierarchies or the role of monogamy as an organizing rationale for regimes of normalcy and social structures of inequality" (2016: 10). Schippers argues that turning away from the monogamous couple through polysexualities offers an opportunity to reorient not just relationships but also gender and race relations (2016: 4). Jin Haritaworn, Chin-ju Lin, and Christian Klesse also argue for an intersectional account of polyamory. They map the progressive political movements from which polyamory emerges, including feminism's critique of marriage, gay male sex culture's forms of nonmonogamy, BDSM's practices of sexual care, commune movements' forms of living outside the nuclear family, and bisexuality's expansion of relationality. They conclude:

> An engagement with polyamory and non-monogamy can provide novel insights into the social construction and organization of kinship, households and the family, parenting practices, sexual identities and heteronormativity. What is more, polyamory opens up new sex-positive terrains for erotic, sexual and relational understandings and practices. ... These new narratives of emotional and sexual abundance and collective care may provide real alternatives to capitalist and patriarchal ideologies of personal ownership and scarcity. (Haritaworn et al. 2006: 518–19)

These scholars are all engaged with the potential of polyamory to deconstruct the normative structures of monogamy, not least its implication in racial and colonial power. But they also see blind spots within polyamory. Christian Klesse's empirical work directly examines the contradictions in poly cultures, in particular the ways in which polyamorists reject the term "promiscuity" and create a distance between their own "respectable" form of nonmonogamy and the less desirable forms of "the bad swinger" or "the promiscuous queer" (2006: 578). In addition to such conservative attitudes to nonmonogamy, Klesse finds that "poly communities tend to reproduce a culture of multiple privileges, namely around class and race/ethnicity" (2014: 204). He concludes that "the socioeconomic inequalities that are prevalent in polyamorous communities can only ever be challenged effectively, if the ambivalent position of polyamory with regard to the cultural dynamics of neoliberal capitalism are fully understood" (2014: 204).

These arguments map onto *Sense8*'s ideological ambivalence: all of these scholars note the dominance of white middle-class people in poly communities, and Schippers counterposes the problem of "polynormativity" (2016: 19) with the potential for poly sexualities to undo normativities. Just as *Sense8* has been criticized for its whiteness and its lack of attention to power hierarchies, so queer theorists have criticized the reflection of systems of privilege in dominant poly cultures. And yet, these theories open up the potential for modes of poly relationality that would not be exclusionary or separate themselves from the "promiscuous queer." Klesse, indeed, notes that his own research failed to sample working-class and non-white people in polyqueer relationships, a gesture that allows us to posit that speculative fiction might be a more successful mode than sociological research with which to stage the possibilities of poly lifeworlds. The Wachowskis might be seen as feeding into modes of normativity across *Sense8*, and yet, the formal ways in which the show is polycentric are more able to refute normativity and to imagine alternative forms of sociality. Klesse concludes:

> Many polyamorists see polyamory as a critical discourse that aims at diversifying intimate and sexual cultures. At the same time, polyamory discourses tend to establish exclusive standards for what should be considered an ethical sexual and relationship practice. Thus, polyamory seems to be positioned ambiguously in the conjuncture of diverse normative and counternormative discourses on sex and relationships. The central role of love and intimacy in polyamory discourses renders them vulnerable to being appropriated by normative and assimilationist ideologies. (2006: 579)

This ambivalence between normativity and antinormativity perfectly describes the ideological tension at work in *Sense8*, and that risky bet on love and intimacy reveals why poly forms the ideal concept with which to engage both the politics and the affect of the show.

In arguing for *Sense8* as constructing a poly imaginary, I aim not only to contribute to the conversations already underway in queer critique of the show but also to advance a different way to analyze the queerness of the cluster form. Lothian speaks positively of the "queer promiscuity" of the show's orgies, in which "the messy, queer possibilities that erupt when bodies meet bodies" is better than the "sterile fantasy of mind-to-mind communication" (2016: 95). I will return to the idea of "queer promiscuity," which is a term with more cinematic resonance than Lothian necessarily intends here, but her valorization of bodies over minds leaves the nonsexual communication of the cluster—their ability to share thoughts, feelings, and bodily experiences—as outside the space of queerness, and on the side of globalized exploitation. Rather than locating the queer parts of *Sense8*'s central premise only in its representations of sex, I argue that the cluster form itself offers an expansive account of queer relationality. Dilyana Minceva's comparison of the cluster to Georges Bataille's "community of lovers" (2018: 36–7) is useful in conceptualizing an intimate assemblage which might evade the strictures of capitalism and in which community is defined by intense intimacy, emotion and bodily pleasure. For Bataille, she notes, "the ecstasy of fusion, which is anarchic and formless, yet productive of an existence not marked by possession, should be the real political principle of community" (2018: 37). *Sense8* does not escape either possession or form, but it does imagine a world in which community and love are radically reconfigured around the cluster. By constructing intimate bonds through a grouping that nurtures and supports desire, love, friendship, care, solidarity, and direct action, *Sense8* imagines a queer transformation of social relations.

How can we theorize a poly media text as a question of form? I turn first to Leo Bersani's "Against Monogamy," and thence to Cüneyt Çakırlar and Gary Needham's application of Bersani to the formal demands of queer film theory. Bersani's article is particularly germane to this project as a foundational text in queer theory that takes nonmonogamy as its central praxis of queer radicality. Written in 1998, the article begins from what Bersani sees as the oddity of campaigns for gay marriage, which he describes as a "rush to respectability" (1998: 3). He cites Foucault's "new ways of being together" (Bersani 2001: 351) in opposition to such retrograde desires. "And yet," he counters, "if the monogamous model seems more firmly established than ever before as the hegemonic model of sexual relations, the very publicity it has been enjoying suggests that its hegemony has been subjected to perhaps unprecedented strains" (Bersani 1998: 3). Even when Bersani was writing this article—not many more than twenty years ago—the possibilities of queer representation on popular television were vastly different. Ellen DeGeneres had just come out the year before, both in person on *The Oprah Winfrey Show* and as her character on her eponymous sitcom *Ellen* (1994–8) in which she came out to a therapist played by Oprah Winfrey. The politics of gay respectability were only beginning to coalesce. *Sense8*'s entire narrative culminating in a triumphant lesbian wedding speaks of a radically different moment in both popular and theoretical conceptions of queer life. Nonetheless, Bersani's argument against monogamy provides us with ways to theorize *Sense8*'s poly project. He writes: "Monogamy has become a subject of reflection—a reflection that is a minor but crucial aspect of a more widespread problematising of the nature and value of community, of the relation between community and identity, and, most profoundly, of the nature of sociality itself" (1998: 4). This shift from the couple toward community, identity, and sociality is very much the project of *Sense8*. Through the cluster form, it imagines a different mode of sociality, one that is deeply threatening to existing human power structures (within the show, concretized as Biological Preservation Organization (BPO)) and that involves forming entirely new types of affective, social, and sexual bonds with groups of other people. The dispersal of monogamy that inevitably attends the cluster form is only one index of its larger promise of queer sociality.

Çakırlar and Needham build on Bersani to propose monogamy and promiscuity as opposing modes of cinematic vision with formal qualities, akin to the ways that feminist theory has analyzed gendered forms of looking relations. Thus, they aim "to explore how cinema could potentially produce alternative optical registers in presenting different modes of intimacy, which we would like to conceptualise by treating monogamy and promiscuity as ideological forces that reify aesthetic practices in film and arts" (3). Translating Bersani's critique into specifically audiovisual terms, they propose a dominant monogamous optic within which film and other visual media structure identification, pleasure, and narrative meaning through the formal construction of the romantic couple. For them, homonormativity in gay cinema consists in using the same monogamous optic as straight cinema does, asserting subjectivity as defined through the couple form and suppressing any sexual dissidence that might find its expression in alternative forms. In contrast to this monogamous optic, they outline what they term a promiscuous optic, which "implies a dispersal of the character's subjectivity and the subject of spectatorship" (Çakırlar and Needham 2021: 17). What is especially productive in this argument is their elaboration of the monogamous and promiscuous optics in terms of audiovisual form. Their examples include the application of what Bersani calls "the couple's oval-like intimacy" (Bersani 2010: 33) in framings of romantic couples facing each other on-screen, versus the way a promiscuous optic breaks apart shot-reverse shot structures in order to disaggregate characters from the couple form. Çakırlar and Needham's choice of "promiscuous" as the opposing term to monogamous indicates how their focus on gay cinematic cruising might be precisely what Klesse's normative polyamorists are afraid of. Certainly, they are more invested in formally radical art cinema than in popular television. Nonetheless, I would argue that monogamy/promiscuity can be more flexibly understood not as a binary but as a continuum, within which texts can construct many visual strategies. Çakırlar and Needham ask: "How can the text engage the spectator in a mode of promiscuous looking, and in a mode of sociability that contests the screen couple as an ethical ideal?" (2021: 19). *Sense8* may not reach the radical edges of formal and sexual fragmentation, but it does reject the dominant visual optics of monogamy and it does develop an ethical vision of sociability that looks beyond the couple form. Drawing on Çakırlar and Needham, I argue that *Sense8*'s formal articulation of the cluster creates a poly optic.

Sense8's Poly Optic

The basic form of polycentricity in *Sense8* is the way in which the cluster share sensations, experiences, and perspectives. From the very beginning, the subjectivity of a sensate is shown to exceed the bodily boundaries of the individual. In S01:E01, Will hears loud pounding techno and thinks that the music is coming from his neighbor's apartment in Chicago, but he discovers that it is empty, because the sounds are actually coming from Riley's DJ-ing in London. Subjectivity is no longer individual, and connection to others penetrates into the body across space. In the polycentricity of the cluster, characters can sense things taking place elsewhere, as the sensorium expands and extends beyond realist limits. This extension is marked formally both between and within shots. When Riley experiences "sharing" Will's body, it is first signaled through an optical point of view shot in which Will's partner shouts directly at the camera, and then through Will's look at Riley reflected in a car window. In the next scene Riley is not sharing but "visiting," so she is able to share screen space with Will, bringing two spaces together within the shot. When she turns, a match on action cut shows what she sees in London, not Chicago, and when Will looks over, he can see them too. Here, continuity editing teaches the audience a grammar of sharing and visiting, and in turn these familiar formal mechanisms are repurposed to stage a subjectivity that is plural in form. Continuity editing conventionally structures identification around heteropatriarchal systems of subjectivity and, according to Çakırlar and Needham, also around monogamous structures. *Sense8*'s cluster subjectivity begins from these dominant forms—Will and Riley will become a romantic couple, for instance—but its polycentricity elaborates a queerly expansive supplement to these modes of being.

In the same way that Amanita protects her romantic partner Nomi in S01:E04 "What's Going On?," so the sensate cluster use their expanded subjectivity to care for and rescue one another. In the first major episode of the cluster visiting and sharing with one another, in S01:E03 "Smart Money's on the Skinny Bitch," Sun and Will use their fighting skills to save Capheus from gangsters. In S01:E04, Nomi requires both the efforts of her girlfriend and her cluster to escape an unwanted brain surgery. As the series develops, cluster subjectivity is articulated across affiliations that are often highlighted as queer. In S01:E09 "Death Doesn't Let You Say Goodbye,"

Nomi visits with Lito in the Diego Rivera museum and shares her experience of transphobia as a way of empathizing with his fear of coming out. Keegan perfectly describes the multiple nature of the cluster form when he writes that

> characters begin in separate, distinctly racialized and gendered narrative settings that the text progressively collapses toward simultaneity, stacking up "nows" until genre becomes the mirrorball surface of a new geometry of global time. Yet rather than collapsing into a singular consciousness, the cluster ripples embodied sensation back upon itself into something far more capacious, complex, and internally expansive. Subjectivity on *Sense8* is plural, enfolded, and unfolding. (Bailey et al. 2017: 6)

This sense of an unfolding and plural sensorium is articulated most clearly in montage scenes like the one in S02:E01 "Happy Fucking New Year," in which we see the cluster swimming underwater together, scored to Avicii's version of "Feeling Good," intercut with their actual locations. Although some of the cluster are in unpleasant or perilous situations (Sun in prison, Will injecting heroin), the emotional tenor of their shared experience is one of fluidity and togetherness. Keegan posits the show's ability to position the spectator "between genders, genres, geographies, cultures, and bodies' as 'an astonishing exploration of trans* phenomenology as it might be formalized by popular televisual narrative" (Bailey et. al. 2017: 6). I see this trans* reading as contiguous to my own and polycentricity as working in concert with a trans* aesthetic. In other words, the queerness of *Sense8* also emerges in its ability to transform and extend from the queerness of individual characters to reimagined modes of collective life.

As with its central trans* narrative, *Sense8* offers direct examples of polyamorous relationships within its central cluster. Wolfgang (in Berlin) falls in love with clustermate Kala (in Mumbai), but Kala is already engaged to non-sensate Rajan. When Wolfgang first encounters Kala in S01:E02 "I Am Also a We," he is in bed with a woman, but locks eyes with Kala through a shot-reverse shot that traverses Berlin to Mumbai. His partner asks what he is looking at and if there is someone else. He says no, but already the cluster form is proposed as a different option for affective relations than existing social and audiovisual forms. The cluster does not preclude outside attachments, but editing extends human vision and cathexis across geographical and narrative spaces. In S01:E05 "Art Is Like Religion," Wolfgang visits Kala's wedding naked, causing her to faint, and in the following episode, "Demons," he again appears naked, this time in her bedroom. In these sequences, visiting works to complicate her seemingly inevitable marriage: both his gaze on her and her desiring gaze on his naked body open out cluster visiting as a promiscuous form. Kala and Wolfgang kiss for the first time in S01:E11 "Just Turn the Wheel and the Future Changes," but she nonetheless marries Rajan. Whereas the first season might have led viewers to interpret the plot as a generically conventional love triangle, in which Kala would choose between love and duty, the second season makes clear that her answer is "both." In S02:E01, Kala's tentative wedding night with Rajan is comedically interrupted by Wolfgang enthusiastically having sex with a woman he met through an app. Through cluster visiting, all four participants seem to be in the same room. Whether played as melodrama or comedy, the poly nature of their connection is formally centered. As the narrative develops, it morphs from love triangle to throuple (Figure 5.1). In S02:E06 "Isolated Above, Connected Below," Rajan bends to kiss Kala awake but a cut reveals that he is actually kissing Wolfgang's face. The cluster form produces and enables poly attachments. By S02:E12 "Amor Vincit Omnia," all three are physically in the same place. Watching Wolfgang exchange small talk with Rajan, Kala exclaims anxiously, "I don't know what rules to follow!" In the next shots, however, Kala embraces first Rajan and then Wolfgang, their kisses intercut in slow motion. Once again, conventional monogamous camera and editing practices are repurposed to elaborate a poly aesthetic.

Sense8's poly optic, though, does not depend on the representation of specifically polyamorous relationships. It is perhaps most capaciously imagined in the series' famous orgy scenes, in which poly desire and affection is at its most joyfully unrestricted. The first orgy, in S01:E06 is limited in scope but it reveals some key features of the show's sexual imaginary. Sexual orientation is structurally loosened within the cluster since, while each member retains their object choice(s) in their primary relationships,

FIGURE 5.1 *The cluster form enables poly attachments, as in the throuple that forms among Kala, Wolfgang, and Rajan.*

the cluster form enables them to have sex with everyone else in the cluster, regardless of gender or sexual identity. The orgy begins with various characters doing physical but not necessarily sexual activities. Will and Lito are both at the gym, and in one of the first moments of sexual visiting, Will lifts a weight out of frame to reveal Lito, who kisses him. Will, who has hitherto been represented as heterosexual, begins his sexual life as a sensate by kissing a man. (The actor who plays Will, Brian Smith, has since come out as gay, adding to the cultural discourse around the queer identities of many of *Sense8*'s cast and creative team.) As the sequence continues, we cut among various pairs of cluster members, most of whom are kissing someone outside their previously narrated identities (a lesbian and a gay man, a straight man and a lesbian, etc.). Moreover, the shared sexual pleasure of these scenes teaches us something about the sexual dynamics of cluster sense perception. Each orgy scene begins by intercutting characters in their own spaces, often although not always having sex in couples. It would be easy to view these shots as conventional cross-cutting among entirely separate entities, and thus as presenting conventional monogamous couples as the material basis for the sensate orgy. In the *Sense8* world, however, montage works to share bodies and sensations, so we already know that each sensate can feel the experiences of the others. Editing performs a new function here by prefiguring the appearance of the sensates together within shots. The most obvious way that *Sense8* shows us the cluster sharing sensation is by placing the actors physically in the same space, but these shared compositions only render visible something that was already occurring diegetically. In other words, the cluster are already fucking one another when all we see are discrete couples: every image that we see of sensate sex is already polyamorous. The cross-cutting that bookends the orgies stages between shots the same poly imaginary that visiting does when viewed within shots. Lito smiles and says, "I just had one of the best orgasms of my life," because being in a sensate poly orgy opens out new forms of queer bliss.

One of the central formal mechanisms of the monogamous optic, for Çakırlar and Needham, is Bersani's "oval-like intimacy" of the couple, which they interpret visually as framings of the romantic couple facing each other on-screen. The orgy sequences illustrate the distinction between Çakırlar and Needham's preferred promiscuous optic (in which oval couple forms are rejected) and *Sense8*'s poly optic in which romantic love is visually affirmed and yet is also formally subsumed within the wider bonds of the cluster. In S02:E01, we begin with some classic oval shots of couples, including Nomi and Amanita undressing each other in a public park, and Will and Riley having sex in the missionary position. Will and Riley's candle-lit sex, in particular, seems to follow entirely monogamous heteronormative representational protocols. But, as I have argued, in these shots, the cluster is *already* experiencing a polysexual orgy, and what looks like an oval is necessarily resignified. One of the couples seen at the beginning is Lito and Hernando, whose shots immediately displace the oval. They are in a bathroom stall, and instead of placing the camera at the same level as the two characters' heads, here the camera is overhead, looking down into the stall where Lito is on his knees in front of Hernando. This (slightly) dirtier act of semi-public sex opens the way for the formal breakdown of monogamy: we return to the bathroom stall at the end of the orgy with another overhead shot of the entire cluster and their partners squeezed into this tiny space. Even when we think we see a couple, this shot emphasizes, it is actually an entire cluster.

The main body of the orgy strikingly breaks down the oval form by staging cluster sex in a tableau that disaggregates couples and bodies. Laura Horak and Rox Samer consider the orgy in S02:E01 to be "reminiscent of Gian Lorenzo Bernini or Antonio Canova sculptures" (Bailey et al. 2017: 10), and the Italian Baroque provides an excellent reference point for the scene's formal emphasis on the multiple curves and movements of flesh. In many shots, we do not know exactly who we are looking at, as quick cuts make it hard to grasp exactly whose body we are seeing. Instead of face-to-face intimacy, these shots focus on fragmented corporeality: Nomi's arm, Capheus's back, someone's ass. When we cut back to a wide shot of the whole group on a San Francisco hill, the tableau is shaped more like a triangle than an oval (Figure 5.2). The varied intertwined body parts build into a whole that produces a spectacular effect that I have previously identified as the pretty (Galt 2011). The ornamental figuration of the Baroque produces an aesthetic of bodily pleasure, but also one of affect and intimacy—which is to

FIGURE 5.2 *In* Sense8*'s orgies, the oval of the monogamous couple is replaced with spectacular and pretty shapes of multiple intimacy.*

say that *Sense8*'s poly optic rejects monogamy but not sentimentality. As we cut back to a wide shot, the cluster begins to move in unison—a harmony that calls back to the previous scene of dancing in time to music, and also a swooping gesture that repeats the motion of the rope swing from an earlier scene. It is a movement that resonates in sex—as in the next shot of Will swinging his body up to meet Riley—but within the orgy it does not seem to indicate a sexual act but rather an ecstasy that emerges out of being together and moving together.

The final orgy in S02:E12 fully integrates the polymorphous sexuality of the previous sex scenes with the cluster's polyamorous relationships. Near the beginning of the scene, Wolfgang appears on the bed beside which Kala and Rajan are standing. He taps the bedspread and raises an eyebrow suggestively. Rajan cannot see him but he knows he is there. In response, Rajan looks to the bed and raises his own eyebrow. When we next cut to them, all three are framed together with Kala between the two men. Wolfgang pulls open Rajan's shirt, indicating that their sex will not only be an MFM threesome but something more open. They form a small diegetic polycule, but this grouping also becomes a visual anchoring point for the polycentricity of the entire expanded cluster. Something similar can be said about the more ambiguous threesome of Lito, Hernando, and Daniela. As we cut among the cluster's couples, Daniela is included with Lito and Hernando. Although the men are represented as gay, Daniela lives with them, sleeps in bed with them, and is included in many of their intimate scenes. Here we see her kneeling as if she is about to go down on Hernando. The cluster orgies are not limited by orientation, but this polymorphous sexuality seems to bleed outward into Lito and Hernando's affection for Daniela. When Rajan and Wolfgang kiss, this is the act that shifts the scene away from the rhythm of cutting among couples (and throuples) to the wide shot with the expanded cluster together in a tangle of bodies. As the camera roams slowly across the orgy, we cut to memory montages of each sensate, in which their romantic histories feed into the present sensation. According to Bersani, "psychoanalytically, monogamy is inconceivable except as something that blocks circuits of desire" (1998: 11). He sees the monogamous couple in Freud as "a unit in continuous dissolution" (1998: 11), and this endless dissolution is what *Sense8*'s cluster form reimagines as bliss. The couple form sustains, but it is always being dissolved into the cluster and reconstituted in revised form, ecstatic and multiple. The cluster does not destroy the romantic couple, but it does visually narrate a claim that love is not exhausted or limited by the dyad. It strips away monogamy's normative social isolation and sexual exclusivity, insisting that love can take multiple queer pathways. As Rajan exclaims at the end of the scene: "My god, I didn't think such things were possible!"

Sense8's polycentricity is at its most utopian in the orgy sequences, but it stakes its claim to a queer politics most vividly in its attempts to imagine a different form of collective life. Bersani considers monogamy to be a kind of reaction formation to the difficulties of being in the world. "Psychoanalysis," he proposes, "with its obsessive concern with the difference between the self and the world, necessarily sees the latter as the repository of everything hostile to the self. It is a place to which, at best, we adapt and from which we retreat and regress to the imagined familial securities nourished by such privileged institutions as monogamy and marriage" (1998: 21). By contrast, *Sense8* stakes its theory of subjectivity on the possibilities of being in the world and imagines the cluster as a form that exists in the world and across the world. Discussions of the show often focus on its many locations, whether to laud its spatial ambition, describe its challenging production schedule, or criticize its too easy appropriation of different cultures. In both its material production and its ideological aims, the project of creating a world is central to *Sense8*'s narration of the cluster. Schippers asks, "What *effect* poly ... relationship choices might have, not just on the individuals involved, but also, if chosen collectively, on social relations more generally" (2016: 4). *Sense8*'s response might be the title of S02:E03 "Obligate Mutualisms," a concept of ethical responsibility to the collective that imagines such an effect on social relations. Within the narrative, mutualism is generally leveraged in action sequences, such as in S02:E11 "If You Want a War?" in which the cluster help Sun chase down her criminal brother and escape from the police. In the larger narrative, however, cluster subjectivity is explicitly presented as a mode of social existence that is a threat to normativity. *Sense8* places polycentrism as central to its critique of inequality. BPO are so afraid of sensates because they recognize that the cluster form is an existential threat to normative systems of social relations. Exiting from normal human subjectivity into the subjectivity of the sensate is not only an opening to other sensations, other bodies and their desires; it is also an opening to different ways of being in the world.

This mode of worldliness is manifested not—as some of the critics I mentioned earlier complain—as realist political representation but as affect. An enlarged cluster of eight sensates plus those with whom they share romantic and non-romantic bonds emerges as a locus of collective care and affirmation. Biological families are not the center of this collective. Instead, *Sense8* privileges friends, from Nomi's long-time hacker buddy Bug to Sun's cellmates in prison to Lito's beard-friend-lover Daniela. These bonds can be not only nonsexual but also nonhuman. For Sun, separating from her beloved dog was one of the worst aspects of going to prison, and in S02:E05 "Fear Never Fixed Anything," she is reunited with him in an emotional, magic-hour reunion. In S02:E01, one of the show's most sentimental montage scenes imagines the expanded cluster as a queer family. The scene is scored to a cover of Leonard Cohen's "Hallelujah," and we discover that this music is (or rather is presented as) diegetic when Nomi and Amanita attend a concert at City Hall by the San Francisco Gay Men's Choir. Some of our sensates share familial bonds: Capheus watches *It's a Wonderful Life* (Capra, 1946) with his mother, while Lito, Hernando, Daniela, and Lito's mother attend a Christmas vigil at Mexico City's cathedral. Sun, by contrast, is in prison because of her brother, and she is cared for instead by one of her fellow prisoners who pushes candies through the bars of the cell in which she is in solitary confinement. Chosen family, biological family, and outlaw solidarities are folded into the ambit of the cluster, in the face of disease, injustice, homophobia, and violence. All of the cluster visit Nomi to listen to the choir, turning to this cultural touchstone of queer community as a reminder of the show's opening gesture toward queer histories, resilience, and affective bonds.

Sense8's finale, "Amor Vincit Omnia," as its title suggests, proposes love as the defining feature of the cluster form and the strength of the world it might create. Love, as Klesse points out, is a defining feature of polyamory discourse, in ways that have both the reactionary potential to disassociate from promiscuity and the radical promise of "blur[ring] the boundaries between the sexual and non-sexual and partnership and friendship" (2006: 566). Love might demand an inward-looking dyad or an outward-looking cathexis to the community, and as much as *Sense8* celebrates the romantic couple, the cluster form never ends there. The utopian scene of Nomi and Amanita's wedding in Paris brings together all of the sensates and their expanded cluster in joyful queer communion. As Riley's father plays a version of The Magnetic Fields' bittersweet song "Nothing Matters When We're Dancing," various configurations of people dance together and kiss. Serena Anderlini-d'Onofrio uses the term "plural happiness" to discuss bisexual and polyamorous imaginaries in cinema, suggesting that this form of collectivity and collaborative love "reconfigures the ecology of queer theory" (2009: 344). I find this to be a somewhat overstated claim, but if I can redirect it, it *does* make sense in regard to *Sense8*, which has very much reconfigured the ecology of queer popular television. In reading *Sense8*'s vision of queer love and polycentric collective life, we can remain cognizant of the limitations of its sentimental politics while also taking seriously its speculative potential. That *Sense8*'s utopian ending was instantly beloved by fans is not a case of queer false consciousness. In S02:E12, the queerness of the cluster reimagines the world: forms of relationality; ways of being; emotional bonds and ethical responsibilities to others; relations of family, friendship, and care, as well as those of lust, romance, and partnership are reformed around a multiple, polycentric imagination. And this polycentric optic frames its vision of relationality around the lessons of queer activism, experience, history, and critique. *Sense8*'s utopian gesture is to imagine that we can reconfigure the world in the forms and affects of what Bersani calls "our promiscuous humanity" (1998: 21).

Works Cited

Anderlini-d'Onofrio, S. (2009), "Plural Happiness: Bi and Poly Triangulations in Balasko's *French Twist*," *Journal of Bisexuality*, 9: 343–61.

Bailey, M., m. cárdenas, L. Horak, L. Kaimana, C. M. Keegan, G. Newman, R. Samer, and R. Sarkissian (2017), "*Sense8* Roundtable," *Spectator*, 37 (2): 77–88.

Bersani, L. (1998), "Against Monogamy", *Oxford Literary Review*, 20 (1–2): 3–21.

Bersani, L. (2001), "Genital Chastity," in T. Dean and C. Lane (eds.), *Homosexuality and Psychoanalysis*, 351–66, Chicago: University of Chicago Press.

Bersani, L. (2010), "Is There a Gay Art?," in *Is the Rectum a Grave and Other Essays*, 31–5, Chicago: University of Chicago Press.

Çakırlar, C., and G. Needham (2021), "The Monogamous/Promiscuous Optics in Contemporary Gay Film: Registering the Amorous Couple in *Weekend* (2011) and *Paris 05:59: Theo & Hugo* (2016)," *New Review of Film and Television Studies*, 18 (4): 1–30.

Galt, R. (2011), *Pretty: Film and the Decorative Image*, New York: Columbia University Press.

Gentleman, R. (2019), "'I'm Not Just a Me but I'm Also a We': Algorithmic Culture and Netflix's *Sense8*," *TDR*, 63 (4): 139–51.

Haritaworn, J., C. J. Lin, and K. Klesse (2006), "Poly/logue: A Critical Introduction to Polyamory," *Sexualities*, 9 (5): 515–29.

Keegan, C. M. (2016), "Tongues without Bodies: The Wachowskis' *Sense8*," *TSQ: Transgender Studies Quarterly*, 3 (3–4): 605–10.

Klesse, C. (2006), "Polyamory and Its 'Others': Contesting the Terms of Non-Monogamy," *Sexualities*, 9 (5): 565–83.

Klesse, C. (2014), "Poly Economics—Capitalism, Class, and Polyamory," *International Journal of Politics, Culture and Society*, 27: 203–20.

Lothian, A. (2016), "*Sense8* and Utopian Community," *Science Fiction Film and Television*, 9 (1): 93–5.

Mincheva, D. (2018), "*Sense8* and the Praxis of Utopia," *Cinephile*, 12 (1): 32–9.

Schippers, M. (2016), *Beyond Monogamy: Polyamory and the Future of Polyqueer Sexualities*, New York: New York University Press.

6

Between Necropower and Erotopolitics: Community and Clusterfuck as Alloerotic Distraction

John Lessard

This chapter analyzes the Wachowskis' clusterfuck sequences alongside Jean-Luc Nancy's phenomenology of the political in order to understand why sense becomes *Sense8*'s privileged figure for understanding the surprise, and therefore the event, of community. Rather than treating Nancy's oeuvre as a theoretical instrument that can be brought to bear on the Wachowskis work, or vice versa, I propose that we consider them according to the model of "quantum entanglement" that Angelica explains to Raoul during a flashback in S02:E03 "Obligate Mutualisms": "Particles respond to the same stimuli across huge distances." Proposed by Albert Einstein, Boris Podolsky, and Nathan Rosen in 1935, quantum entanglement refers to the "correlations" between two quantum systems that remain in effect even after the two systems have separated (Bub 2020).

Consonant with *Sense8*'s simultaneously sexed and speculative species of erotopolitics, Nancy's asymptotic philosophy of touch and exposure seeks to interrupt hegemonic models of community that reduce the political as such to the production of an essence, sameness, or identity (*idem*—the same). For Nancy, as for the Wachowskis, such circuitries of the same remain bound to the earlier sense of *jouissance* in French: "etymologically, there is no special relationship between the word jouir (from the Latin gaudere, 'to rejoice') and sexuality. For a long time, jouissance has had a mainly legalistic sense, designating the effect of complete possession of something, a possession that allows a complete, limitless use of what I own" (Nancy 2017: 4). This older meaning of jouissance runs counter to the more recent sense of intense pleasure, an erotic quivering that announces the coming of joy (and joy of coming). *Jouissance* thus carries a jointly political and erotic charge derived, at least in part, from the manifold pleasures and intensities, even the "co-jouissance" (Nancy 2000: 75) of what Nancy designates as "being singular plural" (Nancy 2000: 37). The particular ways that being singular plural "spaces" the cluster's inherent unities and divisions together constitute the drama and allure of *Sense8* (Nancy 1997: 160).

In their respective bodies of work, both the Wachowskis and Nancy have developed erotically charged philosophies of community that chart out the complexities of being singular plural. Whereas Nancy's philosophy was marked by the political and sexual experiments of the generation of 1968 (Nancy and Engelmann 2019: 40), the Wachowskis rose to prominence during the quite different moment of the Generation X 1990s. Yet they have each pursued the cinematic capacities of philosophy and the philosophical dimensions of cinema along sympathetic, often parallel, routes. Despite the twenty or so years separating their respective journeys, all three are deeply speculative thinkers who have consistently probed the radically ecstatic character of community and commonality. Nancy's elaboration of a "post-deconstructive" ontology of political community has in turn shaped his philosophy of cinema: "the realism of Nancy's touch-as-spacing is post-deconstructive in that it perpetually disperses and defers the immediacy of the phenomenological *corps propre* ('body proper'), thereby interrupting any recourse to a metaphysics of presence" (McMahon 2010: 74). Both drawing on and radically reshaping Heidegger's notion of ecstasy, Nancy understands *ecstatic* being as a standing outside oneself, an *ek-stasis* that is simultaneously a condition of subjectivity and the generative structure of community and communality as such (Nancy 2006: 6). For Nancy, the pervasively ecstatic structure of community requires that we not only rethink Being in terms of "Being-with" (what Heidegger called "Mitsein"), but even further, that we do so in terms of the "with" itself, thus moving beyond Heidegger's limited treatment of it (Nancy and Engelmann 2019: 65). It is this "with" that *Senses8* both inhabits and brings into view.

Despite its monumental production scale and abundant spectacle, *Sense8*'s most distinctive formal achievements include its transnational constellation of settings, generic hybridity, and horizontally dispersed yet vertically integrated narrative structure. *Sense8* has therefore broken new ground in the "new mode of television storytelling" that Jason Mittell refers to as "complex TV" (Mittell 2015: 3). Mittell notes that complex TV has created space for an "operational aesthetic" based more on "narrative special effect" than on the kind of New Hollywood action and VFX-based spectacle with which the Wachowskis had long become synonymous (Mittell 2015: 43). The show combines the generic conventions of global conspiracy-thrillers and multi-story puzzle films (Buckland 2009: 5) with a more speculative sensibility attuned to affective intensities and embodied, yet transsubjective experiences. In this regard, *Sense8* stands as a kind of unofficial follow-up to the intersecting storylines and transsubjective affinities of the Wachowskis' 2012 film *Cloud Atlas*, a transnational production based on a novel by *Sense8* cowriter David Mitchell, and jointly helmed by *Sense8* codirector Tom Tykwer, whose own breakout hit, *Run Lola Run* (1998), features a similarly jigsawed construction and philosophical ethos. One might say that the puzzle principle underlying *Sense8*'s formal construction is precisely the puzzle of community and desire.

This puzzling of the communal unfolds, moreover, within a global imaginary that is more properly a global phenomenology, at least insofar as *Sense8*'s understanding of being is consistently framed in terms of an appearing, or rather of a coappearing. *Sense8*'s phenomenal rendering of world thus recalls Heidegger's rooting of phenomenology in the Greek φαίνεσθαι: "to show itself [and therefore] what shows itself, the self-showing" of beings (Heidegger 2010: 27). By differentiating this more fundamental sense of a self-showing from the diminished sense of phenomena as spectacle or mere appearance, Heidegger grounds phenomena in the relationality of "Mitsein," which is to say, Being-with (Heidegger 2010: 115). For the sensates, too, Being reveals itself to be grounded in the cluster's more fundamental mode of Being-with. It is less accurate to say that the cluster is coterminous with the sensates' existence as subjects than to say that the cluster precedes the sensates' emergence as individual beings, let alone as individual subjects. Born of Angelica's second cluster birth, Will asks Jonas whether "any gender can give birth to a cluster," and Jonas confirms that they can do so repeatedly (S02:E03). As Jonas explains, it is precisely this ontological promiscuity that "terrifies them the most about us. Potential population growth" (S02:E03). The biosocial unit of the cluster is therefore both multiple and multiplying (see Figure 6.1).

The sensates are born of an originary communality that aligns with Nancy's account of "a primordial plurality that co-appears, and is also anterior to the order of [mere] appearance, manifestation, phenomena, revealing, or some other concept of becoming-visible" (Nancy 2000: 67). Much as Marx argues that the bourgeois subject is both preceded and made possible by collective existence, not the other way around, Nancy argues that being itself is fundamentally plural. This plurality is not only prior to, it is indeed the condition of, any notion of a distinct individuality. *Sense8*'s representation of transsubjective and transnational phenomenality generates a thick topography or areality that carries a simultaneously geopolitical and ontological weight. As McMahon explains, Nancy understands the "politics of space as non-unitary and non-identitarian," and therefore as

FIGURE 6.1 *Imaging ontological promiscuity and the coming community.*

"the inexhaustible delineation of co-exposure, the inoperative opening of the political" (McMahon 2011: 625). In the case of the sensates' evolving experiences of identity and community, it is critical that their growing exposure to one another is organized as an unexpected interruption or irruption—a distraction from the immediacy of their surrounding world that takes the form of a transsubjective mediacy. Much like the time traveler of Chris Marker's proto-modernist sci-fi short, *La Jetée* (1962), the protagonists of *Sense8* experience each other as a phenomenal interruption or irruption that fractures their sense of the immediacy and unity of their surrounding worlds, and therefore too their familiar communities of relation.

But in contrast to the ideological and discursive machineries that serve to both produce and reproduce a nationalist essence or identity, the sensates' sense of mutual connection is generated instead by intense states of erotic distraction and pleasurable phenomenological surprise. *Sense8* thus draws on two different understandings of world and transcendence that converge, and therefore come into conflict, around questions of the proper mode of community. As erotic distractions in a very fundamental sense, *Sense8*'s orgies or clusterfuck sequences provide a valuable index of the show's larger imaginings of community and commonality. These orgiastic sequences—one can't really call them scenes in the usual sense due to their distinctive folding of narrative space-time—pleasurably disrupt the coercive unities of subject and community undergirding identitarian politics. Borrowing the distractive structures of erotic daydreams, *Sense8*'s telepathic orgy sequences feature an aleatory eroticism that becomes in turn aligned with the pleasures of unanticipated, and by conventional logic, unimaginable community. The alloerotic ethos of these clusterfuck sequences is charged with the unintended *jouissance* and desirability of remaining open, or as per Nancy, "exposed" to the eros and orexis of alterity, including self-alterity. The clusterfuck sequences thus embody, in the most literal sense, a trans*/queer challenge to the Biological Preservation Organization (BPO), and by extension, to an ultraright imaginary steeped in the centuries-old toxicity of racism, eugenics, homo- and transphobia, and virulent nationalisms.

How then are we to understand *Sense8*'s interweaving of these two elements: the political and the erotic? Should we view the clusterfuck sequences as a privileged form of the political in *Sense8*, or even as its defining image? Or is clusterfucking but one of the many forms or modes of community that we encounter in *Sense8*'s psycellium-powered diegesis? In contrast to the more frequent and sustained storylines devoted to conventional-looking cis-hetero romantic alignments (e.g., Will and Riley), the relative scarcity of clusterfuck sequences raises additional questions regarding the narrative role and political implications of the show's full range of intimacies and interactions. Are the clusterfuck images meant to be exceptional to, or exemplary of, sensate community? Rather than probing *Sense8*'s politics of gender and sexuality directly and as such, I propose a more oblique approach that focuses instead on the implications of the clusterfuck sequences for our sense of the show's political imaginary. While *Sense8*'s clusterfuck sequences are remarkable from a purely formal perspective, they also illustrate and perform the show's erotopolitical co-constitution of sense and community.

It is therefore *Sense8*'s interest in erotic distraction that most powerfully grounds its erotopolitical imaginary within the ethics and temporalities of becoming. To think the other according to a phenomenology of the event is to imagine community according to an ecstatic temporality that outstrips the subject and resists the appropriation of community as essence. To speak of community in terms of the event is therefore to acknowledge that its sense or meaning lies in the asymptotic temporality that structures it: event as a coming that is always either not yet here or already arrived. The ecstatic temporality of the event as such is precisely what lends it its force, being, or sense: an erotopolitical event that announces what we might call (per Agamben) a coming community.

The Birth of Community

Nowhere is *Sense8*'s conjugation of the erotic and political more visible than in the show's use of both procreative and orgiastic imagery to embody the generation and communalization of the cluster. In their different ways, images of natality and clusterfuckery reinforce the eventality and surprise of community. Community is treated not as substance or essence but as happening or event. The event of community, the clustering of the cluster, is organized as the spontaneous autoproduction of a new sense and its intangible correlates: contact, touch, exposure. By conjoining number, sense, and identity in its very title, *Sense8* lends an unavoidably political dimension to its discourses and iconographies of sense. *Sense8* celebrates the irruptive character of community from the beginning, and as beginning, in the most literal sense: as birth, as becoming, as novum. Angelica's psychic birthing of the cluster provides the initial narrative disruption that sets the rest of the story in motion. In S01:E01 "Limbic Resonance," the sensates' opening to their telepathic abilities, and therefore to each other, is staged as a haunting. Disturbing images of a woman (Angelica) giving both birth (to the cluster) and death (to herself) merge with the suggestively Gothic tableau of an abandoned church, which thereby accommodates both maternal trauma and the withdrawal of presence associated with Deus absconditus, the absent (spiritual) father. This ideologically saturated mise-en-scène serves as the launching ground for what might have been a conventional narrative of Oedipalized subject formation. But those conventional narrative contours are quickly exploded by both the show's generic excesses and its more interesting premise of singular-plural subjects coalescing around, but also as, community.

The other appears, but precisely as an appearance or apparition: an image that initially haunts or unsettles the sensates' very sense of sense, which is to say, their common sense. The sensates are drawn out of their commonsense experiences of the world by the urgency of a call or demand to which they have been inexplicably opened, or toward which they have somehow opened themselves. At the same time though, this coming of the other often reveals itself to be in fact a kind of return, a second coming. Angelica's spiritual birthing of the cluster is preceded by their natural births and the first breath that each of them unwittingly shared (and later represented in S01:E10 "What Is Human"). The surprise of the other is less an event of pure arrival than the return of a forgotten or estranged community, the recollection of an originary communality. Insofar as these traumatic birthing images recover the forgotten truth of a common origin, the cluster's very constitution as a cluster functions like Heidegger's truth as αλήθεια (alethia) (Heidegger 2009: 102–4), which is to say, truth as a kind of unforgetting or disclosure.

The sensates awaken to their telepathic abilities at the same time as, and by virtue of the fact that, they awaken first of all to each other (and therefore to themselves). Yet this telepathic opening introduces a phenomenological shock or surprise that fundamentally disrupts their phenomenal world, which is to say, the world as given, and above all, as given to common sense. While a sensate's apparitional other destabilizes the immediacy of sensory perception, and also of common sense, the other nevertheless carries the weight of the real. The other's standing as phenomenological interruption foregrounds questions of community and political experiment even as it privileges various forms of erotic possibility and play.

Talking with Will in front of Rembrandt's *The Night Watch* in Amsterdam's Rijksmuseum, Richard Croome (Clive Wood) surprises Will with his view of Homo sapiens and Homo sensorium as "obligate mutualisms," a view that puts him at odds with Milton Brandt's genocidal faction within the BPO. Intent on salvaging the possibility of a human-sensate collaboration, Croome reframes their shared battle against intolerance in terms of a historicity of sense. Croome asks us to see the historicity of sense not as a question of history per se, but as an index of the communality underlying common sense: "How we see changes. The same is true for our ears. ... Why? Because our senses, including *our common sense* [my emphasis] are constantly evolving." Croome's singling out of the senses of sight and hearing identifies the very channels of communication through which Whispers pursues and murders the sensates. With Whispers, however, intentionality kills, but intentionality in the phenomenological sense according to which every thought (noesis) is a thought of something (noema). The potentially asphyxiating structure of intentional thought—an intentional object forced to disclose itself as a pure presencing of a self-evident givenness—is imaginatively magnified through the murderous gaze that Whispers's deploys to occupy and annihilate his fellow sensates. To capture Whispers's attention is to be captured, annihilated.

Whispers's weaponization of intentionality to lobotomize and thus kill other sensates, those within his own cluster above all, earns him the nickname of "The Cannibal," which is an apt term for a sensate insofar as killing the other is not only killing one's own kind, but also experiencing it as if it is one's own death. Despite the existential terror involved in experiencing an act of murder from the perspective of both killer and killed, Milton's willingness, even willfulness, to undergo that pain is organized not by his recognition of human finitude or even of the other, but rather the denial and negation of each. Insofar as Milton murders his clustermates in the hopes of negating his own finitude, this gesture is founded on his dangerous conflation of humanness, and therefore consciousness, with the infinite. In that sense, the finitude of the other functions as a kind of ersatz for Milton's own, and thus allows him to indulge in a ritualistic staging of the death of his own death. It is fitting, perhaps, that Whispers's own death unfolds only in S02:E12 "Amor Vincit Omnia," his death reinscribing the *fin* or *fine* of finitude into the show's own finale, the production and financing of which Netflix offered on condition that the 2-hour episode would indeed constitute the end—but also, perhaps, *telos* (amor vincit omnia)—of the show.

For *Sense8*, then, as indeed for philosophy, the death of the other provides a kind of limit case for understanding the nature of finitude and transcendence, without which any thinking of consciousness, communication, or community would be foreclosed. If the death of the other galvanizes and invigorates what Achille Mbembe has termed "necropower," and by extension, "necropolitics," it is on the condition that the other be reduced to the enemy as such, but enemy "understood in its concrete and existential meaning, and not at all as a metaphor or as an empty and lifeless abstraction" (Mbembe 2019: 49). To the extent that the necropolitical state constitutes itself through a declaration and liquidation of the enemy, and therefore through the construction and policing of borders, its counter lies precisely in opening oneself to the touch of the other. The disruptive potency of touch or contact is evident in young Will's telepathic contact with Sara Patrell. Will's childhood encounter with Sara upends his sense of self and world, exposing him to the stakes of mortality on a timeline that either slightly precedes or roughly coincides with the toxic transformation of the BPO that Croome describes to Will in S02:E03. To Will's question about the sinister perversion of the BPO's original mission under founder Ruth El-Sadaawi, Croome replies, "The same thing that changed for the rest of the world. 9/11. The end of the Cold War mutated into the endless War on Terror" (S02:E03). By inserting the BPO's diegetic corruption into the real-world history of a recent cultural past, Croome thereby recasts the BPO's genocidal transformation as a parallel to real-world hostility and intolerance. Whether we see Sara's appeal to Will as a call for help or as a call that helps, or both, Sara's ability to touch other lives long after her passing becomes evident when Nomi and Amanita visit Sara's mother, and bring Will along telepathically. Even though this gnoseological event in some ways resembles the theological structures of revealed religion, the show ultimately grounds the cluster's access to the suprasensible phenomena within a distinctly evolutionary-biological, rather than supernatural, idiom for thinking about finitude.

The Attentional and Intentional Economies of Necropolitics

In an earlier, much-debated essay "The Inoperative Community" (1983), Nancy locates in the fascist orgy an image of the work of community transformed into "works of death" (Nancy 2006: 24). Whether it be in the more romantic form of the "joint suicide or death of lovers" or of fascism's fascination with "communal fusion" and sacrifice, Nancy argues that "political or collective enterprises dominated by a will to absolute immanence have as their truth the truth of death" (Nancy 2006: 12). Rather than cede community as such to this destructive drive and its attendant fantasies of the sovereign subject, Nancy pivots from the community as work of death to an idea of "community [that] is calibrated on death as on that of which it is precisely impossible to make a work" (Nancy 2006: 15). The limbic modes of community conjured by *Sense8* challenge and destabilize the work of death carried out by Whispers and the BPO, agents of a will to absolute immanence the truth of which is precisely death. Instead, *Sense8* elaborates a philosophy of sense according to which community becomes thinkable as event and therefore as a matter of contingency and finitude rather than of essence, substance, or identity.

As an extension of colonial violence and erasures, necropower "proceeds by a sort of inversion between life and death, as if life was merely death's medium" (Mbembe 2019: 38). However, far from lending death great symbolic power, the global ascendancy of necropolitical regimes reveals an "indifference to objective signs of cruelty" because the death of the enemy "has nothing tragic about it [which] is why necropolitical power can multiply it … using an implacable logic of separation, strangulation, and vivisection, as we see in all the contemporary theaters of terror and counterterror" (Mbembe 2019: 38). Necropower operates through a global network of state and non-state actors, each of whom makes a claim on "modes of domination without responsibility, as capital confiscated for itself the right of life and death over those it subjugated" (Mbembe 2019: 34). Within *Sense8*'s diegesis, Fuchs and the BPO operate within similar kinds of necropolitical networks, for which the liquidity of global capital both requires and reinforces the power to liquidate any life whatsoever. And as is the case with the necropolitical regimes Mbembe describes, the BPO's power and will to decide the life or death of the other runs counter to our cluster's empathic openness, vitality, and jouissance. Insofar as the show generally confirms Jonas's belief expressed in S02:E03 that "there's always an 'us and them,'" its characterization lends the show a melodramatic quality that the rest of Jonas's pronouncement nevertheless complicates: "There's always an 'us and them' even inside a tightly controlled 'them' like BPO." This fragmentation of every us, including that of the sensates, into an us and them lends greater depth to the *show's* examination of the ethos and ethics of community.

There is in fact a strongly melodramatic quality to the show's sharp delineation between the disciples of Eros and Thanatos. In contrast to the constitutive excesses of the cluster's common sense and sensing, a sexual encounter between Wolfgang and Lila Facchini illustrates instead the destruction of sense meted out by both the BPO and late-stage global capitalism. During a meeting with Lila and Sebastian Fuchs, Wolfgang experiences his first out-of-cluster tryst while Fuchs offers a chillingly didactic account of global capital's impervious desires and extra-legal fluidities. Playing the part of the dispassionate *condottiero*, Fuchs lectures his guests on the difference between the "old world [which is] tribal, it's primitive" and the "interconnected world of global finance. Capital exists beyond the auspices of ethics, morals, or even law." The submerged wordplay of juxtaposing Fuchs and fucks is more properly a kind of worldplay that pits the world of capitalist liquidities and liquidations against our sensates' autoproliferating psychic and libidinal flows. (I say *our* sensates since it is clear that not all of the sensates or clusters share their utopic energies). Although Wolfgang seems initially befuddled by this contradiction, he increasingly relaxes into the pull of Lila's erotic seductions.

I have used the term seduction rather than distraction here because it best captures Lila's intent and the power differential between them. The main cluster's erotic encounters often warrant the term erotic distraction insofar as they are organized according to unpremeditated yet not unwanted tractive forces that both interrupt and enrich the sensates' inner and outer lives. To dramatize this important difference between seduction and distraction, one need only compare Lila's seduction of Wolfgang to Wolfgang's awkward yet playful interactions with Kala on her first night in bed with Rajan. Here, as elsewhere, the editing of the sequence uses intercutting to convey actions unfolding in two different spaces at the same time, only here the two spaces are two dimensions of the same material space. When Wolfgang and Felix first arrive at Fuchs's apartment, a series of shot-reverse shots sees Sebastian drawing them further into his apartment where Lila remains laid out on the corner of a sofa at the far end of the room. An implicitly subjective close-up pans from her feet up to her face, thereby slowly filling in her elongated pose. Shortly thereafter, Lila's body leaves the room momentarily, but as her body departs Wolfgang's presence, she begins seducing him telepathically. By intercutting shots of Wolfgang's external and internal experiences of the dinner, the scene is also intercutting images of an ideological and a sexual seduction. In other words, the editing establishes an opposition or perhaps parallel between the heartless exertions of pan-capitalism, and the utopian worlding accomplished through pansexual openness and polyamorous clusterings. Amid the almost Eisensteinian barrage of contradictions he encounters at Fuchs's pad, Wolfgang has no problem understanding the kind of person Fuchs is, but is bemused and a little bewildered by his simultaneously real and virtual, bodily and disembodied, encounter with Lila. A surprised Wolfgang asks Lila, "How can I feel you touching me if I am not touching myself?"

Lila's reply belies an almost Socratic patience: "When you jerk off do you think about your hand or do you think about something else? I am something else." We are cued to the fact that Lila is a compromised or at least complicit sensate by the fact that she says, not "I am someone else", but "I am something else." As sensate, Lila translates Fuchs's mercenary capitalism into a kind of neoliberal sexual morphology that siphons libidinal energy off with the same rapidity, omnivorousness, and ontological violence as digital-era capitalism. And with characteristically Wachowskian aplomb, Lila's almost didactic explanation reduces Adam Smith's invisible hand of capitalism to the inveterate palm of a tireless wanker.

Erotic Play and Common Sense

Although "to sense" is usually understood as transitive, one can only sense another thing or person if one also senses oneself at the same time. Sensation is always therefore an act of both allosensing and autosensing. Sense belongs to both the infinities of inner life and to the material exigencies and necessities that determine the inner life's outward conditions of possibility. *Sense8*'s fascination with sense stems in part from sense's inherent categorical instabilities, and therefore its potential to resist, short-circuit, or transform the metaphysics of substance and subject. As a counter to these ideological traps, *Sense8* looks instead to sense and to the logic, or perhaps counter-logic, of copulation in order to stage the event or coming of community as precisely a coming community. Steeped in the appropriative logistics of identity, substance, and subject, Whispers and the BPO reduce community to the production and policing of an identity or essence, and therefore to the liquidation of difference. By contrast, *Sense8*'s phenomenology of the cluster simultaneously traverses and destabilizes those rifts between subject and world, matter and perception, self and other, subject and substance. Although *Sense8*'s clusterfuck sequences do not exhaust the show's political imaginary, they lend it a distinctively trans*/queer potential that destabilizes our ability to draw a sharp line between the erotic and political. To talk about *Sense8*'s community ethos is therefore to talk about its communal eros, the one to the extent, and by virtue of, the other. By treating the literal (figure of the body) and figurative (body as figure) as coextensive, *Sense8* invests the show's bodily imaginary with an erotopolitical force that is further amplified by the clusterfuck sequences. At stake is our understanding of the relationship between *Sense8*'s erotic sensibility and its reflections on the nature of community, identity, and alterity.

As its specular clusterfuck sequences suggest, the link between propositional copula—that is, the form of "to be" linking subject and predicate—and sexual copulation is more than just wordplay. In each case it is the ontological force of connection as such that is at stake. And it is precisely from the pleasurable (if also painful) *enjambment* of the two that *Sense8* draws its libidinal force and cultural consequence. The cluster *is* not except insofar as it is sensed and sensing. Since a cluster can only be sensed, in diegetic terms, by a sensate, a sensate is only a sensate by virtue of that sensing. Even further, the cluster can only be sensed in the first place because of the sensing through which the cluster itself comes to be; it is therefore the sensing itself that clusters. This autoproductive, and therefore autosensing, dimension of the cluster presents us with fundamental ambiguities that both embody and undercut the utopian ethos of the show. As the twisted trajectory of Whisper's sensate identity reveals, the erotopolitics of the cluster are always in danger of collapsing back into a metaphysics of identity and therefore an exclusionary politics of the same.

In a 2017 interview with Cáel M. Keegan, Lana Wachowski describes *Sense8* as not only "super complicated [but also] full of sex! What director has shot as much sex as me?" (Keegan 2018: 149). *Sense8* is indeed "full of sex," but what differentiates it from a more lurid approach is its communication of the fullness of sex, its saturation in sense but also as sense. *Sense8*'s euphoric orgy sequences are as much affective, perceptual, and intellectual as they are sensual in a bodily and embodied sense. As a result, the fullness or saturation of sex functions as a privileged form of sense, the sensus communis. As Sun declares in S02:E01 "Happy Fucking New Year": "We exist ... because of sex." And nowhere (utopia) does *Sense8* visualize sexual modes of being together more spectacularly than in three major clusterfuck sequences that punctuate the show's arc (in S01:E06 "Demons," S02:E01 and S02:E12 "Amor Vincit Omnia"). Cutting across familiar oppositions between inner and outer, mind and matter, subject and object, *Sense8*'s clusterfuck sequences instead exemplify the show's search for a sensus communis grounded not in the abstractions of intellect but in the constraints of finitude and the capaciousness of love. While other essays in this volume explore the ramifications of montage and polyamory, respectively, this essay addresses *Sense8*'s attentional and intentional structures of desire alongside its organization of a diegetic multiverse that traverses both res cogitans (or res sensorium) and res extensa. Due to the complicated nature—in the sense of *complicare*, to fold together—of the sensates' inner lives and interactions, which double as inner-actions, montage principles are thus central to *Sense8*'s narrative worlding and erotopolitical mobilizations of affect and attention.

By interlinking the political with the amatory and erotic, *Sense8* shifts the stakes of truth and being from copula to copulation, which is to say, from the fundamental solipsism—the "solus ipse"—constraining Husserl's transcendental egology (Husserl 1970: 89) to a sensus communis born of a shared and sharing exposure to others and to the world. In the lecture on the Homo sensorium species that Nomi and Amanita attend in S02:E02 "Who Am I," Professor Kolovi underscores the historicity of sense, but also the possibility of a state shift in our sense of being and world: "There was a time we thought our place in the world was the will of the Divine. As that rationale fell out of favor, it was the science of the Enlightenment that provided any number of answers to our ascendancy." Kolovi thus clears a space for Homo sensorium as the key to a transformation of sense and world from which all can benefit. With their empathic faculties, the sensates' promise or capacity to renew the world is grounded in their heightened sensitivity to contact and touch, physical as well as emotional and intellectual. In keeping with Croome's discussion of sense with Will in S02:E03, *Sense8* offers fucking and sensing as exemplary because they each express a kind of common sense or communing of sense. And both fucking and sensing are structured according to an impossible excess in which there is always more and less than the one of the subject (Nancy 2015: 9). It is this more and less than one that the cluster both embodies and virtualizes.

The Inoperative Cluster as Coming Community

First published in the journal *Aléa* in 1983 (Nancy 2016:4), Nancy's essay "The Inoperative Community" sought to "theorize about a post-sovereign notion of the political community [that can provide an alternative to] the place that has been traditionally occupied by the 'political community' in leftist theory" (Bird 2008: 4). Kristin Hole notes that Nancy's sustained engagement with the question of world and community can be seen as part of an attempt to "respond to the perceived failure of political communities in the twentieth century and reflect[s] a desire to recuperate community in a non-oppressive way" (Hole 2013: 104). And as Nancy's more recent texts attest, that is, *The Disavowed Community* (Nancy 2016: 4) and *Democracy and Community* (Nancy and Engelmann 2019; 63), "The Inoperative Community" provoked a public, and for Nancy, unsettling rejoinder from Maurice Blanchot, whose *Unavowable Community* was published in response to Nancy's essay (Nancy 2016: 12). The long cultural life of the resulting debates has nevertheless given Nancy's essay a pronounced visibility within post-Cold War philosophies of community and commonality. But to what extent does *Sense8*'s erotopolitical sensorium ultimately align with Nancy's notion of an ecstatic mode of being singular plural that resists the metaphysics of identity and community? At the very least, we can say that *Sense8* reveals a shared desire to reshape our sense of the world according to a "coming community" that is both on its way and always already underway (Nancy 2016: 2). For the same reason, this coming community can escape the reduction of community to a project or work that reinforces the ideological mirroring of subject and state (Balibar 2014: 24). By contrast, the coming community always comes as a surprise even when anticipated or expected. In *Sense8*, as in Nancy's philosophy, this coming of community is also always a matter of time, but not the messianic time that Mbembe has shown to be complicit with the "Dark Enlightenment" of contemporary necropolitical regimes (Mbembe 2019: 105). *Sense8*'s ethos of the cluster, which is also the ethos of the clusterfuck, instead posits a coming community whose place is not some transcendent beyond of time, but instead our own here-and-now. Community comes by taking place, and it is this taking place that constitutes what Nancy calls the "spacing" existence (Watkin 2015: 222–3).

But it is only in the here-and-now of our world that *we* can take place at all, and precisely as the embodied "spacing" of our shared "exposure" to each other, and therefore to our shared finitude.

Sense8's most radical challenge is to think cluster or community without accepting the double bind according to which community must either be a suffocatingly univocal essence or a mere aggregation of atomized individuals. In light of its etymological affinities with clot (*OED* 2020), cluster suggests a gathering or accumulation that echoes Nancy's analysis of "struction," and its etymon, "'*struo*,' meaning 'to amass,' 'to heap' [and by extension] the heap, the non-assembled ensemble" (2015: 48–9). Yet by Nancy's account, struction—which underlies structure and construction, but also destruction—constitutes a kind of pure accumulation grounded in "contiguity and copresence, but without the principle of coordination" (2015: 48–9). Is a cluster then a mere heaping or ingathering, no matter which? And in what ways or to what extent is community a function of number?

Whereas "socius" suggests, per Nancy, "the 'with' or *cum* around which or through which something akin to a sharing plays out," struction comes closer to a "pure and simple juxtaposition *that does not make sense*" (Nancy 2015: 49, my emphasis). If jouissance can be thought of as an abundance or excess of sense, then the jouissance that drives *Sense8*'s cluster imaginary would seem to exceed the terms of a mere struction or accumulation. The cluster should rather be conceived according to the with or *cum* of community, the unity of which is both a more and less than one, and such that "*World* means at least being-to or being-toward [être-à]; it means rapport, relation, address" (Nancy 1997: 8). In *Sense8*, the coalescence of the cluster, its clustering, enacts or performs this shared exposure that in turn constitutes the event of community, and therefore our shared exposure to each other. The clusterfuck sequences pit the jouissance of community, in both its fragility and persistence, against the sinister machinations of Whispers and the BPO. Indeed, the BPO exemplifies what Mbembe has characterized as the ultraright's feverish embrace of a "technomillenarianism that "seeks not ... community," but instead "purity and self-separation as ways of staving off the disasters of a 'crackup civilization'" (Mbembe 2019: 106–7). In sharp contrast to such identitarian enforcements of separation, isolation, and distinction, the figure of the cluster privileges instead the jouissance, indeed the event, of touch, contact, and shared exposure.

Put differently, the coming of community is coming precisely insofar as community is neither a thing nor essence, but instead an event or happening whose horizon is that of our shared finitude. Nowhere is this evental nature of community more visible than in the erotopolitical event of the clusterfuck sequences. Both *Sense8* and Nancy's philosophy of community thus "involv[e] a rethinking of unity and a rethinking of origin in such a way that these seminal metaphysical principles do not exclude plurality" (Brogan 2010: 295–6). *Sense8* dramatizes the conflict between two different understandings of world and the proper mode of community. In the first, world stand as a unified field of intended sense that operates in a normative fashion to establish its terms as those of a common sense. Here, world functions as regime of concentrating, or concentering, intentionality that filters, focuses, and delimits; its proper mode is that of a closed or exclusive universum of sense that privileges identity and unity as the grounds of knowledge, if also of the subject and of community. In the second, world names a horizon of familiar sense that is nonetheless open to ruptures and surprises that disrupt or interrupt the metaphysics of subjective intentionality and attention; its mode is that of an ecstatic, transcendent distractability that opens itself to being drawn out or attracted, thereby creating space for non-identitarian forms of community and being-in-common.

Sense8's jouissant clusterings seek to reimagine the very terms upon which community is configured. *Sense8*'s intrigue consists in the fact that its imagined alternative to oppressively identitarian politics takes the form of an eroto-phenomenological distraction. By that I mean an erotics of distraction that both invokes and challenges the dominance of rationalist models of subjective intentionality, and therefore of the epistemological gulf or abyss that metaphysics has erected between a subject and her surroundings, between subject and world. Whereas *Sense8* aligns a sense of world-as-totalizing-unity (or closed universum) with a subplot about global terror, it explores a quite different sense of world-as-transcendent-openness with an ecstatic, allocentric eroticism, a state of fundamental distractability in which noetic intentionality is deferred and the coercive unities of subject and community are pleasurably interrupted. *Sense8* tries to imagine new forms of transnational community that exceed the terms of identitarian politics and the neoliberal global imaginary. *Sense8*'s erotopolitics of the cluster thus resonate with Nancy's sustained attempts to theorize a rigorous political ontology that "exscribes" the very roots and terms of community and communality as such (Nancy 1997: 9). *Sense8* celebrates the possibility and desirability of remaining open, "exposed" to the distractions of alterity, which is to say, the opening, rupture, or interruption posed by manifold singularities (Nancy 2006: 31–2).

It is ultimately *Sense8*'s investment in erotic distraction that most powerfully grounds its erotopolitical imaginary within the ethics and temporalities of becoming. To think the other according to a phenomenology of the event is to imagine community according to an ecstatic temporality that outstrips the subject and resists the appropriation of community as essence. To speak of community in terms of the event is therefore to acknowledge that its sense or meaning lies in the asymptotic temporality that structures it. Community is enacted through and as an erotopolitical event, a coming that is always either not yet here or already arrived, the privileged form of which is equally the collective mouth taking its first breath, and the shared kiss's manifold lips parting to announce the coming community.

Works Cited

Agamben, G. (1993), *The Coming Community*, trans. M. Hardt, Minneapolis: University of Minnesota Press.
Bird, G. (2008), "Nancy Responds to Blanchot;" *Angelaki*, 13 (1): 3–26.
Brogan, W. (2010), "The Parting of Being: On Creation and Sharing in Nancy's Political Ontology," *Research in Phenomenology*, 40 (3): 295–6.
Bub, J. (2020), "Quantum Entanglement and Information," Stanford Encyclopedia of Philosophy (Summer Edition). Available online: https://plato.stanford.edu/archives/sum2020/entries/qt-entangle/.
Buckland, W. (2009), *Puzzle Films: Complex Storytelling in Contemporary Cinema*, Maldon: Wiley-Blackwell.
OED Online (2020), "cluster, n." Oxford University Press. Available online www.oed.com/view/Entry/34883.
Heidegger, M. (2009), *The Essence of Truth: On Plato's Cave Allegory and Theaetetus*, trans. T. Sadler, New York: Continuum.
Heidegger, M. (2010), *Being and Time*, trans. J. Stambaugh, revised by D. J. Schmidt, Albany: State University of New York Press.
Hole, K. (2013), "The Ethics of Community: Nancy, Blanchot, Esposito," *Angelaki*, 18 (3): 103–18.
Husserl, E. (1970), *Cartesian Meditations: An Introduction to Phenomenology*, trans. D. Cairns, The Hague: Martinus Nijhoff.
Keegan, C. M. (2018), *Lana and Lilly Wachowski*, Urbana: University of Illinois Press.
Kornhaber, S. (2015), "*Sense8*: The Premise Is Not Enough," *The Atlantic*, June 5. Available online: http://www.theatlantic.com/entertainment/archive/2015/06/sense8-the-premise-is-not-enough/394898/#article-comments.
Mbembe, A. (2019), *Necropolitics*, trans. S. Corcoran, Durham, NC: Duke University Press.
McMahon, L. (2010), "Post-Deconstructive Realism? Nancy's Cinema of Contact," *New Review of Film and Television Studies*, 8 (1): 73–93.
McMahon, L. (2011), "Jean-Luc Nancy and the Spacing of the World," *Contemporary French and Francophone Studies*, 15 (5): 623–31.
Mittell, J. (2015), *Complex TV: The Poetics of Contemporary Television Storytelling*, New York: New York University Press.
Nancy, J. L. (1997), *The Sense of the World*, trans. J. S. Librett, Minneapolis: University of Minnesota Press.
Nancy, J. L. (2000), *Being Singular Plural*, trans. R. D. Richardson and A. E. O'Byrne, Stanford, CA: Stanford University Press.
Nancy, J. L. (2006), *The Inoperative Community*, trans. C. Fynsk, Minneapolis: University of Minnesota Press.
Nancy, J. L. (2016), *The Disavowed Community*, trans. P. Armstrong, New York: Fordham University Press.

Nancy, J. L., and A. Barrau (2015), *What's These Worlds Coming To?*, trans. T. Holloway and F. Méchain, New York: Fordham University Press.

Nancy, J. L., and P. Engelmann (2019), *Democracy and Community*, trans. W. Hoban, Medford, MA: Polity Press.

Nancy, J. L., and A. Van Reeth (2017), *Coming*, trans. C. Mandell, New York: Fordham University Press.

Watkin, W. (2015), "Spacing," in P. Gratton and M. E. Morin (eds.), *The Nancy Dictionary*, 222–3, Edinburgh: Edinburgh University Press.

7

Sing a Song of *Sense8*: Musicality, Multiplicity, and Synchronicity

Rob Stone

The Spanish poet and playwright Federico García Lorca cherished a concept of empathetic transcoding between different languages, music, art, and people. In his lectures "Un poeta en Nueva York" (Poet in New York) in 1932 (1994: VI: 343–53) and "Juego y teoría del duende" (Play and Theory of *duende*) in 1933 (1994: VI: 328–39), Lorca analyzed the music and songs of multifarious cultures and asserted that flamenco *cante jondo* (deep song), Cuban *son*, and Black American gospel were all distinct but congruent expressions of a *cante universal*, a universal song that was a vehicle for compassion, solidarity, and protest. Finding affined sentiment in disparate song styles from distinct peoples, Lorca identified unexplored avenues of understanding different cultures by means of radical empathy that was best expressed in song and best explored in civil disobedience, for which singing could be a potent weapon. "Quiero llorar porque me da la gana" (I want to cry because I feel like it), wrote Lorca in "Poema doble del Lago Eden" (Double Poem of Lake Eden) (1994: II: 278), but his explanation of repressed homosexuality was withheld until "El poeta cuenta la verdad" (The Poet Tells the Truth) was published in *Sonetos del amor oscuro* (Sonnets of Dark Love) in 1981, long after his murder by Francoist forces. In this poem equating desire and death, Lorca sounded his cry of anguish along with the songs of oppressed others and called for a reciprocal chorus of the similarly frustrated and impassioned:

Quiero llorar mi pena y te lo digo
para que tú me quieras y me llores
en un anochecer de ruiseñores,
con un puñal, con besos y contigo. (1994: II: 402)

[I want to cry my sorrow and I'm telling you
so that you will love me and cry for me
amidst a dusk of nightingales,
with a dagger, with kisses and with you.] (author's translation)

These nightingales in partial darkness were for Lorca a hidden universal choir and he exhorted the active, creative process of their singing together as a way of proclaiming and realizing kinship. Synergy between orality and performative manifestations, which included recital, dance, song, and film, seemed to Lorca to offer conduits for transcoding emotions and ideas between cultures and communities and across geographical borders. His ideas were humanistic and focused on self-actualization through collective endeavor and they chime with what Georg Sørensen theorized as the creation of a community of sentiment (2003), which is an extended cluster formed by its members subscribing to an ungovernable flow of shared feelings that extends along a strata of similar cultural, social, linguistic, economic, and identitarian concerns and conditions. Their coming together enables "a historical identity based on literature, myths, symbols, music and art, and so on" that has nothing to do with the citizenship of one country or another and everything to do with radical empathy (Sørensen 2003: 83). Lorca would have loved *Sense8* because of the convergence of musicality, synchronicity, and multiplicity by which the cluster of sensates are called forth and united, and because of its characters' freedom to express themselves sexually, unimaginable in Lorca's Spain. Proudest when loudest, *Sense8* illustrates by embodiment the meaning, function, and advocacy of universal song. Beginning with Lorca's ideas and building on recent scientific research into music and cognition, this chapter subscribes to Carl Plantinga's definition of empathy in relation to spectatorship as an ability and willingness to share our own and someone else's "congruent feelings" (2009: 10). It then analyses the montage sequences in *Sense8* that are triggered by diegetic songs and music in order to contend that radical empathy, which turns feeling into action, may be transfigured by listening amid so much white noise to the songs that other people are singing.

Listening is a rebellious and subversive act in *Sense8*. Amid all the hacking and spying, with a good guy named Bug and a bad guy called Whispers, sounds are like secrets that can reveal a sensate's location and bring about their doom. In S02:E02 "Who Am I?," for example, when Riley and Will are in their Amsterdam hideaway, the merest mention of a memory by Riley prompts Will to demand another heroin-induced coma so as to silence their risk of exposure. In contrast, when the music plays and songs are heard diegetically from often multiple, disparate but synchronized onscreen sources, they sound a declaration of difference and defiance. By these means, music is signaled as both the medium and the message in *Sense8*, eliciting and delivering empathy in a sensorial loop. This is not without the predominant English lyrics causing a risk of Anglocentrism in the series' experimentation with universal song, but it is consanguineous with the way that certain songs and music videos have gone viral on the internet. And it is cognizant too of the distinctions between telepathy and empathy and sympathy. Whereas telepathy is the supposed communication of the content of thoughts by means other than the known senses, empathy demands the sharing of congruent feelings and is so sensorial as to resemble form, which *Sense8* embodies in music, song, and dance. And whereas sympathy is feeling for a character amid the ephemeral activity of a scene, empathy is feeling what a character feels and thus a process that calls for further emotional and temporal investment in the way a character or series arc plays out. That is to say, sympathy is a one-way expression without reciprocity, whereas empathy feels like a two-way transaction based on sharing and "affectively congruent but different in both strength and kind" (Plantinga 2009: 100), which informs analysis of the *Sense8* fanbase and how it would not and will not let go.

The first occasion of a song proving itself to be the key to transnational cluster empathy in *Sense8* is when "What's Up?" by 4 Non Blondes inspires a plot-based thematic example of a song being the medium and the message of a sonic and symbolic equivalence between races, genders, sexualities, and performance systems, particularly when these emerge from distinct cultures but share an understanding of suffering. "What's Up?" is heard in S01:E04 "What's Going On?" for which Tom Tykwer takes directorial credit. The song's title does not appear in the lyrics, but "What's going on?" is repeated in the chorus in a way that brings the plot and meaning of *Sense8* into focus after three fragmented and confusing episodes. The lyrics are apt even though the song's deployment in *Sense8* requires suspension of disbelief in order to accept the utopian, transnational, musical encounter of eight characters from eight countries where the song is apparently equally well known, including Korea and Kenya, despite or because of its origins in a US band and its popularity in European pop charts. Consequently, the song both establishes and emblematizes the problematic compromise of English as the vernacular of the sensates and so the series. Riley in London is the sensate who chooses the song, selecting "What's Up?" on her iPod as shown in Figure 7.1, while Wolfgang reacts to it popping up as his karaoke turn in a Berlin bar, Capheus in Nairobi sings along to it on the radio while driving his *matatu*, Sun in Seoul dances to it in her shower, Lito in Mexico City mouths the words so as not to wake Hernando and Daniela, Will in Chicago murmurs the lyrics in his apartment, Nomi handcuffed to a bed in a San Francisco hospital mutters it in her anaesthetized state, and

FIGURE 7.1 *Riley selects the music that will play in multiple, synchronous ways around the world.*

Kala in Mumbai, peculiarly, appears to be in two places at the same time, listening to it on the rooftop of her apartment building and simultaneously dancing to it on her bed. A predecessor is perhaps the scene in *Magnolia* (Paul Thomas Anderson, 1999), wherein nine characters are shown in their particular isolation to be synchronously singing along to a non-diegetic Aimee Mann's "Save Me." In *Magnolia* the meaning is opposite, however, because although the characters all feel the same, each of them suffers alone. In contrast, the sensates discover that the song, which is diegetic in multiple synchronous ways, enables them to appear in each other's worlds—Kala in Wolfgang's karaoke bar, Will in Nomi's hospital bed from which he then (as her) escapes, Wolfgang on Kala's rooftop and on her bed, and the rescued Nomi on the bench in London next to Riley—as the lyrics declare their first collective glimpse of their unity:

> I realized quickly when I knew I should
> That the world was made up of this brotherhood of man
> For whatever that means. (Linda Perry 1992)

It is fitting that Wolfgang is soon belting out the song in Berlin because this is also where the modern concept of empathy was formulated by philosopher Theodor Lipps as *Einfühlung* or "feeling into" something or someone as a way of explaining aesthetic experience (Lipps 1907). For Plantinga, the way that audiences "feel into" films and television "is always differently inflected, typically more sympathetic than empathetic

[and] fraught with ambiguities and contradictions" (2009: 72, 99). But the fan response to *Sense8* contradicts this because its fervidity is triggered by identification with the characters and ethos of the series. This suggests an empathetic response on the part of the audience, which invested so much time and emotion in the series that it triggered a worldwide campaign for proper closure following the cliffhanger of S02:E11 "You Want a War?" and subsequent series cancelation. Refusing to countenance anything but its own success, the fan campaign anthemized the song "What's Up?" in their protests, launching numerous tribute videos ("Be Part of *Sense8* Tribute Videos" 2017), and duly brought forth S02:E12 "Amor Vincit Omnia" from Netflix as well as social media groups, such as "Sense8 (Netflix)" on Facebook that boasts over forty thousand members, wherein watch parties and singalongs are a prominent part of the ongoing campaign for a third series. Opportunities for sympathy abound in response to characters who experience suffering and embody marginalization, but the mutual, reciprocal, centrifugal experience of empathy by the eight sensates in this scene of a song uniting their cluster not only makes them feel a certain way but also makes them feel it all together. Moreover, it explains and drives the plot, enabling the rescue of Nomi, as well as inspiring identification with their incipient unity and incoming clarity by the audience. "What's Up?" in effect goes viral among the diegetic sensates and between them and the non-diegetic audience, not in the sense of carrying a pathogen but of distributing an antibody: that is, by using the same channels or veins of a hyper-connected media culture against itself, to counter its tendency toward toxicity by sharing empathy and beneficial resilience instead.

Riley selects the song because its title seems to ask an appropriate rhetorical question, which suggests she does not expect any answer, let alone the response her choice inspires from seven distant strangers. Her selection prompts Wolfgang to grimace on recognizing its first notes in his karaoke bar, but he very quickly leans into the performance as a way of connecting with the "visiting" Kala. Will wakes up in Chicago to find himself Nomi in San Francisco and promptly escapes the handcuffs that chain her to her hospital bed. An addled Nomi then manages to escape the hospital with the timely assistance of Amanita, who concludes their getaway by bundling her into a taxi. Trying to make sense of her breakout, Nomi mumbles "I've had this song stuck in my head all day" as Amanita commiserates, calling it "the perfect soundtrack for a lobotomy." The song and this sequence thereby tie all the loose threads of the first three episodes of *Sense8* together, including its main characters and key locations, while acknowledging the differences of the sensates and voicing crucial questions about their interaction. The initially begrudging performance of Wolfgang in Berlin, the joyful chorus of Capheus in Nairobi, the quavering of Sun in Seoul, the tentative attunement of Kala in Mumbai, the lonely hum of Will in Chicago, the sedated lullaby of Nomi in San Francisco, and the whispered lyrics of Lito in Mexico

City are all heard by Riley, who actively chose the song, which marks her as the unifying presence and nascent mother of the cluster, as will be discussed further. The song clarifies plot, theme, character dynamics, and ethos by anchoring them all to a shared experience *of* sharing. Indeed, it also enables the cluster to instinctively rescue Nomi, who, finding herself safe and somehow in London next to Riley, concludes the sequence by singing an off-tune *a capella* version of the song that Riley is listening to on her earphones. At the point where embodiment of empathy is rendered musical, synchronous, and multiplicitous, made of equal parts confusion, wonderment, and compassion, *Sense8* issues a catchy refrain that sounds a barbaric yawp, calling for a group hug that invites the audience in.

The function of diegetic songs is foreshadowed prior to "What's Up?" in S01:E01 "Limbic Resonance," when Wolfgang takes a break from safe-cracking to watch a talent show and declares one competitor's song to be "the language of pure emotion" (which also foreshadows the flashback in the final episode to him and his beloved mother watching a similar talent show). The first intuitive notions of the sensates sharing a communal headspace are also musical and necessarily loud enough to be heard: Will hammers on a neighbor's door because he hears Riley's rave in London and Wolfgang's rave in Berlin interrupts Kala in Mumbai. The karaoke machine, Riley's iPod, the various raves, and Capheus's radio are distinct from the non-diegetic score by Tom Tykwer and Johnny Klimek and the extra-diegetic soundtrack, which is not heard by the characters on-screen. Instead, the global singalong encapsulates not only the ambitions of *Sense8* but also the literal aim of the Netflix distribution model, which offers simultaneous international distribution or worldwide "drops" of series and shows that suggest equivalence with the simultaneity of the sensates hearing "What's Up?" and their global audience watching and listening to it happen. Indeed, several recent viral videos have illustrated matters of world music as it is consumed and shared as well as the contagion of outrage and its channeling into political protest via the conduit of song. In the first instance, an early attempt at capitalizing on the potential of streaming platforms to show the world through music was Matthew Harding's 2005 video of himself entitled "Where the Hell Is Matt?" that showed him performing simple dance moves in front of twenty global landmarks (2006b). After this video went viral, sponsorship led to Harding visiting thirty-six locations for the 2006 version (Harding 2006a), sixty-nine for the 2008 edition (Harding 2008), and seventy-eight for the 2012 episode (Harding 2012). Despite the spectacle, however, the original 2005 video only demonstrated the privilege and entitlement of a white, Western male failing to interact with anyone local on his travels. Instead, the video shows him performing exactly the same dance moves everywhere, reveals no sharing in either direction, and suggests a colonizing attitude to tourism. The 2012 edition starts with shots of him copying local, popular dance moves that include a cheerleading routine in

Pennsylvania, a flamenco flourish in Seville, juggling in Kabul, and a tribal dance in Papua New Guinea, but quickly surrenders to the familiar banality of Harding spasmodically raising his arms together and knees alternately no matter his location. Far more illustrative of how music can bring citizens of the world together and create a community of sentiment is the Playing for Change multimedia music project founded in 2002 by music engineer Mark Johnson and film producer Whitney Kroenke. This movement bills itself as coming from "a common belief that music has the power to break down boundaries and overcome distances between people" (Playing for Change 2020a). It begat a nonprofit foundation dedicated to building music schools for children worldwide and has communicated its ethos via music videos in which myriad musicians performing popular songs in manifold locations are seamlessly edited together, thereby illustrating musical multiplicity and synchronicity. The Playing for Change video of Marvin Gaye's "What's Going On," for example, integrates musicians in American states and African countries (2020g), while "Guantanamera" combines seventy-five Cubans playing in Havana, Miami, Barcelona, Tokyo, and elsewhere (2020d). Moreover, the project is polyglot with videos such as "Guantanamera" and "La Bamba" in Spanish (2020e), "Ahoulaguinbe Akaline" in Tuareg (2020b), "Pemba Laka" in Portuguese (2020f) and "Chanda Mama" in Telugu (2020c). In addition, significant hybridization is demonstrated in the videos, with "Ahoulaguinbe Akaline" including an Italian harpist (Giuliana de Donno) and a Japanese sanshin player (Ayano Uema), "Satchita" moving from Brazil to India by way of the Caribbean, and "Chanda Mama" fusing Indian and African rhythms with a touch of New Orleans jazz.

Playing for Change, like *Sense8*, ultimately challenges cultural theorist Stuart Hall's theories of coding/encoding, which he applied to television discourse. Hall claimed that when human communicators engage in coding (producing messages) and encoding (receiving them), "what are called 'distortions' or 'misunderstandings' arise precisely from the lack of equivalence between the two sides in the communicative exchange" (2005: 131). But both Playing for Change and *Sense8* posit a utopian world based on equality in diversity, where all participants share the same musical code and use it to transmit undistorted empathy. Like the widespread musicians, the cluster of sensates deploys songs as an ideal forum for communication among themselves and others capable of reciprocal empathy via sharing in the lyrics (content) and colluding in their synchronous multiplicity (form). The utopian cluster thereby liberates communication from operating solely within a framework of power, politics, and economics by exploring cross-cultural translation and intermedial adaptation in terms of a universal cure for Hall's diagnosis of "distortion in the origins and destinations of communicated messages, with the humans that encode and decode them" (2005: 158). Whereas Hall maintained that the stages of coding/encoding are not relatively autonomous because each stage limits the possibilities of meaning in the next, thereby encasing the semiotic paradigm within a social framework that is hierarchical, centripetal, and exclusive, *Sense8* functions on the principle that codes operating within the syntagmatic chains of intercultural, cross-language, and transmedial discourses create discursive forms that, when fueled by radical empathy, lead to a complex array of actions and meanings that, though worldwide and centrifugal, exhibit an affined, inclusive essence in their aesthetics, impact, and affect. Musical, synchronous, and multiplicitous, the cluster of sensates embodies an active transnationalism in being in up to eight places at once, allowing some to explore this and their transmediality in creative ways, such as Riley with her music, Lito on film, and Nomi on the internet. In the problematic but practical lingua franca of "telepathic" English, the sensates engage in simultaneous translation, immediate transmediality, and the transnational interaction of performance systems, as well as the exchange of beliefs, sexual impulses, fears, and skills. Their communication of meaning is by no means dependent solely upon the lyrics, moreover, but also carried by rhythm, tone, and melody: a conceit explained in the diegetic aural motif of "Nothing Matters When We're Dancing" by The Magnetic Fields (Stephin Merritt 1999), which is deployed both intimately, when Riley's father plays it to her on his ukulele, and spectacularly, when it sets off the fireworks at the end of Nomi and Amanita's wedding in Paris and thus concludes the entire series. Working (dancing) together as a group, the sensates discover they can circumvent hierarchy, overthrow its divisiveness, and realize a unified sense, sensibility, and sentiment instead, thereby becoming what Sørensen theorized as a community of sentiment as opposed to a community of citizens. That is, a group or cluster that finds belonging in feeling the same, not one that is formed by the imposition or withholding of criteria for inclusion or exclusion. As for the members of a community of sentiment, the sensates recognize that their differences are both convergent (with each other) and oppositional (to fanaticism, homophobia, sexism, corruption, censure, and so much else), particularly in their affined representation of the disenfranchised and marginalized, which emphasizes those afflicted by prejudice, poverty, stigma, and social conditioning. Interconnectedness and solidarity are inevitable themes of the series, wherein it assuages Lito's anguish as a closeted homosexual, Capheus's immersion in violence-ridden poverty, Kala's struggle to reconcile fidelity to her husband with her passion for Wolfgang, the transgender Nomi's rejection by her mother, Sun's suffering on account of her father's dismissal of her gender, and Wolfgang's abusive and violent childhood as an East German immigrant in West Berlin.

For Lorca as for Playing for Change and the Wachowskis, it seems, musicality, multiplicity, and synchronicity are essential for empathy. Songs are emotional stimulants as well as carriers of meaning that inspire a feeling of consensus and point to the potential of protest. The power of songs to encapsulate, symbolize, and galvanize movements is most evident when linguistic differences are no impediment to the sharing of feeling. A recent example is the protest song "Un Violador en Tu Camino" (A Rapist in Your Path) about rape culture and victim shaming penned by LasTesis, a Chilean feminist collective, that has become an anthem for feminists worldwide ("This Chilean anti-rape song is now a viral feminist anthem," 2019; Martin and Shaw 2021). Its chanted lyrics and forceful dance movements, which incorporate the enforced crouch of a rape victim undergoing internal examination in police custody, have been adopted by protestors worldwide from Santiago to Beirut, Barcelona, Berlin, London, Paris, Mexico City, and New York ("A Rapist in Your Path," 2019). The feeling of the song was encoded and decoded along a single "frequency" by protestors, some of whom did not speak Spanish but learnt the lyrics by imitating the sounds, while others translated its anger into their own language. In January 2020, for example, an English-language version was performed by protestors outside the New York courthouse where Hollywood producer Harvey Weinstein was on trial for sex crimes (Aratani 2020): "And it's not my fault, not where I was, not how I dressed / And the rapist was you! / And the rapist is you!" The language was different, but the feelings expressed by their chant and dance were similar to those in Chile, prompting Chilean lawyer Belén Saavedra to tweet that this was "now a global song for all women" (Saavedra 2020). The sharing of the song therefore challenges Hall because its semiotic paradigm operates within a social framework that is not "hierarchical, centripetal and exclusive" but anarchic, centrifugal, and inclusive. Crucially, what this song shares with those in *Sense8* is the fact that "its real power lies in how it feels" (Hinsliff 2020). Furthermore, allied to this exhortation of radical empathy based on equivalence is the idea that although grammatical language has superseded the spontaneous expressions of nature, people still express their strongest emotions in song. Charles Darwin wrote in *The Descent of Man* that "the sounds uttered by birds offer in several aspects the nearest analogy to language, for all the members of the same species utter the same instinctive cries expressive of their emotions; and all kinds that have the power of singing exert this power instinctively" ([1871] 2010: 30). As Darwin concludes, "I cannot doubt that language owes its origin to the imitation and modification of various natural sounds, the voices of other animals, and man's own instinctive cries, aided by signs and gestures" ([1871] 2010: 31). In other words, evolution may have refined our eloquence but the repetitious, unifying cries of "What's Up?" can still cut through linguistic differences to become the worldwide anthem of *Sense8* fandom:

> And I scream from the top of my lungs
> What's going on?
> And I say, hey yeah yeah, hey yeah yeah
> I said hey, what's going on?
> And I say, hey yeah yeah, hey yeah yeah

I said hey, what's going on?
Oh, oh oh
Oh, oh oh. (Linda Perry 1992)

At the level of plot and character, moreover, it is inevitable that Riley should evolve throughout the two seasons of *Sense8* toward the maternal role and assimilate to some extent the characteristics of the deceased Angelica as the surrogate mother of the cluster, even "becoming" Angelica in her attempt at suicide in S01:E12 "I Can't Leave Her." Riley's role in the cluster is compounded by her tending compassionately to Will, masterminding the deception that safeguards the group in Amsterdam, communicating on behalf of the group with the Old Man of Hoy (Sylvester McCoy), who leads a network of other clusters, most often having the final word in her cluster's deliberations and, primarily, by being the sensate most associated with music. As a DJ Riley dedicates herself to communicating through songs, summoning Yrsa (Lilija Þórisdóttir) by singing a nursery rhyme, for example, and sharing ideas and feelings with people via music too, just like her father, a concert pianist himself, who tells her, "you make music, Riley, and for a moment people forget the troubles in their lives. It's no small thing." Riley's ubiquitous blue headphones are a part of her, seemingly absorbed into the blue streak of hair that she performatively applies. The blue streak thus symbolizes her sensitivity to sound and emphasizes her ability to feel for rhythmic patterns and motifs in the cluster, such as actions that are repeated in the past and in the present and will be in the future. Crucially, Riley works as a DJ blending songs into each other in a manner similar to her handling of the cluster, because the skill of mixing songs at a rave has parallels with the way the sensates exist separately like different songs, but pick up on each other's biorhythms until they inhabit each other's spaces and take over, such as when Sun "becomes" Nomi in her alley-way scrap with cops and Lito "becomes" Sun when his bartending skill at making "the best sidecar in the world" is required in order to maintain her disguise as a waitress. This overlapping of the sensates is attuned to the way that DJs like Riley play two or more songs simultaneously and find the ideal moment to create seamless transitions between them, thereby developing unique mixes. Knowing how to align the distinct beats so their tempos do not clash in order to achieve a constant flow of music and thereby preserve, temper, and control the energy on the dance floor is the same skill that Riley applies, albeit unknowingly at first, to her cluster. Cueing, equalization, beat-matching, and mixing are how Riley empathetically transcodes her fellow sensates, selecting "What's Up?" the first time in S01:E04 and performing a remix (actually by Gabriel Mounsey) in S02:E05 "Fear Never Fixed Anything" at Amsterdam's Ruigoord, a repurposed church, where she not only calls forth her own sensates but also prompts their "mixing" with others like The Old Man of Hoy and Puck in the audience. Finally, in S02:E12, Riley sets the concluding act in motion by calling all the friends and members of her cluster to Naples by cueing up "I Feel You" by Depeche Mode on her iPod on the train. Although Riley listens through earphones and the carriage is silent, Will and Lito start nodding in synch, prompting Daniela to ask "You can hear her music?" "If I want to," admits Lito. Riley passes earphones to Dani, Hernando, and Detective Mun (Will and Lito, of course, do not need them) and the song claims the soundtrack and the headspace of the disparate sensates.

> I feel you
> Within my mind.
> I feel you,
> Your heart, it sings.
> I feel you,
> Your precious soul.
> And I am whole. (Martin Gore 1992)

Riley's cue prompts Nomi to channel it from her phone to the media player of the van in which she's driving to Naples with Bug, and Capheus to turn the song way up on the radio in the car in which he's driving Rajan, Wolfgang, and Kala. The cutting between Riley's sleepy train carriage and its muted chirruping of headphones and her same carriage as the simultaneous venue of a riotous rave involving all the sensates and their favorite non-sensates, as shown in Figure 7.2, proves that Riley is the DJ of their evolution and shared destiny. Cueing is sensates acknowledging each other, equalization

FIGURE 7.2 *Riley cues, equalizes, beat-matches, and mixes her cluster.*

is their visiting, beat-matching is synchronization allowing sharing, and mixing is their embodied becoming.

Several theorists after Lorca have considered such empathetic transcoding. Barbara Lüneberg applies a praxeological approach to this social phenomena, meaning that she sees it as deliberate and purposeful rather than reflexive, holding that knowledge of an entire "network of practices, experiences, narrations, rearrangements and historical accounts" is necessary in order to inform "investigation of interactions between artists and their audiences" (2019: 161). Lorca's poetry exhibits his transcoding of the metalanguage of flamenco into his own poetic forms as a result of the empathy he felt for the singers of flamenco deep song called *cantaores*, whose rhythms, imagery, symbolism, and performance system informed his reinvention in the guise of poet-*cantaor*. His example suggests that empathetic transcoding occurs when a creative, receptive person—a sensate—deliberately operates between two or more systems, media, languages, or worlds in order to purposefully carry something over such as an emotion, philosophy, meaningful protest, or all three. In Lorca's case, he carried over the existential despair of the Gypsy *cantaor* into his poetry, whereby and wherein he performed the role of *cantaor* for and on behalf of those whose essence, in this case their homosexuality, lacked other forms of expression. And just as radical, empathetic transcoding can function across different media such as recital, song, dance, and film, so it functions between the sensates. That is to say, when the form of Sun, Nomi, and Lito changes (when Sun becomes Nomi to fight the cops and Lito becomes Sun to mix the cocktail), the essence of the cluster is expressed and heightened in the same way that confirmations of solidarity and interconnectedness enhance campaigns for recognition, equality, and diversity.

Neither Lorca nor the Wachowskis made any attempt to develop their theory in formal scientific terms, relying instead on rich but ultimately speculative narratives illustrated by their creativity. However, recent research into cognitive psychology has focused on transnational and transmedial creativity by investigating empathy between languages, cultures, and peoples; between media, performance systems, and audiences; and between art and social and political protest. In relation to songs as examples of musicality that can inspire worldwide synchronicity and engender multiplicity, for example, experts have investigated "the cognitive and affective underpinnings of musical preferences" and concluded that individual musical preferences are related to variation in empathy traits and that multiple people with similar degrees of empathy tend to like the same music (Greenberg et al. 2015). Their research suggests that because people with a high degree of empathy tend to like the same kind of music, so listening to that same music can make people who are less empathetic more so. Findings point to the conclusion that listening to songs involves perceptual processing (taking the song in) and affective reactivity (experiencing emotional and psychological responses) as well as intellectual interpretation (a holistic attitude to what takes place inside the event of listening) and prediction (anticipation of melody, duration, and a conclusion to the narrativization of the event) (Greenberg et al. 2015). The common link between these is empathy in response to music, which is herein defined as "the ability to identify, predict, and respond appropriately to the mental states of others [...] when perceiving musical content [and] reacting emotionally and physiologically to it" (Greenberg et al. 2015). Concluding that "the associations between empathy and musical preferences are robust and independent of the links between preferences and personality," this research recognizes a neurological basis of differences and similarities between listeners, with the measurement of "activity in the medial orbital frontal cortex and nucleus accumbens" of subjects capable of indicating a likelihood of empathy between them (Greenberg et al. 2015). The use of songs in *Sense8* corresponds to this alignment of cognitive "reasoning" about another's perspective and affective "resonance" with another's experience, while suggesting that within its fiction the radical empathy and collective identity of the sensates have a neurological basis that is unique to them. Nomi and Will both have scans that reveal how their medial orbital frontal cortex, which is crucial to emotion, memory, and empathy, is changing, not because, as Will fears, "I'm losing my mind" but because, as Jonas explains, "it's just expanding."

The fact that empathy can be inspired by songs and that certain songs can identify those with empathy may be essential to pro-social behavior such as building collaborations and communities through understanding, enhancing identities, and developing strong bonds and a conscience. As Riley learns of her cluster's place in the Archipelago—a network of sixteen such clusters—the context of communication between the original eight and all the other sensates broadens and the distinctions between diegetic and extra-diegetic songs dissolve. This suggests that any sensate capable of thinking of a song can claim the soundtrack, which is then heard telepathically by all sensates, extending across all edits regardless of temporal or spatial differences, suturing their actions regardless of their physical place in the world. Indeed, there is a vital correspondence between the rule of eight sensates in a cluster and there being eight notes of the so-named octave on the musical scale. On a C scale, for example, the notes from low to high are C, D, E, F, G, A, B, and C with the final note (the octave or eighth) given the same name as the first but having double the frequency. The octave is the "basic miracle of music [and] common in most musical systems" (Cooper 1981: 16). It is thus the basis of Lorca's concept of universal song and the corresponding number of sensates. In S02:E01 "Happy Fucking New Year," as the sensates acknowledge their shared birthday, as Wolfgang goes shirtless in a Berlin rave and Kala delights at music on the Amalfi coast, the burgeoning montage is anchored to Riley sharing a bath with Will in their hideaway. On the occasion of his/her/their birthday, Riley encourages Will to temporarily set aside the heroin block that keeps Whispers out of his mind and he finds himself hearing the music heard by his fellow sensates, making those vital connections, and recognizing the function and meaning of radical empathy via Riley's mixing of their embodied, synchronous, celebrations of becoming:

RILEY: Can you hear the music?
WILL: It sounds like a radio … keeps changing stations …
RILEY: We shared our first breath and now it's time to celebrate that breath together.

The ensuing revelry includes scenes from Lito's birthday party in Mexico City, Kala's on the beach in Positano, and Sun alone in her cell, with both the music and these scenes and the sensates within them being mixed by Riley "changing the radio" inside Will's head as she beat-matches all the sensates. Thus, as Steve Aoki's "Home We'll Go (Take My Hand)" becomes Banda Caio Rodriguez's "Chan Chan" and then Just a Band's "Huff + Puff," the location-switching becomes less erratic as the scenes of the cluster visiting each member's location are all rendered as smooth transitions that cohere in slow-motion when they all join Sun in her cell. This visual synchronization of all images to a single rhythm suggests a coincidence of heart beats that returns us to the concept of universal song, which quietens in the silent cell of Sun, where her solitary tai-chi is assumed by all members of the cluster, whose slow-motion movements emulate a single heart's rhythm. Again, the guiding hand of Riley in this synchronization is identified as she is shown ahead of the cluster as it performs tai-chi while simultaneously stepping up to request control of the DJ's platform in Positano. Raising the beat with Dave 202 and Gino G's "Knockdown," Riley cues, equalizes, beat-matches, and mixes into the second of the series' three orgies, which she fittingly scores to Jetta's "I'd Love to Change the World." At the close of S02:E01, the musicality, synchronicity, and multiplicity of the sensates is confirmed with Leonard Cohen's "Hallelujah" being sung by Daniel Moore and the Apollo Choir of Chicago, which plays over separate scenes of the scattered sensates before the San Francisco Gay Men's Choir is featured and the song is anchored diegetically (albeit by the Daniel Moore version which was overlaid in postproduction due to licensing complications) as the cluster convenes alongside Nomi and Amanita to hear the choir perform in San Francisco City Hall (Tunefind 2017).

Sense8 contains further examples of songs stimulating the radical empathy that inspires the sensates to embody each other, unite in defense, or succumb to sensual and sexual pleasures. Several achieve an overarching fluidity in the editing that meaningfully blurs and erases any distinction between diegetic and non-diegetic sources. Some even "go viral" within the cluster, such as "Demons" by Fatboy Slim and Macy Gray, which inspires the orgy of S01:E06 "Demons," and Avicii's cover of "Feeling Good," which spurs the synchronized swim that starts S02:E01. Most emotive of all is Beethoven's Piano Concerto no. 5 in E-flat Major, which draws all the sensates to successively assume the position of Riley in the concert hall in Reykjavik in S01:E10 "What Is Human?," whereupon they each relive their own births. This montage is also triggered by Riley listening to music, in this case that of her father playing the Beethoven onstage, which inspires her primal memory of being born to the piano music that her absent but joyous father played over the telephone to her mother. The concerto, Beethoven's last, shifts from the Allegro of the opening section, when Riley and the sensates are thrilled by the flamboyant piano solo of her father, to the Adagio, which accompanies their births, with the music taking on a propulsive theme. The sequence underlines Riley's status as mother to the group and foreshadows the revelation in S01:E12 "I Can't Leave Her" that she lost the child to whom she gave birth in a crashed car in Iceland, thereby indicating, moreover, that her maternal role was postponed until her role in the cluster fulfils it. As the music heightens their empathy, each sensate's birth reveals a similar foreshadowing of their destinies. Will is born in the back of his father's police car and is thereafter on course to become a cop. Kala next, born in the monsoon under the watchful eye of the elephant god Ganesh, and then Lito, whose birth coincides with a madly melodramatic moment on a Mexican soap opera that has his entire family screaming at the television and seals Lito's actorly ambition for life. Then Sun, born in a graveyard to her suffering and lonely mother, and then Nomi, untimely ripped from her mother's womb by a C-section that emphasizes the surgical aspect of the first birth of a character who will be reborn when she has gender reassignment surgery in later life and wakes to the sound of her sister singing "Happy Birthday" and holding a cake with one candle. Wolfgang slips joyfully into water as he does so often in the series and, finally, Capheus is born into poverty and boundless love. As the sequence ends, however, Riley rises distraught, blood pouring from her nose and collapses. "Her father was playing music and it triggered something in her," explains Will, but what he misses is that this is the point where empathy becomes its own character in *Sense8*. Here the cluster becomes its own sentient being because of it, able to cue, equalize, beat-match and mix itself in infinite ways by its members appearing alongside each other, embodying each other, becoming each other, with the cluster evolving holistically as they do.

As research from the Ahmanson-Lovelace Brain Mapping Center at UCLA has recognized, the sharing and spread of radical empathy via music "may indicate that music is being perceived weakly as a kind of social entity, as an imagined or virtual human presence" (Wallmark et al. 2018). As the authors of "Neurophysiological Effects of Trait Empathy in Music Listening" explain,

Music is a portal into the interior lives of others. By disclosing the affective and cognitive states of actual or imagined human actors, musical engagement can function as a mediated form of social encounter, even when listening by ourselves. It is commonplace for us to imagine music as a kind of virtual "persona" with intentions and emotions of its own. (Wallmark et al. 2018)

This idea of music imagining a virtual human presence into being is given its own, strong, logical destiny when the premise, characters, plot, aesthetics, and form of *Sense8* combine to explore the potential of musicality, synchronicity, and multiplicity in realizing its cluster of sensates. It even suggests that their combined empathy can be radical, fueling a community of sentiment that might protest, take action and even overcome prejudice, discrimination, marginalization, injustice, and oppression. *Sense8* might be fanciful but it nonetheless illustrates a long-standing and increasingly scientifically grounded theoretical framework for exploring empathy as a much-needed human trait that is stimulated by music and songs. Musicality, synchronicity, and multiplicity are thus the essential, evolutionary stages of empathy by which the cluster evolves and by which anyone with an innate sensitivity to music might move toward a sharing of congruent feelings among a multitude of others. In other words, as Lorca recognized in "Réplica" (Rejoinder) and had known all along,

> Un pájaro tan solo canta.
> El aire multiplica.
> Oímos por espejos. (1994: I: 396)

> [Only a single bird is singing.
> The air multiplies it.
> We hear through mirrors.] (author's translation)

Works Cited

"A Rapist in Your Path: Chilean Protest Song Becomes Feminist Anthem" (2019), *The Guardian*, December 6. Available online: https://www.youtube.com/watch?v=s5AAscy7qbI.

Aratani, L. (2020), "More than 100 Women Protest Trump and Weinstein with Anti-Rape Anthem," *The Guardian*, January 10. Available online: https://www.theguardian.com/us-news/2020/jan/10/more-than-100-women-protest-trump-harvey-weinstein-anti-rape-anthem-new-york.

"Be Part of *Sense8* Tribute Videos!" (2017), June 5. Available online: https://renewsense8.com/2017/06/05/sense8-tribute-videos/.

Cooper, P. (1981), *Perspectives in Music Theory: An Historical-Analytical Approach*, 2nd edn. New York: Harper & Row.
Darwin, C. ([1871] 2010), *The Descent of Man*, Mineola, NY: Dover.
Fitzpatrick, K. (2006), *The Anxiety of Obsolescence: The American Novel in the Age of Television*, Nashville: Vanderbilt University Press.
García Lorca, F. (1994), *Obras completas*, Madrid: Akal Bolsillo.
Greenberg, D., S. Baron-Cohen, D. Stillwell, M. Kosinski, and P. Rentfro (2015), "Musical Preferences Are Linked to Cognitive Styles," *PLoS ONE*, July 22. Available online: https://journals.plos.org/plosone/article?id=10.1371/journal.pone.0131151.
Hall, S. (2005), "Encoding/Decoding," in S. Hall, D. Hobson, A. Lowe, and P. Willis (eds.), *Culture, Media, Language: Working Papers in Cultural Studies, 1972–79*, 117–27, London: Taylor & Francis.
Harding, M. (2006a), "Where the Hell Is Matt? 2006," YouTube, June 21. Available online: https:// www.youtube.com/watch?v=bNF_P281Uu4.
Harding, M. (2006b), "Where the Hell Is Matt? 2005," YouTube, June 24. Available online: https:// www.youtube.com/watch?v=7WmMcqp670s.
Harding, M. (2008), "Where the Hell Is Matt? 2008," YouTube, June 20. Available online: https:// www.youtube.com/watch?v=zlfKdbWwruY.
Harding, M. (2012), "Where the Hell Is Matt? 2012," YouTube, June 20. Available online: https:// www.youtube.com/watch?v=Pwe-pA6TaZk.
Hinsliff, G. (2020), "'The Rapist Is You!': Why a Chilean Protest Chant Is Being Sung Around the World," *The Guardian*, February 3. Available online: https://www.theguardian.com/society/2020/feb/03/the-rapist-is-you-chilean-protest-song-chanted-around-the-world-un-violador-en-tu-camino.
Lipps, T. (1907), *Ästhetik*, Berlin: B.G. Teubner.
Lüneburg, B. (2019), *TransCoding: From "Highbrow Art" to Participatory Culture*, Austria: Transcript-Verlag.
Martin, D., and D. Shaw (2021), "Chilean and Transnational Performances of Disobedience: LasTesis and the Phenomenon of 'Un violador en tu camino,'" *Bulletin of Latin American Research*, January 20. Available online: https://doi.org/10.1111/blar.13215.
Plantinga, C. (2009), *Moving Viewers: American Film and the Spectator's Experience*, Berkeley: University of California Press.
Playing for Change (2020a), "About Us." Available online: https://playingforchange.com/about/.
Playing for Change (2020b), "Ahoulaguine Akaline." Available online: https://playingforchange.com/ahoulaguine-akaline-songs-around-the-world/.
Playing for Change (2020c), "Chanda Mama." Available online: https://playingforchange.com/videos/chanda-mama/.
Playing for Change (2020d), "Guantanamera." Available online: https://playingforchange.com/videos/guantanamera/.
Playing for Change (2020e), "La Bamba." Available online: https://playingforchange.com/videos/labamba/.
Playing for Change (2020f), "Pemba Laka." Available online: https://playingforchange.com/videos/pemba-laka-songs-around-the-world/.

Playing for Change (2020g), "What's Going On?." Available online: https://playingforchange.com/videos/whats-going-on/.

Saavedra, B. (2020), "The Song and Lyrics Are from Lastesis in Chile! Not Argentina. Though Right Now I Feel Like It's a Global Song for All Women. It's Amazing to See How Far It Got," Belén Saavedra@MabSaavedra. Replying to @Kate_Kelly_Esq, January 10. Available online: https://twitter.com/MabSaavedra/status/1215700626727997440?s=20.

Sørensen, G. (2003), *The Transformation of the State: Beyond the Myth of Retreat*, Basingstoke: Palgrave Macmillan.

Stone, R. (2004), *The Wounded Throat: Flamenco in the Work of Federico García Lorca and Carlos Saura*, New York and Lampeter: Edwin Mellen Press.

"'This Chilean Anti-Rape Song Is Now a Viral Feminist Anthem'" (2019), *VICE News*, December 12. Available online: https://www.youtube.com/watch?v=Bgmq3BpKNvc.

Tunefind (2017), "Scene & Heard: Behind the Music of *Sense8* S2," *Tunefind*, May 15. Available online: https://blog.tunefind.com/2017/05/behind-music-sense8-season-2/.

Wallmark, Z., C. Debliek, and M. Iacoboni (2018), "Neurophysiological Effects of Trait Empathy in Music Listening," *Frontiers in Behavioral Neuroscience*, 12. Available online: https://www.frontiersin.org/articles/10.3389/fnbeh.2018.00066/full.

8

Sense8 and the City: Frontier Cosmopolitanism

Luis Freijo

From the first montage sequence in S01:E01 "Limbic Resonance" during which the eight sensates are "born" to the final orgy in Paris, *Sense8* constructs its diegesis through a complex dynamic in its depiction of space. On the one hand, its scope is global: the eight protagonists are scattered across the world, bridging the differences that can arise between citizens of far-flung places. Yet, on the other hand, each of these characters rooted locally in a major city—Mexico City, Berlin, Mumbai, Nairobi, Seoul, San Francisco, Chicago, and London/Reykjavik—is narrated through the lens of their respective sensate inhabitants. Because the basic spatial unit of *Sense8* is the city, this chapter evaluates how the cityspace is constructed in the series around "global/local" coordinates in the sense described by Wilson and Dissanayake. These authors posit that such a convergence can "refigure one-way models of domination to the social formations of the modern nation-state and, in its more optimistic formulations, activate multiple lines of social invention, contestation, mobility, reimagining, coalition, and flight" (1996: 2). To map these intersections between global and local, this chapter blends theories of urban space with those theories of cosmopolitanism that have become prevalent in the fields of international ethics and international relations. Moreover, in *Sense8* the violence surrounding the sensates' struggles throughout the two seasons causes the urban and cosmopolitan aspects of the series to orbit around notions of violent frontiers, which shapes its take on global/local configurations. This chapter therefore examines how these urban spaces are constructed around their native or related characters (in the specific case of Riley and London) and analyzes how the violence of each of the cities configures different urban frontiers. I argue that the series adopts a cosmopolitan stance and deals with the problems arising from this, and I ask how this cosmopolitanism at the frontier might become a frontier cosmopolitanism.

A Tale of Eight Cities: Space, Place and the Construction of Identity

From an urban theory perspective, *Sense8*'s approach to the city echoes one of the principles of critical regionalism in architecture, namely that "the form is a space and when the space is provided with an identity it becomes a place" (Mistra et al. 2018: 104). City grids, urban design, and touristic sites are constructed spaces that do not acquire an organic category of place until, as Giuseppe Licari explains, they "exist as a spatial moment, as named locality" (2011: 47). Licari advocates for an anthropological method in the study of the cityspace, whereby a twofold process of configuration of identities ensues: the city's borders determine the relations, affiliations and movement of those living inside them, but at the same time the city is "narrated" by its inhabitants, to the point that narrating a city becomes "a constructive performance" (2011: 49). This is what *Sense8* comprises at its core: a tale of eight characters who live in eight cities, and a tale of eight cities mediated by their eight protagonists.

Mexico City is the first urban space to appear when the sensates are "born" from Angelica Turing. Lito Rodríguez is a B-movie star in the Mexican film industry who conceals his homosexuality. Through Lito, Mexico City is initially presented as an unreal space, that of the film set on which he performs macho acrobatics, seducing and saving the leading lady. Yet this unreality includes layers of reality because Lito is both performing an identity as a professional actor and performing heteronormativity in his public persona. This has consequences for the depiction of the city as a place: any authentic view of Mexico City is denied, just as Lito denies his sexual identity, and this eventually responds to the choice made by the series' makers to show Lito's privilege and wealth rather than that of less affluent characters or areas of Mexico City. An oppositional dynamic is established between the film set, the premiere and the fancy restaurant, on the one hand, where Lito performs his public identity as a straight film star with a glamorous girlfriend (Daniela), and on the other, the penthouse where he lives with his life partner Hernando and which functions as a fortress—at least until Daniela recognizes the dynamic, is aroused by it, and sutures the two worlds in her performance as Lito's "beard."

The vantage point of Lito's penthouse as the center of *Sense8*'s depiction of Mexico results in a "gentrified" view of the city, in the sense of Neil

Smith, who claims that gentrification works to create a Barthesian myth of the urban space through de-territorialization, whereby history and geography are rendered cliché (1996: 11). Smith criticizes the use of this myth of gentrification as a neoliberal strategy that ignores urban social conflict, which is "not so much denied as externalized" (1996: 16). In *Sense8*, the penthouse is a cityspace as refuge, constructed without history, geography, or memory through Lito's own choice, adopted because of the pressure of homophobia and the aspirations of a young, upper class. Lito's living arrangements present a de-territorialized and gentrified Mexico City, obscuring its social conflicts. This approach is supported by the make-believe violence of the film set on which Lito vanquishes his fictional foes, which is deliberately shown to be achieved by filmmaking tricks, including slow motion and pyrotechnics, despite the ironically excited claims of the director in S01:E05 "Art Is Like Religion" that the scene is "so natural, so real." Irony extends to the juxtaposition of this fake violence with the few occasions on which Lito leaves his penthouse and enters a "real" space in which the violence of the city appears, displayed mostly by Daniela's boyfriend Joaquín but also by nasty journalists and paparazzi. Even if this violence is real, it still occurs in rarefied celebrity spaces or in Joaquín's palatial garden, which he has created with the profits of his drugs business. It is not coincidental, for instance, that Lito has lunch with Joaquín in S01:E03 "Smart Money's on the Skinny Bitch" with the iconic Plaza del Zócalo as a background, since the violence threatened by Joaquín is related to the "real" spaces of the city, albeit through a tourist gaze that corresponds with the media stereotypes of "narco" crime embodied by Joaquín. Lito is the sensate whose ability to act is both a blessing and a curse, enabling and obliging him to embody lies and divergent realities through performance in both his professional and personal life, and his arc (and thus that of Mexico City throughout the series) consists of reconciling performativity with reality, discovering, and deciding which Lito and which Mexico City are presented as authentic within the diegesis.

The opposite process occurs in Wolfgang's Berlin. A safecracker from East Berlin, Wolfgang's identity is marked by the weight of his familial history as the son of a prominent gangster who controls a large area of the city. *Sense8* does not dwell on touristic or gentrified views of Berlin (with the exception of fleeting shots of the Brandenburg Gate in the credit sequence and of the Siegessäule in S01:E02 "I Am Also a We"); rather it focuses on the street cafés, abandoned warehouses, parking lots, and night clubs where Wolfgang and his friend Felix work and play. Yet *Sense8* does refer to the violent history of East Berlin, presenting indications of its communist past, of the criminal underworld that has evolved since the postwar black market and of the Holocaust, which is emphasized by the sequence in the Memorial to the Murdered Jews of Europe that suggests an analogy with the persecution and intended genocide of sensates by Whispers. All this is interwoven with

Wolfgang's history as his own sister's son, due to her rape by his father, who Wolfgang killed when he was just a boy. In contrast to Mexico then, history is prominent and present in Wolfgang's Berlin, as is made explicit in S01:E04 "What's Going On?," when Abraham, the Jewish diamond dealer (a problematic stereotype) meets Wolfgang and Felix at the memorial and lectures them: "We, like these books or these diamonds, have the secret of our past hidden inside us." Wolfgang's arc in S01 has parallels with his city, then, as it consists of liberating himself from his violent family and, in S02, dealing with his heritage.

The main cities of *Sense8* are linked by more factors than mere interaction between the sensates. In S01:E01 the diamonds that Wolfgang steals and which trigger the chain of events in Berlin come from Mumbai, the city of origin of the sensate with whom Wolfgang has the deepest connection—Kala. Arjun Appadurai has described Mumbai's position as a global capital since the beginning of the twenty-first century as being influenced by "images of globalization that are cracked and refracted" and which bear the imprint of British colonialism, postindustrial capitalism, the remnants of Fordist manufacturing, and "varied political cultures of citizenship and rule" (2002: 54). Accordingly, both Kala and Mumbai are split in a conflict between Hindu tradition and Westernized modernity, in which the refraction of those images of globalization add multiple layers to the cityspace. For instance, Kala is at the same time a proficient chemist with a secure professional position in a pharmaceutical company and a firm believer in the god Ganesha, often praying at a temple. Furthermore, she struggles to reconcile her doubts about her love for her husband Rajan, the son of the pharmaceutical company's owner, and her initial belief in monogamy with her newfound passion for Wolfgang. Kala navigates a cityspace organized into highs and lows, in which postindustrial capitalism exists in both her post-wedding luxury penthouse and the pharmaceutical company's skyscraper of identical white coats, while her father cooks traditional food in his street-level café, and the temple of Ganesha anchors her experience of the city in its ancient, local culture. Kala tries to reconcile these cultural crossroads by not bifurcating her city into a set of zero-sum choices between Western and Indian options, but rather by refusing to choose and preferring liminal spaces such as the roof of her parent's small house or that of the street-level temple, where she is usually depicted praying, thinking, singing, or having conversations with other sensates. Kala's arc, therefore, consists of repairing the cracks and refractions of globalization by trying to achieve a complete image that reconciles all of Mumbai's inputs.

The linking of cities and sensates continues when the unethical practices of the pharmaceutical company where Kala works are revealed as directly affecting the impoverished district of Kibera in Nairobi, where Capheus lives. Kibera is a district in which Capheus and his mother arrived after fleeing tribal conflicts. Capheus works there as a *matatu* driver, providing a public bus service to Nairobi's city center. Capheus's Nairobi is designed in a horizontal hierarchy: the cement city center of Nairobi is the core and the destination of Capheus's pendular movements with the bus, while the muddy streets and low buildings of Kibera constitute the periphery. The relation of Kibera with the center of Nairobi is layered through Capheus's aspirations for "upward" social mobility but the trajectory of this aspirational mobility is actually shown to be horizontal, or rather, concentric—from the periphery to the center. Rather than moving upward, Capheus goes underground as his need to obtain AIDS medicine for his mother leads him to navigate Kibera's criminal underworld. As with Lito in Mexico City, there is a performative element to Capheus's experience of Nairobi's underworld through his admiration of action star Jean-Claude Van Damme, which suggests an aspiration to emulate European and US cultural figures. Capheus's adoration even leads him to assume the star's identity, thanks to his borrowing of Sun's fighting abilities in an illustration of a complex, transnational, transcultural configuration. Nairobi's hierarchy is complicated by *Sense8*'s portrayal of Kibera's inhabitants, however, because instead of a stark image of underdevelopment, *Sense8* shows, on the one hand, the district's low income levels and its problems with the supply of both water and medicine and, on the other, a strong sense of community and solidarity. *Sense8* does not condemn Kibera to the misery of poverty but rather suggests some of its causes and effects (corruption, crime, drugs, AIDS, the commodification of water) and the potential that Capheus and his fellow citizens could achieve if they were not subject to these negative life constraints (a thread that might well have been continued in S03, as discussed later).

Meanwhile, Sun, in Seoul, is also damaged by criminal dealings involving pharmaceuticals: she takes the blame for her brother's manipulation, for personal gain, of the price of medicines in the family company (Bak Enterprises). Seoul does not, like Mumbai, stage a conflict between colonial modernity and tradition; rather, the conflict is between the different gender roles that Sun must adopt in her navigation of the city, marked by her dying mother's request that she look after her brother and her passion for martial arts. Seoul's hierarchy is organized with irony: the heights are depicted as male spaces of corruption and gender discrimination; for example, the skyscraper owned by Bak Enterprises, where Sun is ignored by her father, mocked by her brother and rejected by the company's clients who will not do business with a woman. Conversely, the ground-level cityspaces are welcoming regardless of Sun's gender, including the underground boxing ring where she is admired for her fighting skills and the park where she practices with her teacher, as shown in Figure 8.1. This division is expressed visually in S01:E05 when Sun is shown against the street-level green of the park with the financial district's skyscrapers looming over her to the right,

FIGURE 8.1 *A split, even fragmented Sun as/and Seoul.*

and when her teacher diagnoses her problem as being that she is "of two minds," Sun replies "At least."

The depiction of Bak Enterprises as male-dominated contrasts with the female character of the jail where Sun spends most of the series imprisoned for her brother's embezzlement. Sun's convict status turns Seoul into a corrective space in a Foucauldian sense, in which "punitive methods are … specific techniques of the wider field of power procedures" ([1975] 1998: 30; author's translation), but also into a site of misogynist oppression, because most of the female inmates are imprisoned for having defied male violence and abuse of power, as evidenced by the fact that the "reeducation" activity policed by the guards is sewing. Irony persists, however, as Sun finds herself belonging to a community formed by strong ties of friendship and solidarity, in which feminist collectivity makes imprisonment tolerable compared with a male world of privilege based on corruption and misogyny. Sun's imprisonment also converts Seoul's hierarchy of power from a vertical one into a concentric one, as she must make her way back from the periphery of the prison to the Bak skyscraper in the center of downtown Seoul, to expose the truth about her father's murder. Sun traverses a hostile cityspace in which she adopts and subverts gender stereotypes, including dressing as a sexualized waitress, to confront her brother's male power. Ultimately, the fact that Sun is in her underwear during the final chase and naked at the climax of her arc suggests a performativity that echoes those of Mexico City and Nairobi, with the difference that it is a gendered one: surrogate mother, aggressive businesswoman, and chased convict are impositions that Sun rejects through her contradictions. Sun is the sensate that challenges categorization in the most defiant manner, by both inverting and ironizing power in Seoul, overthrowing the superficial truth of its traditional male power by advancing its underlying female potential and a transgender aesthetic in which she is embodied in male bodies, such as Capheus.

Like Seoul, San Francisco is a city threatened by corrective places related to gender performativity, in this case the hospital where Nomi is due to have brain surgery at the beginning of S01. The city is initially presented as a welcoming space for LGBTQ identities: the Pride flag waves prominently, the streets play host to Pride parades and there is a strongly articulated community of queer activists and hackers that gives shelter and assistance to Nomi throughout the series. However, this network must function against a set of institutions that conform to the idea of a "punitive city," where the "functioning of the penal power [is] divided up in the entire social space" (Foucault [1975] 1998: 135; author's translation). These include, first, Dr. Metzger's hospital, then the policed areas and zones prowled by Whispers, and then the suburbs where the human-hunt is conducted by FBI agent Bendix. The layout of San Francisco's city grid echoes Licari's assertion that "the spatial context is at the same time what the identity of a group expresses and what a group has to defend against external and internal threats" (2011: 51). Like Seoul, then, San Francisco suffers from a hierarchy of power that is organized in concentric circles around its characters. This hierarchy is structured in the winding, steep streets of the city, layered in narrow alleys and different levels, which both help Nomi and Amanita in different moments to physically escape and provide refuge to the network of shelters and helpers that enable them, and ultimately stage a conflict between identity and control.

The other US city in the series, Chicago, is also presented as a policed space, with the difference that in this case it is its sensate, Will, who patrols it alongside his partner Diego and assumes, therefore, a semblance of authority. Will's background and heritage as both a city cop and the son of a cop influence the way in which the city is presented in S01. The space of Chicago is divided into legitimate and illegitimate places, depending on the authority the police force wields. Both Will's father and Diego support a Manichean view of the police's role as law enforcers that bifurcates Chicago in a battle of cops as legitimate wielders of violence versus criminals, whose violence is illegitimate, which is underpinned by a racial divide between both groups. From the security of their police cruiser, Will and Diego are shown attempting to cross the spaces of the city in the name of "urban safety" (Licari 2011: 51), but they encounter secluded "no-go" areas in the ghetto, whose gunshot victims assume no right to be treated in a public hospital. In Chicago, the space of the city is turned into a "control tool" and its streets are constructed around a "new discriminating factor: fear" (Licari 2011: 51). The violence between police and gangs can thus be understood as constructed, and its "fictional" aspect from a social point of view is highlighted when, in S01:E05, the scene of Lito shooting an evidently fake action sequence overlaps and alternates in the editing with Will and Diego chasing a young boy through Chicago's ghetto, suggesting that the violence exerted by the police is as subject to performativity as Lito's character shooting blanks and being suspended by wires, only with all too real consequences for the Black victims of police violence. Although *Sense8* conceives of this violence and fear as constructed, its controlling effects are very real since, in S02, Will takes center stage in the fight against the Biological Preservation Organization (BPO) and, consequently, the cityspace as a control tool turns against him. Chicago becomes a space haunted by the memory of both Will's exile and of Sara Patrell, the child murdered by Whispers, as Will's father lies dying and Will is branded a criminal, which is confirmed and exacerbated by his addiction to heroin (taken to protect him from Whispers).

The last sensate to be discussed in this cluster is uniquely split between two cities: London and Reykjavik. Riley flees from a traumatic past in Iceland to London, where she performs as a DJ. Riley's London is usually depicted at night, focusing on the clubs where she works, and is presented as an unwelcoming space, with tourist sites such as St. Paul's Cathedral and the Millennium Bridge shown as menacing locations. With the exception of Primrose Hill, where she goes at dawn to vape and think, Riley is granted no safe haven in London from her inner traumas. When Riley returns to Reykjavik, she must face the trauma of the accident that killed her husband and newborn baby. More than any other of the series' cities, Reykjavik is remote and is rendered with ambivalence: the city wears an image of naturalness and beautiful perfection—utopia when compared with the concrete outskirts of Wolfgang's Berlin—but Riley's trauma and the BPO base at which she is imprisoned at the end of S01 reveal the dark underside of the city, suggesting that the trauma takes the form of BPO violence in Reykjavik, and that even such a remote and natural location as Iceland can be sullied by the BPO's reach.

Finally in this section, a few words must be dedicated to the key role that Paris and Naples play in S02:E12 "Amor Vincit Omnia." In this final episode, the sensates are physically regrouped in these two European cities, with which none of the protagonists are familiar. In Naples, the city is narrated by the antagonist Lila Facchini, Mafia queen and BPO collaborator, and the visual experience of the city is equated to the portrayal of the character. Lila is presented as conventionally pleasurable for Wolfgang's male gaze through nudity, transparent outfits that highlight her physical qualities, and her depiction as a stereotypical femme fatale. Symmetrically, Naples is subject to a tourist gaze in which picturesque and pleasurable views of the coastal resort and its Renaissance palaces are offered. Through the identification of Lila with Naples, the tourist gaze is identified with a sexual gaze, albeit in a problematic way since, in contrast to the complexity achieved with the rest of the cities, Lila and Naples offer a clichéd notion of Italianness focused on the bodies of Italian women, the heritage sites and the danger presented by the Camorra. This is complicated by the climactic dynamics of the narrative, since it is in Naples where the big-budget violence is ramped up even as the touristic perspective endures, with, for example, the spectacle of Wolfgang, bearer of the gaze, blowing up a helicopter, which equates the masculine hero fantasies of control and destruction with the kind that can be sampled in spectacular holiday adventures such as hunting, extreme sports, and, as here, a parodic combination. The sensates even pose as tourists to infiltrate the Palazzo Forcello, where the villains have their base. Regarding the second of the cities in this episode, Paris, the cityspace does not reflect the narration of the city performed through the identity of any particular sensate, and the final wedding at the Eiffel Tower thus responds more to the tourist fantasy of getting married in Paris than to any identitary resolution of the sensates' conflicts with the BPO.

Sense8, then, narrates all these global cities through their protagonists, as Licari argues that "through the creation of stories, people are therefore attributing meaning to events and their own (internal and external) world both at an individual and a collective level, and by doing so, they attribute it mainly to their living space" (2011: 50). More than mere representation, however, the combined meanings of these cities are congruent with a grand narrative that centers upon frontier theory and its relation to cosmopolitanism.

You Want a War?: Violence and the Creation of a Global Frontier

The connection between the different cityspaces described above can be interwoven to uncover further strategies of meaning, specifically the grand narrative of the frontier. More than a century ago, Frederick Jackson Turner conceptualized the frontier in relation to the history of the United States as "the meeting point between civilization and savagery" and as "the line of most rapid and effective Americanization" (1998: 32–3), which served to justify the nationalistic and colonialist operation of expansion into and domination of the American West as predicated by the assumption of a Manifest Destiny. In contrast, I aim to create an abstract formulation of the urban frontier that de-roots the notion of frontier from Turner's nationalistic project and can be applied to a cosmopolitan analysis of *Sense8*. The frontier is conceived in this chapter as an unformed political space due to the existence of a violence that is not controlled by the institutional state. This idea stems from German philosopher Max Weber's early-twentieth-century writings about the formation of the nation-state, in which he posited that "violence is the means specific to the State, [particularly] the monopoly of legitimate physical violence" (2004: 33). There is a distinction here between border, the line that physically demarcates two political entities, and frontier, a political space where violence appears not to be controlled by the institutional state. As such, the frontier space can exist around a borderland that separates two nations but it can also exist in cityspaces such as the ones depicted in *Sense8*, determining their political and social conditions without necessarily splitting them into two differentiated territories.

In *Sense8*, however, the concept of nation, as an actual place wherein Weber rooted the state, is turned into an obsolete notion. The names of the different countries inhabited by the sensates are mentioned only in passing, as a larger context for where the relevant space, that is, the city, is situated. It is therefore vital to recognize the existence of violence in the city as the condition for the creation of the frontier, which in the case of *Sense8* is not that of the nation-state, but a violence that is repurposed to signify the global/local dynamics of the series. The concept is underpinned by Michel Foucault in his writings about power and resistance, wherein he delocalizes Weber's rooted conception of power by positing that "power must be understood ... as the multiplicity of force relations" that extend globally in the "formulation of the law, in the various social hegemonies" and encompass a "grid of intelligibility" in which the state and its instruments are only "terminal forms power takes" ([1976] 1990: 92–3). Crucially, however, this is not a vision of power that becomes univocal, because power fosters contestation: "Where there is power, there is resistance, and yet, or rather consequently, this resistance is never in a position of exteriority in relation to power" (Foucault [1976] 1990: 95). Resistance, like that of the main cluster of sensates, is then likewise de-rooted as a "multiplicity of points of resistance" (Foucault [1976] 1990: 95). In *Sense8* the frontier space is the meeting point between power and resistance.

Initially, the violence in the city is represented by the different manifestations of the criminal underworld in the series' cities. In Riley's London, Capheus's Nairobi, and Wolfgang's Berlin, the violence between gangsters creates contested frontiers. In Kala's Mumbai these battles are between politicized religious groups and corrupt business practices, and in Will's Chicago there is racial conflict. Here the term "underworld" suggests a vertical organization of the frontier, within which criminality is relegated to the cityspace *below* the frontier line of "legality," from where violence can "erupt" in gunfights, machete battles, and car chases. In *Sense8*, however, there is another source of violence and power that bears down from the legitimate space *above* the frontier line on those beneath it and resembles a kind of criminality that can only be described, symmetrically, as the "overworld," where the underworld criminality of street gangs and drug dealing is mirrored in capitalist-sanctioned corrupt practices, Big Pharma off-loading drugs past their use-by dates, and sexual and gender oppression through social mores.

As such, the "overworld" in Mexico City takes the form of homophobic and misogynistic culture and laws, which are embodied in the physical violence of Daniela's ex-boyfriend Joaquín, and in the symbolic and economic violence exerted by Lito's agents on his career when his homosexuality becomes public. In Mumbai, Kala is caught up in the violence of religious fanaticism and Big Pharma's illegal practices of selling expired medicines to low-income countries—Kenya, for example, where their supply has a direct effect on the contestation of frontiers in Kibera. San Francisco is the city where the power of the overworld most clearly takes the form of state surveillance, while in Chicago cops deploy violence to police a thin strip of no-man's land between law and lawlessness that is ridden with racial conflict. The powerful BPO overlooks these global/local instances of violence for the sake of a racist, homophobic, misogynistic overworld and deploys those employed by the states it controls (medical staff, police forces, federal agents, the media) in its hunt for the sensates.

Power becomes a grid in these cities, wherein the dynamics of the underworld and the overworld function locally as an interpretive framework for their navigation, but the "string-pulling" of the highest power at the global level is obscured until the sensates interact and confer. Only then, when the extent of the grid as a vertical and horizontal structure is understood, can the resistance exerted by the sensates come into play by means of an equivalent grid of global collaboration created through their "visiting" abilities. This grid reveals a multiplicity of pressure points that the sensates' visiting abilities condense into a porous frontier space through which they pass. And this frontier space spans the world in the form of infinitely spiraled, concentric spheres that are generated at the locations of the eight sensates like radio signals, redirecting the issues they face outward with centrifugal force, overlaying and rendering obsolete any significance of the national border and relocating citizenship from the nation to the global city. The global scope of the frontier and the lack of relevance of the nation demand, therefore, a consideration of cosmopolitanism as an explicative philosophy of these global ethics.

I Am Also a We: Cosmopolitanism as Resistance

The global scope of the urban frontier that transcends the nation-state and the "global/local" reconfigurations of Wilson and Dissanayake renders cosmopolitanism a viable organizational form that represents a philosophical stance. Cosmopolitan theory and practices orbit the idea of world citizenship, which entails "a commitment to a notion of moral equality of human beings beyond existing borders, with the responsibilities implied by it" (Parvu 2017: 785). Cosmopolitanism means "addressing problems of global governance, management of the environment, maintenance of peace, equitable global distribution of social goods and resources, humanitarian assistance, intercultural tolerance and understanding, and the protection of human dignity around the world" (van Hooft 2009: 1–2). Van Hooft understands the necessity of extracting the idea of cosmopolitanism from its Western origin in the Cynic and Stoic schools of Ancient Greece and Immanuel Kant's formulation of the world state as perpetual peace, so that it does not become a form of covert ideological colonialism but rather "a form of ethical thinking that is itself global in resonance and appeal" (2009: 2). Other less positive formulations of cosmopolitanism have also warned about the potential for elite cosmopolitan perspectives to "shore up social and cultural privileges in unequal power relations" (Deleyto 2019: 26). However, when Gerard Delanty argues for the cultural encounter at the center of the cosmopolitan attitude, where "the perspective of others is incorporated into one's own identity, interests and orientation in the world" (2011: 634), he is also describing the main feature and consequence of the sensates' empathic abilities and the potential for a form of cosmopolitanism that can be ethical, collective, and, as shall be discussed below, contestatory.

Angela Taraborrelli identifies three lines of enquiry: a political-legal cosmopolitanism—which "proposes the creation of a *cosmopolis*, a cosmopolitan institutional order under which all persons have equivalent rights and duties and are therefore citizens of a universal republic" (2015: 47)—a moral cosmopolitanism, and a cultural cosmopolitanism. The problem with the first is that a world state could be used to advance the agenda of multinational companies in the context of a globalized economy or to impose a specific (e.g., neoliberal) political and cultural model (Taraborrelli 2015: 81–2). *Sense8* identifies the BPO as a constrictive and homogenizing proto-world state that responds to the previously discussed notion of "overworld" as invisible power, and pursues a "globalization of domination" (Koukouzelis 2017: 747) by means of its monopoly of the "sanctioned" use of violence worldwide. The violence of the sensates resists this, however, thereby creating the global frontier space. It is at this point that a definition of frontier cosmopolitanism can be essayed, for this chapter conceives of frontier cosmopolitanism as the network of global/local configurations of solidarity in which the sensates are included, and which they strengthen and solidify. It is a frontier cosmopolitanism because the attitude, ethics, and practice behind that network are uncompromisingly cosmopolitan, and because they can be born only in the frontier conditions that are created globally by contesting the global monopoly of violence on the part of the BPO. This section, therefore, discusses the capacity for change and action on the global stage that the combination of the concepts of frontier and cosmopolitanism conveys, compressed between the sensates' empathy, which is built around a class-transversal cluster including upper-, middle-, and working-class members, and the BPO's state-like violence.

Lila Facchini states as much in S02:E12, when she asserts: "BPO is like any government. To deal with them you have to speak their language: force." The BPO's overworld power is violent, corporate and all-pervasive, built on a blend of public and private money that seeks the homogenization of diversity and the atomization of resistance by sensates. *Sense8* suggests a connection between the BPO and neoliberalism, because the persecution of sensates is also the persecution of the empathic collectivity that sensates represent, and which threatens the individuality of a neoliberal political rationality based on "an all-encompassing economic judgement" (Parvu 2017: 780). *Sense8*'s response to this model of political-legal cosmopolitanism is one of deep distrust, as it bears the elite implications suggested by Deleyto (2019: 26) and aims to hold a transnational controlling power bent on suppressing freedom and connections. This distrust prompts the question of how to create a union of peoples from the baseline of the city without their having recourse to the law or its enforcement.

Sense8's response involves Taraborrelli's other two schools of cosmopolitan thought: first, moral cosmopolitanism, because its "various forms ... share the idea that every human being has equal moral worth and that this equal moral worth gives rise to certain moral responsibilities having universal scope" (Taraborrelli 2015: 1), which translates into an ethical mandate that works at the three different levels of the individual, the national and the supranational; and second, cultural cosmopolitanism, which attenuates the importance of the individual in cosmopolitan thought and calls for a contextual understanding of cultural and historical backgrounds, thus countering the danger of Western rootedness. Cultural cosmopolitans (like the sensates) observe that communities and nations "are becoming increasingly multiethnic and multinational; that individuals are characterized by forms of multiple membership which often transcend the limits of national boundaries" (Taraborrelli 2015: 88). Consequently, these cosmopolitans champion "difference, diversity and hybridity while learning how to reason from the point of view of others and mediate traditions" (Taraborrelli 2015: 91), a utopian premise embodied by the sensates, albeit not without problems—for instance, the predominance of Western cultural references such as Van Damme, the Christmas iconography and the use of popular English-language music. Sheldon Pollock and his colleagues call for a conception of "cosmopolitanisms" in plural, in order to "leave open the question of the center and periphery in intellectual debates, and ... to avoid the imposition of practices and histories that do not necessarily fit interpretations for historical situations elsewhere" (Pollock et al. 2002: 8).

The main cluster of *Sense8* can be positioned at the forefront of this frontier cosmopolitanism. Because the eight characters in the cluster are connected by radical, simultaneous empathy and can also feel and think simultaneously, they embody Delanty's cultural encounter: when you are encountering the other, you are encountering yourself. *Sense8* correlatively applies the notions of queerness to the realm of cosmopolitan politics, rejecting any normativity that is based on the development of constricting legal frameworks and oppressive police forces and, instead, unfolds an idea of "worlding" as theorized by Schoonover and Galt in relation to "queer cinema's ongoing process of constructing worlds, a process that is active, incomplete, and contestatory and that does not presuppose a settled cartography" (2016: 5). Queer television such as *Sense8* does not presuppose a settled legislation either, for its mechanism of constructing a world also queers cosmopolitan politics through the rejection of state-generated rules. *Sense8*'s worlding even resembles "contestatory cosmopolitanism," a neologism that has described social movements since the 2010s, including 15-M in Madrid, Occupy Wall Street, and the protests in Istanbul's Taksim Square (Parvu 2017: 776). These protests are not only against neoliberalism but also *for* a "gradual development of an alternative form of political rationality that is, to a significant degree, cosmopolitan in substance" (Parvu 2017: 776). Against the homogenizing neoliberal force of the BPO, the contestatory cosmopolitanism of the sensates proposes, like these social movements, an ethical form of political rationality that envisages a "worlding" based on collaboration, collectivism, empathy, and diversity, a process that in *Sense8* is located in the realms of identity and sexuality rather than class.

Sense8's strategies of worlding are explored not only in its narrative but also in its editing. In this sense, editing allows the visiting abilities of the sensates to create "transparent interstices" (Licari 2011: 53) that connect their cities globally. Licari defines these transparent interstices in urban spaces as "spatial realities that open the door to a dialogue among the cultures present in the same context, overcoming exclusions and indifference" (Licari 2011: 53). *Sense8* constructs them in its editing through shot-reverse shot structures, in which cuts take the narrative back and forth between different cities, and also in camera movement that often encircles the characters or pans in different directions, thereby enabling centrifugal transitions. Examples of actions that are initiated by one character in one place and are finished by another character in another space can be found when Sun throws a punch and Capheus knocks his assailant out in S01:E03 and when Sun drops a cocktail mixer and Lito catches it in S02:E10 "If All the World's a Stage, Identity Is Nothing but a Costume." As these examples suggest, transparent interstices can resolve a variety of problems for the sensates, but they can also reveal causalities and consequences in the background. In S01:E01, for example, Kala attends a meeting at the pharmaceutical company where, unknown to her, her fiancée Rajan is facilitating the distribution of defective drugs. The next scene is in Nairobi, where Capheus is trying to purchase medicine for his HIV-positive mother. This is rendered

FIGURE 8.2 *Capheus's reaction constitutes a cosmopolitan expression of the moral worth of all human beings.*

personal when, in S02:E07 "I Have No Room in My Heart for Hate," Kala confronts Rajan about his offloading of defective medicines to "Africa," a word Rajan uses out of the ignorance and arrogance that consider the African continent as a single country homogenized by underdevelopment. Kala looks to her right, and a cut to Capheus shows his expression of dread as he realizes the connection: "Like Kenya?" (Figure 8.2). While Rajan sees only Kala's (local) dismay, the audience sees that of Capheus and his mother and also that of Kenya, asserting its specific place instead of being subsumed within the construct of "Africa." Through these editing strategies, *Sense8* conveys complex political ideas that differentiate between economic globalization, which also entails Rajan's unethical cosmopolitanism, and moral cosmopolitanism. Yet this transparent interstice is also where change is possible: faced with Kala's rejection of his excuse, Rajan apologizes, changes company policy, and collaborates with the police to expose the racket, while Kala begins to feel love for Rajan at last, and Capheus decides to go into politics.

Demons: *Sense8*'s Cosmopolitan Limitations

Sense8's cosmopolitanism is not without its problems. The series is excessively rooted in the Western hemisphere and its narrative is overly prone to resolving matters with violence, which entails the risk identified by Tamara

Cărăuș that "cosmopolitan initiatives conceived of and created by a counter-hegemonic character can later come to assume hegemonic characteristics" (2016: 99). That is to say, the cluster's victory only confirms the importance of violence in maintaining their cosmopolitanism. By the end of the series, even Kala, an indecisive pacifist, joins their killing spree in Seoul and Naples. The exception is Capheus, who gets involved with the Kenyan Democratic Reform Party during S02. Capheus embodies here some of the traits of political populism, such as the contestation of cultural elitism and "the privilege of elites" (Cărăuș 2016: 83), and points to a uniquely nonviolent form of resistance that might have been explored in S03. Disappointingly, Capheus's ambitions are curtailed not only by the violence that ruins his political rally but also by that of the final episode, which shows the sensates fighting the BPO with guns and rocket launchers, thus granting a narrative privilege to violence and to the Western characters that have been driving this aspect of the series. Furthermore, Capheus is also shown to benefit from violence (via Will and Sun "visiting" him in S01 to combat the gangsters) and from the drug trade too, with the ruthless ganglord Kabaka of S01 turning into a well-meaning philanthropist in S02, who woos Capheus's mother and gifts him a new *matatu*, bought with the profits of that bloody trade. These contradictions might have come into play in S03 with Capheus being challenged about his past during further electioneering, but political action in Nairobi and Kenyans' agency regarding their own improvement are halted.

Indeed, the closing down of all narrative threads in the final episode has the peculiar effect of reversing the centrifugal force of the frontier dynamics of power and resistance that are fundamental to the construction of the cosmopolitanism of the series. Instead of dispersing, all the sensates come together in Naples first and then Paris, both of which are experienced by them as tourist sites. The series thus ends by becoming centripetal. Contradictions abound: the speech about unity delivered by River El-Sadawi (the daughter of the woman who established the BPO for benevolent causes), the marriage between Amanita and Nomi, and the final orgy all consolidate *Sense8*'s cosmopolitan stance, thus suffusing frontier cosmopolitanism with a sexual quality. However, by conceiving of Paris as a fantasy and resolving all conflicts in a narrative bottleneck that dilutes the complexity with which the global cityspace had been constructed, an unreal quality triumphs.

Conclusion: A Frontier Cosmopolitanism

Sense8 constructs a unique stance for worlding by blending the urban space, the use of violence associated with the frontier space and the equality of a cosmopolitan sensibility. It matters, not only because of its willingness to pick a fight with the ugliness and violence that take refuge in the global cityspaces of today and not just because it opposes the domination of neoliberalism, but because it reimagines an alternative through its cosmopolitan approach, albeit through frequent recourse to violence as explained above. By the end of S02:E12, the sensates have rebooted and reorganized the BPO at its root, turning it into a cosmopolitan-oriented organization. They have also tackled with different degrees of success the homophobia, transphobia, criminality, and corruption of their cities. Ultimately, *Sense8* prefaces the disappearance of the need for violence, which would in turn eliminate frontier spaces worldwide.

Finally, however, *Sense8*'s most important achievement is its ability to portray a world in which collective problems are addressed through collective solutions, which is the most radical stance against the atomization and homogenization of the neoliberalism that the BPO has been shown to represent. The open-hearted collaboration between the sensates rehearses a form of "global civil society" (Taraborrelli 2015: 60) capable of exerting changes that bypass the imposition of national borders. Cosmopolitanism in *Sense8* is conceived not as a reified theoretical stance but as a practice that is constantly configured through "unity in diversity" (Delanty 2011: 651), with worlding potential. The problems with the series' political project outlined above can be seen as an open diagnosis of what even a well-meaning cultural product cannot achieve. Even if the final victory of the sensates and their reunion in the Eiffel Tower forces the perspective of tourism to appear in the series, the process of construction of a cosmopolitan attitude at the frontier explored throughout the two seasons demonstrates that *Sense8* conceives of frontier cosmopolitanism as a progressive and ethical model built out of transnational, transgender, and transformative connections between people. No longer the meeting point between civilization and savagery and a justification for colonial genocide, a cosmopolitan frontier is radically converted into a site of unity in diversity, where *amor vincit omnia*.

Works Cited

Appadurai, A. (2002), "Spectral Housing and Urban Cleansing: Notes on Millennial Mumbai", in C. A. Breckenridge, S. Pollock, H. K. Bhabha, and D. Chakrabarty (eds.), *Cosmopolitanism*, 54–81, Durham, NC: Duke University Press.

Cărăuş, T. (2016), "Cosmopolitanism and Populism: From Incompatibility to Convergence, and Back," *Analele Universității din București. Seria Ştiințe Politice*, 18 (1): 83–102.

Delanty, G. (2011), "Cultural Diversity, Democracy and the Prospects of Cosmopolitanism: A Theory of Cultural Encounters," *British Journal of Sociology*, 62 (4): 633–56.

Deleyto, C. (2019), "Performing Cosmopolitanism: Julie Delpy and Ethan Hawke in Richard Linklater's 'Before' Trilogy," *Transnational Screens*, 10 (1): 23–33.

Foucault, M. ([1975] 1998), *Vigilar y castigar*, trans. A. Garzón del Camino, 11th edn. Madrid: Siglo XXI Editores.
Foucault, M. ([1976] 1990), *The History of Sexuality. Vol. 1: An Introduction*, trans. R. Hurley, Harmondsworth: Penguin.
Koukouzelis, K. (2017), "Climate Change Social Movements and Cosmopolitanism," *Globalizations*, 14 (5): 746–61.
Licari, G. (2011), "Anthropology of Urban Space: Identities and Places in the Postmodern City," *World Futures*, 67 (1): 47–57.
Mistra, S., M. Chakraborty, and N. R. Mandal (2018), "Critical Regionalism in the Post-Colonial Architecture of the Indian Subcontinent," *Journal of Architecture and Urbanism*, 42 (2): 103–11.
Parvu, C. A. (2017), "Contestatory Cosmopolitanism, Neoliberal Rationality and Global Protest," *Globalizations*, 14 (5): 776–91.
Pollock, S., H. K. Bhabha, C. Breckenridge, and D. Chakrabarty (2002), "Cosmopolitanisms," in C. A. Breckenridge, S. Pollock, H. K. Bhabha, and D. Chakrabarty (eds.), *Cosmopolitanism*, 1–14, Durham, NC: Duke University Press.
Schoonover, K., and R. Galt (2016), *Queer Cinema in the World*. Durham, NC: Duke University Press.
Smith, N. (1996), *The New Urban Frontier: Gentrification and the Revanchist City*. New York and London: Routledge.
Taraborrelli, A. (2015), *Contemporary Cosmopolitanism*, trans. I. McGilvray. London: Bloomsbury Publishing.
Turner, F. J. (1998), *Rereading Frederick Jackson Turner: "The Significance of the Frontier in American History," and Other Essays*. ed. J. M. Faragher, New Haven, CT: Yale University Press.
van Hooft, S. (2009), *Cosmopolitanism: A Philosophy for Global Ethics*, Stocksfield: Acumen.
Weber, M. (2004), *The Vocation Lectures*, trans. R. Livingstone. Indianapolis, IN: Hackett.
Wilson, R., and W. Dissanayake (1996), "Introduction: Tracking the Global/Local," in R. Wilson and W. Dissanayake (eds.), *Global/Local: Cultural Production and the Transnational Imaginary*, 1–18, Durham, NC: Durham University Press.

9

The Common Good: Birth, Death, and Self-Sacrifice in/of *Sense8*

Will McKeown

The cluster is a felt, multi-presence network that blends sentiment on a psychic level and on a transnational scale. Self-sacrifice in *Sense8* therefore finds contextual resonance in how it integrates notions of selfhood, meaning that the multiple subjectivities of the cluster reconfigure how the self can be sacrificed and what the sacrifice can signify to audiences in contemporary contexts. As will be demonstrated, the mutuality of self-sacrifice within the cluster is a much needed actualization of empathetic solidarity that challenges damaging social and political assumptions. Transgressive meetings of minds and bodies in Berlin, London, Reykjavik, Nairobi, and other global locations defy the binary of unity and separateness because the sensates experience contact and connectivity as a flow that fosters an eternal becoming based on the form and content of a vivid togetherness. The notion of a seamless, cooperative, and empathetic community is a challenge to the dividing influence of corporatism and post-truth politics. It is also because of this sense of community that the sensates perceive actual and potential harm, compromise, and the psychic invasion of the self as mutual threats. These collective dangers demand a constant reevaluation of what the eight sensates are and what their cluster is, and in what ways they/it can be sacrificed. The notion of self-sacrifice encapsulates this challenge in its representation because the cluster of sensates not only responds to the pressures that are applied to communities to make sacrifices, but also transcends this pressurization through solidarity and by understanding the mutual sacrifices of others. In other, often apocalyptic texts, self-sacrifice is an internalization of survival drives to the point that the sacrifice is rendered unworthy of survivor status by its own failures. But *Sense8* offers a different stance, one in which the communal self-sacrifices of the cluster are compensated for by solidarity between individuals.

Accordingly, this chapter analyzes the essential mutability of the cluster in terms of spatial and emotional closeness and with reference to theories of the self-other binary (Lacan [1949] 2006; Verhaeghe 2014). Building upon the "elasticity" of the collective and the self (the idea that the self can be distributed across the globe and yet the cluster can be gathered emotionally and psychically in one place), this chapter explores the sacrifice mechanism that is at the heart of the series. All of the characters in *Sense8* make sacrifices at key points in the series, Nomi endures an e-death to sacrifice any electronic record that she ever existed in order to facilitate her hacktivism. Lito sacrifices his career as an actor, Kala comes close to dying before being saved by her connection to Wolfgang and her husband Rajan (and a Taser repurposed as a defibrillator), Will sacrifices his health to addiction, Sun sacrifices her freedom, Caepheus sacrifices his security, Riley sacrifices everything but her life before having her maternalism reinstated as the cluster-mother, and Wolfgang, who seems most impermeable to all threats, comes closest to sacrificing his life itself in the cliffhanger ending to S02 (and possible series closer before the series was renewed). Like the self, the act of sacrifice, in its various degrees, is also mutable in and around the cluster. Sacrifice unites them in empathy and may be examined in terms of a balance/negotiation between the risks of deep connectivity and the transgressive, spontaneous, and empathetic survival instinct of the network itself. Finally, self-sacrifice in the truest sense—as with the suicide of the original cluster-mother Angelica—will be discussed in terms of the cinematic closeness of birth and sacrifice in *Sense8*, which is not only bound up in the montage of births that culminates in S01:E10 "What Is Human?" (and will be examined in depth) but also bound with the way that Angelica's suffering appears to mask and blur the trauma/serenity of both birth and death, creating a loop (the circle of life) that ultimately binds the cluster together. Even so, the residual representations of Angelica that appear to transgress death itself suggest that the psychic nature of the cluster even challenges the sacrificial aspect of the process by positing transcendence in response to death, much like the series transcended its own cancelation.

Solidarity in Self-Sacrifice: (H)ac(k)tivism against Corporatism and Patriarchal Forces

Self-sacrifice as it is explored in *Sense8* is not absolute but must be understood as an incremental concept that does not necessitate the death of a character. Because each sensate feels both their own and each other's grief, each instance of sacrifice would be emotionally damaging to the point that, even if a member of the cluster did instigate their death via self-sacrifice, the act's benefits would be somewhat undermined. Moreover, because Whispers hunts telepathically and can use a connection to the mind of a single sensate to locate the rest of the cluster, the discovery (i.e., sacrifice) of a single sensate compromises the whole cluster. It is proposed, however, that reciprocated self-sacrifice (and psychic assistance) within the cluster brings with it a solidarity that embodies a resistance to ubiquitous attitudes of division, ignorance, and intolerance, which must be extrapolated from the narrative world to its real counterpart. By this logic, cluster-centric self-sacrifice provides a means of disrupting the dominant social order. The cluster's propensity to transmit states of feeling, information, and skills thousands of miles across national boundaries defines it as transcendent, but also alters how identity occurs within it. Because sensates are at once themselves but also psychically the other members of the cluster too, their transnational connection becomes the embodiment of their multifaceted self-identification(s). *Sense8* provides many instances of geographic and spatial transportation through editing whereby a cut to reverse shot can travel between distant locations, from Delhi to Berlin or from Chicago to Reykjavik. The moment of the cut represents the unique transportational abilities of the cluster or "composite" because the psychic visitation becomes a temporal moment that embodies a state of being in-between. It is an ambiguous geographic marker that oscillates through time, visually mapping the cluster and transcending the established rules of communication, travel, ownership, class, authority, and science. By extension, sensate notions of identity change concurrently. They are no longer of a single country, town, city, race, gender, or religion; rather they are a single "composite" self with multiplicitous configurations of identification and self-awareness. The cluster therefore distorts or complicates representations of identity because it allows for a more diverse, more eclectic, and more unified actualization of self-identity than could ever be possible without radical empathy. Yet the exchange between the cluster goes beyond empathy and incorporates the transfer of otherwise unknowable sensations and skills such as the extreme heat of Nairobi from a different continent (as Riley meets Capheus in S01:E05 "Art Is Like Religion") or the mercurial technique of blisteringly effective martial arts (from Sun to Capheus in S01:E03 "Smart Money's On the Skinny Bitch"), which are direct transgressions or transcendence of what each individual should be (and has been) capable of or able to experience. But it is important to recognize that these acts and instances are each a communal transgression. For each self-sacrifice made among the members of the cluster, which in the early "learning" episodes tends to mean stepping into danger when needed, there is always a corresponding and reciprocated helping hand that materializes psychically in these times of peril. It is this symbiosis that disrupts representations of authority: how often do BPO (Biological Preservation Organization) agents, federal officers, and Nigerian gangsters fall victim to some iteration of Sun's fist? How often are government and BPO databases hacked by Nomi? The coming together of the cluster and each derivation of its emotion, communication and identification posits a challenge to the established status quo that seems set on classification, separation, and eradication.

To gain further understanding of self-identification and how this process can be altered in the situation of the cluster, it is useful to consult Paul Verhaeghe's model of a simplified but no less pertinent theory of identity that follows both Empedocles and Freud:

> These two fundamental tendencies would seem to be typical of every living being: we want to be part of a greater whole, and at the same time we long for independence. As far back as the fifth century BC, the Greek Philosopher Empedocles wrote of two elemental powers that held universal sway: Philia, Love, and Neikos, Strife. Freud saw these as two primal urges: the life instinct, Eros, which seeks to dissolve in love, and the death drive Thanatos, which aggressively seeks separation. Sameness and difference, in other words. (Verhaeghe 2014: 13)

Verhaeghe contends that the basis of individual identity operates as a continuance of sameness and difference: that what someone identifies with, be it a place, person, culture, status, belief, or otherwise, can be cross-referenced against preexisting identifications and mapped in degrees of similarity or discrepancy. The comparative aspect of this identification is what clearly defines the self and the other as two fundamental but separate elements of social identification. The sensate cluster is a clear exception to this rule because the constitutive selves of the cluster do not register a cluster-based other; they are all incorporated into a collective, connected consciousness whereby identity is derived from the coming together of multiple connected selves. As will be seen, however, this does not mean that notions of collective selfhood cannot resist "othered" forces outside of the cluster. This is because the collective identity of the cluster, in line with Verhaeghe's definition, embraces unity and compassion and distances itself from prejudice, intolerance, and ignorance through acts of civil disobedience. Moreover, cluster-based self-sacrifice resembles a movement against the assumptions, pressures, and obligations of corporatism and, in many cases, patriarchal demands, which becomes a reciprocated symbiosis that supports and is supported by other sensates within the cluster. This reframes the notion of survival drives, as outlined by Jonas (Naveen Andrews)—"We have to look forward. If we don't, we won't survive"—from the perpetuation of survivor status to a constant state of mutual assistance, of surviving for others instead of in place of them. It is this shift in dynamic that is the single most important challenge to the established social order in the series, but also in the world around it.

Understanding Violence in *Sense8*

In this consideration of survival, moreover, it is important to note that even though *Sense8* is centered on the issues of global understanding and transnational empathy, it still features many violent sequences. The cooperation of the cluster routinely produces swathes of dead gangsters, bloody-faced misogynists, homophobes, and incapacitated BPO operatives. So how can a series devoted to unity between people engender so many casualties? Characters such as Sun (attacking her brother in S01:E11 "Just Turn the Wheel and the Future Changes") and Lito (defending Daniela from Joaquin in S01:E10) posit endangerment as self-sacrifice in response to social pressures applied by patriarchal corporatist organizations. In many cases, sensates are exposed to forces that are beyond the law, beyond government, and beyond the social order of non-sensates. In the case of Riley and Nomi, an otherwise unremarkable trip to the hospital is always going to end disastrously because the BPO are notified as soon as someone with signs of the sensate genome is taken in. Therefore, the cluster too must transcend the law and exist within a fugitive space, defying criminal syndicates, enlisting hacktivists, and incapacitating armed police. *Sense8* therefore proposes that the only counterpoint to patriarchal and corporatist agendas that transcend the law, such as BPO's obsession with the sensate genealogy and Bak Joong-ki's ability to prevent his father from testifying against him, is not only to match them but also to transgress laws on a transnational scale. Correlatively, the transgression of the justice system from civil disobedience to outright fugitivity is in itself an act of self-sacrifice, but one that is made necessary by the threat posed by the BPO. Nomi's e-death in S02:E05 "Fear Never Fixed Anything" is a self-sacrifice that simultaneously overcomes her fugitive status at the cost of her virtual existence; the sacrifice points to the limits and flaws of the capitalist system and outlines the need to transgress them. Following this logic, the rebellious positioning of cluster-based self-sacrifice, with the telepathically transmitted skills it demands and revels in as well as the risks it may entail, is framed as a composite challenge to the established hierarchies of late capitalism.

The many sacrifices made in the cluster are brave, often against the law and operate at great personal risk. They therefore function to make clear the flaws in a system in which individuals of extreme influence can flout the judicial system. Simultaneously, self-sacrifice within the cluster demonstrates the extreme understanding of the cluster's limbic resonance as an aggressive and visceral challenge to social and political division instigated by race, class, and gender prejudice, in combination with corporate nepotism. It does so in resistance to established notions of patriarchy and corporatism that are founded on the enforcement of division and are equally cultivated by it. The case could be made for an exception to this rule through the opposition between Homo sapiens and Homo sensorium, between "us" and "them". However, "them" is not all other humans. Amanita first and eventually Hernando, Daniela, Rajan and Bug, for example, are sapien extensions of the cluster, meaning the only "them" are those who wish harm to the cluster. Indeed, because harming the cluster is anti-empathetic, the cluster is always positioned in opposition to political powers that seek to propagate the distanciation between the self and the other. There are many non-sensate characters that offer their absolute support to the cluster: Capheus's best friend Jela, Nomi's old partner in crime Bug, Daniela, and Wolfgang's "chosen brother" Felix. Perhaps the most supportive person outside of the cluster is Amanita, who consistently follows and trusts Nomi through increasingly dangerous situations and, in doing so, evidences how the cluster is truly a promoter of unity as it is also made up of compassionate people who love and assist sensates in whichever way they can. It is also true that many of these characters contribute to and interweave with the collective self-sacrifices of the cluster as Jela is threatened, Bug is pursued, Daniela is beaten, Felix is shot and Nomi's fugitive status is shared by Amanita in support of her partner.

To understand the specifics of how the self-sacrifices within the cluster move against modern agendas of patriarchy, corporatism, and post-truth social divisions, the opposition of the individual and the collective may be examined in reference to the work of Verhaeghe. Verhaeghe contends that neoliberalism is the definitive contemporary condition and that its action is centered on the quantification of qualitative experience that polarizes the individual and the organization:

> Diametrically opposed to the individual stands the organization, that wants to restrict the individual rights—in more accurate terms: the demands—of the individual, and this in the name of the benefits of a hypothetical general interest, which is in reality the interest of that organization itself. (Verhaeghe 2015: 7)

The representation of organizations in *Sense8* is focused on the BPO and Bak Enterprises (Sun's family's company), both of which are revealed to be corrupt. Such organizations are in operation by Verhaeghe's logic because they separate themselves from the individual, removing accountability and dividing it into departments and branches, each with various levels of micromanagement allowing for the diffusion of responsibility for any action. As seen in Sun's narrative, this comes about unfairly; she is a less prominent figure in the company (as determined by prevailing prejudicial attitudes to gender) and as such she takes responsibility and blame for the company's embezzlement charges so that the organization can continue: the individual is conditioned to submit to the authority of the organization. And it is this opposition to the individual that allows for the creation of post-truth narratives. Again, Sun exemplifies this: her self-sacrifice is simultaneously a post-truth. She informs the media that she is responsible for the embezzlement in the company in an attempt to uphold her family's honor. A further post-truth is realized when her brother kills her father just as he is about to admit the innocence of his daughter. In both cases, it is the unruly reasoning of influential men in positions of power that criminalizes Sun's resistance to the organization and the patriarchy it represents. Sun did make a promise to her mother that she would look after her brother and safeguard the family's legacy, and Sun's self-sacrifice is therefore also tied into her family's code of honor; but there are flaws in this reading because Sun taking the blame for her brother's crime is built on the assumption that she is less visible in the corporate sphere because she is female. Her sacrifice honors her promise to her mother, but only because it suits a system in which women like Sun and her mother are subordinate to men. The question of family dishonor is reframed, however, when her brother kills her father and Sun is compelled to respond by fighting back against outright criminality, albeit initially on the wrong side of the law—at least until Detective Mun allies his authority with her strategy.

Many similar instances of post-truths can be identified in the interactions of the sensates with the BPO. Jonas is branded a terrorist to the police department because he is a sensate, and Nomi is diagnosed with a supposedly life-threatening illness because her brain scans identify her as one. Both are examples of how influential corporations like the BPO disseminate post-truths that inveigle public services such as the police and the health service in their nefarious strategies. Nevertheless, it is important to note that each self-sacrifice is an example of the intertwining of selfhoods within the strengthening cluster, which opposes the perpetuation of divisions between people and between their notions of self and otherness. Consequently, noticeable parallels to modern right-wing politics can be recognized. The incursive search for weapons of mass destruction in Iraq was one such post-truth that has been pointed out to be in the interests of oil companies (Dekhakhena 2017: 18), while the rise of anti-European Union narratives in the UK were partly supported by the propagation of post-truth reports by various right-wing parties of an influx of legal and illegal immigrants (Greven 2016: 3). On the other hand, self-sacrifice in *Sense8* is centered on the understanding of the other, of a reciprocated emotion that fuses notions of selfhood together and in solidarity with each other. The series offers an alternative to the prejudices that are sown so often by people in positions of influence and power. Instead of collaborating on the dissemination of hate and fear, *Sense8* challenges this sharing of divisive post-truth narratives and demonstrates the socially transformative potential of radical empathy; that is, empathy as precursor to real action and, if necessary, violence. In sum, the sensates form a cluster because their self-sacrifices are all made in support of and in defense of each other, even if this requires preemptive attacks.

Connective Self-Sacrifice: Against Pressurized Survivalism

To further understand the integration of selfhood and otherness that defines the cluster and the transnational empathy that this induces, we must follow the framework of Jacques Lacan's mirror stage. The personal advent of selfhood could be outlined for any one of the sensates, with each of them thereby revealing correspondent insights into their race, culture, gender, sexuality, class, and upbringing as contributing factors in the unifying formation via empathy of the cluster-selfhood. This is signaled by the self-sacrifice of Angelica, whose suicide is the recurring site of reflection for the cluster's sense of collective self, appearing frequently in subjective flashbacks, dreams, and objective recreations throughout the series. Lacan's theorization of the mirror stage is relevant because it outlines the infant's very first conception of itself as a cohesive unit, and, crucially, the suicide of Angelica immediately follows her giving birth to the series' primary cluster and is identified as the first moment of shared awareness of their condition and their cluster for the eight main sensates. Lacan considers an image that looks back at itself, being and doing as it does, and he supposes several repercussions:

> This development is experienced as a temporal dialectic that decisively projects the individual's formation into history: the mirror stage is a drama whose internal pressure pushes precipitously from insufficiency to anticipation—and, for the subject caught up in the lure of spatial identification, turns out fantasies that proceed from a fragmented image of the body to what I will call an "orthopaedic" form of its totality—and to the finally donned armour of an alienating identity that will mark his entire mental development with its rigid structure. (Lacan [1949] 2006: 78)

Following Lacan, the mirror stage recalls the abject for Kristeva because it makes evident the primordial separation of birth and thus the boundary of self/other (Kristeva 1980: 9), whereas Lacan notes the importance of the moment in which the subject sees itself for the first time as a functioning, albeit limited, agent. Both readings can coexist but what matters most are the lasting effects of the first encounter of selfhood. The temporal dialectic that Lacan describes is founded on an infant sense of insufficiency.

By recognizing the materialization of the reflected self, the subject can in turn realize what it lacks and confront its incoordination. The subject can anticipate growing, walking, interacting, and talking by, according to Lacan, an unconscious method of projection and identification, from past inadequacies to future anticipations, which forms a structure that shapes subjective identity for the rest of the subject's life. In *Sense8* the same temporal dialectic is present in representations of self-sacrifice. The sacrifice admits past shortcomings and projects beyond a subject's own self-compromise to transfer survivor status onto those who benefit from the act of self-sacrifice. In other words, the sacrifice looks to the past and the future, generating the present, while gauging perceived insufficiencies from both temporal directions. Self-sacrifice is a moment of clarity in which survival acquires a status that is underpinned by the assumption that it is the optimum outcome of self-sacrifice. Somewhat ironically then, it might be posited that self-sacrifice works towards survival. Indeed, it is often the case that self-sacrifices function as part of a chain whereby a prior self-sacrifice necessitates the demand for further self-sacrifices as a means of vindicating antecedent self-sacrifices. The accumulation of pressure over-determines the need to survive, transferring its emphasis from the prolongation of life to the preservation of status. Nevertheless, the fetishization of survival, where survival is synonymous with selfishness, does partake of the sociopolitical conditions within which it exists, meaning that it can reinforce the position of dominant classes that have access to better healthcare, for example.

On the other hand, when self-sacrifice is in the service of the common good, it internalizes the fetishization of the survival drive and derives pleasure from the survival of others. In *Sense8*, Angelica's self-sacrifice (her death) is paired so closely with her giving birth to her cluster that the two actions are indistinguishable—as one. Moreover, the temporal dialectic that Lacan describes is reconfigured with this self-sacrifice because in giving birth Angelica transcends her own death. Consequently, the psychic connection that defines sensates disintegrates the status of life as well as death, thereby calling into question the value ascribed to survival. Between life and death, Angelica visits the cluster after her sacrifice as a psychic residue, as an irrepressible maternal spectre made evident by the paradox that her sacrifice enabled the cluster to survive, while, at the same time, their birth generated a resultant psycellic network that enables her reemergence. This establishes a precedent whereby self-sacrifice is less concerned with survivalism and more about prioritizing mutual, reciprocal support. Angelica's self-sacrifice does not fetishize survival, but it does manifest the future projection of self-sacrifice, bringing the cluster into existence (a different notion to survival) and giving its eight members a purpose. In the moment of giving birth to the cluster, Angelica individually greets each new sensate in their respective locations, thereby indicating the unification and dispersal of her life-force into the cluster. This means that Angelica's self-sacrifice does not facilitate the assumption of inadequacy or anticipation of deferring future sufficiency; instead it revels in the connections it creates. There is no internalization of selfish survival drives; instead the self-worth of survivors and non-survivors alike move toward equilibrium. This, in turn, breaks down the prestige of survivor status and challenges the notion that the fetishization of survival can be a means of reinforcing the position of the dominant class. The meaning and workings of self-sacrifice within the nascent cluster therefore challenge social inequality through the cluster-based actualization of solidarity and empathy. In S01:E12 "I Can't Leave Her," for example, Will and Riley realize their efforts to escape are futile because Whispers has previously looked into Will's eyes and is now able to see through them remotely as long as Will is aware of his surroundings. Only by sedating himself can Will negate Whisper's telepathic surveillance and grant Riley a chance to escape, albeit by confronting the trauma triggered by being alone on the road on which her husband died in the car crash that induced Riley to give birth to a baby that soon froze to death. Overriding Riley's personal trauma, however, is the knowledge that evading Whispers is crucial because if he reaches a single sensate the entire cluster becomes compromised. Thus, Will's self-sedation is an imperative action but also one of trust because he believes in Riley's strength of character, which is subsequently demonstrated in her ability to relive and overcome her past trauma and save Will, who thereafter becomes reliant on Riley to maintain his drug-induced state in order to ensure the safety of the entire cluster. The chain of self-sacrifice from Angelica to Will to Riley and the rest of the cluster endures and is demonstrated by the empathetic solidarity between the cluster in the eloquent final shot of S01: Riley and a comatose Will are escaping Iceland as passengers on a fishing ship and are "magically" joined by the other six sensates in representation of both telepathic visitation and radical empathy that refrains from granting survivor status and instead outlines the importance of a mutual and transcendent understanding (Figure 9.1).

Empathetic Solidarity and Breaking the Mirror

Another relevant concept in Lacan's framework of the mirror stage is that of an "alienation" that is said to come about through the "lure of spatial identification," which refers to the discrepancy between the knowledge of the self, its felt existence, and what it looks like in the mirror (Lacan [1949] 2006: 78). The reflection is a specular image, a cohesive body that appears complete but, to the person it reflects, it is only a fragment of what they actually are; it omits their memories, feelings, beliefs, and relations. Lacan maintains that the seeming fixity and completeness of the reflected image

FIGURE 9.1 *Telepathic visitation as radical empathy.*

generates alienation because it suggests the extrapolation that identity too is both fixed and complete. In reality, however, when considered on a wider chronological scale, both identity and the specular image are in a state of flux. Moreover, identity is a fragmented construct that originates from multiple social sources, which makes for a stark contrast with the single source that faces the subject in the mirror. Once again, the presence of the sensate cluster complicates this process of alienation and even negates it. This is because the cluster is definitively fragmented in terms of its identity: eight sensates comprise its physicality and its multiplicity and, as such, the cluster eludes the sense of alienation that is generated by any attempt to view it as a singular specular image. The illusion that is maintained by the mirror stage is that identity is fixed and singular but the introduction of the telepathic cluster subverts this as it is a literally represented translation of identity as multifaceted, multiply sourced yet fragmented, albeit in a state of acceptance and togetherness. This is even represented in a literal manner on-screen in S01:E05 when Lito and Sun see each other "in" and touch fingers "through" a mirror.

Identity in *Sense8*, instead of being structured by the damaging temporal dialectic of the mirror stage, is characterized as a state of flow, as a dialogue of emotional states that weave into each other transnationally, becoming a collective consciousness that is mutually supportive and understanding and diametrically opposed to discriminatory oppressive sociopolitical interests. It is for this reason that a Deleuzo-Guattarian framework can help to further understand the meaning of the cluster in relation to self-sacrifice. Dan Smith holds that "*Anti-Oedipus* does not contain a single negative comment about

Lacan" (Smith 2004: 639) and further claims that Deleuze contributed to the Lacanian field "a whole new set of concepts to describe the inverse side of the symbolic structure" (Smith 2004: 648). What may be inferred is that, while Lacan is concerned with the alienating illusion of the mirror stage, Deleuze and Guattari inspect the underlying reality (Real) of multiplicitous identity, which is sourced from various different sites of identification and defined by a state of flow. Deleuze and Guattari's description of how the connection between desiring-machines gives the impression of the subject reveals how the notion of cluster identity can be situated in accordance with Angelica's self-sacrifice:

> Let us trace it along a first path (the shortest route): the points of disjunction on the body without organs form circles that converge on the desiring-machines; then the subject—produced as a residuum alongside the machine, as an appendix, or as a spare part adjacent to the machine—passes through all the degrees of the circle, and passes from one circle to another. This subject itself is not at the center, which is occupied by the machine, but on the periphery, with no fixed identity, forever decentered, defined by the states through which it passes. (Deleuze and Guattari 1983: 20)

If the mirror stage presents an illusion of fixed identity that is subverted by Angelica's self-sacrifice and its production of the cluster, Deleuze and Guattari reinforce this idea by outlining the continuous fluctuations of identity and propose that subjectivity is the product of (and therefore secondary to) overlapping desires. It may therefore be posited that desire is the driving force of identification and, moreover, that desire is therefore also equally fragmentary, both directed at and derived from various sources—an idea which may now be conclusively applied to the sequence in S01:E01 in which Angelica first meets each of her eight sensates.

Angelica sits up, looking into the indeterminate gloom and whispers: "I see them ...." This is captured in a slow and gradual circular tracking shot. The same gradual circulation incorporates Riley vaping in London and Sun in Seoul. Will and Capheus are encountered along the same circumference as the camera tracks their respective vehicles. This generates a sequence that is as fluid as it is interconnected; on the one hand, it is spatially continuous, with each shot melded into its successor through the coordinated movement of the camera as evidenced by cuts from Angelica to Riley, to Angelica, to Sun, just after Nomi appears in Angelica's location. Yet, on the other hand, it is spatially discontinuous with many of the cuts to successive locations indicative of extreme geographical and transnational jumps. This creates a tension between visual and geographic fluidity that stylizes the interactions of the cluster, sets up their capacity for psychic visitation, and binds their respective identities in a mutual encounter with Angelica. At the same time, there are several shots in this sequence that are set up with a more static camera, with the movement in the shot coming from objects in the foreground: for example, the dancers in the scene that introduces Wolfgang in a nightclub. This interrupts the circularity of the sequence but, at the same time, the recurrence of a dynamic composition channels the circular momentum along vertical axes with the use of incremental or slow zooms (as seen with Will, Capheus, and Kala). This is important because it positions the members of the cluster as desiring-machines aligned in circular formations along the duration of the sequence. The subjectivity of the cluster is therefore a by-product of the connection of desiring-machines (sensates) and, therefore, the collision of their pre-cluster identities. Angelica operates as a visual hypostasis in this sequence, her appearance in each of the scenes pinning them together and activating the flow of consciousness, emotion, and empathy that defines the cluster. She is an interruption to each sensate's subjectivity but at the same time the reason their idea of selfhood is to be changed irrevocably.

In many ways Angelica is the body without organs, not just in so much as she reappears to the cluster as a psychically preserved being devoid of a physical body but also in a sense that she is "crisscrossed with axes and thresholds, with latitudes and longitudes and geodesic lines, traversed by gradients marking the transitions and the becomings" (Deleuze and Guattari 1983: 19). Consider the intersections of her instantaneous psychic transport around the world, the coming into being of the cluster for each one of the unknowing sensates she visits, the versions of space they will go on to occupy and transcend. Each connection between the cluster produces desire (as depicted in the telepathic orgy scenes) and brings into existence the collision of worlds and cultures. Each iteration of collective selfhood is also a challenge to the false impression of fixed identity and the eventual assumption of future inadequacies from a point of insufficiency (as outlined in the mirror stage). The mirror in *Sense8* is broken but each fragment houses a different face looking back. Such multiplicity is indicative of acceptance instead of division, and each acceptance is reciprocated because of the telepathic and empathic connections facilitated by Angelica's self-sacrifice. The transfer of sentiments, desire, knowledge, and abilities is realized not only through a solidarity of mutual understanding but also through a visceral challenge to the established order. Deleuze and Guattari similarly denounce the establishment of a dominant class. They contend that the foundation of a class system "involves deliberately organizing wants and needs (manque) amid an abundance of production; making all of desire teeter and fall victim to the great fear of not having one's needs satisfied" (Deleuze and Guattari 1983: 28). This means that the fear of not having one's needs satisfied, which equates to the mirror stage assumption from a point of potential insufficiency, is an oppressive social construct that ensures social stratification. By extension, the movement from fixed identity and the

Lacanian mirror stage to multiple identity and the subject as a by-product following Deleuze and Guattari positions the self-sacrificial birth of the cluster in opposition to the hegemony of dominant classes, fighting the corner for minorities in empathetic solidarity.

Collective Birth as Concert of Self-Acceptance

Finally, having established that the self-sacrifice and coming together of the cluster generates a unity that is positioned as a network of protests against corporatism, right-wing post-truth politics, the patriarchy, and the cementation of social strata, other aspects of the representation of pure empathy can be examined. It is proposed, for example, that pure empathy as the medium of telepathic and transnational social activism evidenced in the workings of the cluster also cultivates self-acceptance. This comes about in each and every mutually supported instance of self-sacrifice throughout the series but is never clearer than in S01:E10 in the scene at the Reykjavik Opera House. Riley's father is a virtuoso pianist who contributes the lead to a performance of Beethoven's Piano Concerto no. 5 in E-flat Major that melds the sequence together. Riley is the only sensate to be physically present, but the intensity of her psychic response summons each of her cluster to take her place. As the music plays, each sensate is depicted in close-up before their subconscious memories become active reimaginings of their simultaneous birth(s). The perspective of these recollections is transgressive because, in sequences such as Kala's and Sun's, the moments that predate the birth of the sensates are also articulated. This clearly positions the births as a collective reimagining but also locates their interaction outside of the constraints of linear time. It therefore holds that the births transgress the construction of time but are also inextricably bound to it: each sensate has been on this earth for an identical amount of time, housing them in an intimately unified timeframe, yet completely beyond the authority of transnational time zones through instantaneous psychological travel. What is vital to recognize here is that it is not only space that the cluster is able to collectively transcend but also time and memory. As ambiguously represented recollections are woven into the fabric of the cluster's experience of exchange, each sensate generates a birth narrative that allows them to reclaim the advent of their existence, promoting a sense of self-acceptance based upon the empathetic action/reaction to which the cluster is integral.

The spatial composition of the audience is also a means of capturing the empathetic unity of the cluster. A close-up frames Riley from behind, out of focus in the foreground, with the emphasis of the shot on the lower galleries and the stage. In contrast, both Will and Kala are the sole subjects of their close-ups with much of their location blurred out. The effect of this is that, while it is clear that they are "in the audience" because of the diegetic musical cues and the color palette of the blurred periphery, the positions of each of the sensates are unverifiable in relation to Riley. The other sensates are "present" but in a vague sense that characterizes togetherness without making it so explicit that spatial direction distracts from the sense of unity. Moreover, it is the concert that causes the gravitation of the cluster, the welling of emotion, and the surge of feeling that brings the birth scenes into being. The spatial construction of the sequence draws attention to the mechanics of the majestic opera house, from the rich fabrics of the seating galleries to their acoustic depth. The glossy timber of the stage and the fanatical enthusiasm of the musicians all contribute to the sense that the imagined births are countermelodies stitched into the orchestral performance. Percussive flourishes that both empower and support the soaring intricacies of the piano playing liken the formation of the cluster to the workings of the orchestra, with each instrument benefiting from the unique timbre and identity of all other parts. Indeed, the co-aligned construction of mutual support defined by diversity and the conjunctive fusion of differences is a fitting description of both the cluster and the orchestra. Moreover, the spatial composition of sensates in the audience locates the psychic transfer of imagined births in support of, and also mutually supported by, the performance of the orchestra. Capheus can be seen laughing and crying simultaneously in a euphoria of reciprocated pride at this collision and collusion of identities and cultures being openly and psycho-communicatively screened as works of art. Indeed, the cluster is set up in, and as, the viewing of a work of art, in a symbiosis of appreciation, acceptance, and emotional liberation that contributes to an emotional solidarity, one that is a violent antidote to the established prejudices of late capitalism. But, at the same time, the cluster, as positioned among a dialogue of births and the musical exchange of harmony and dischord, enables the purest form of empathy as a vehicle of self-acceptance. This sequence is therefore a dialogue and a performance of self-acceptance; for an additional means of harnessing pure empathy to challenge damaging norms and assumptions is understanding that empathizing with others is also means of harnessing, and ultimately propagating, self-love.

Radical Empathy as Self-Love

In conclusion, self-sacrifice in *Sense8* has a number of iterations that revolve around mutual support and reciprocated states of feeling. The cluster's facilitation of instant psychic visitation means that sacrifices can be made as and when they are needed; they transcend time and space to bring together transnational versions of selfhood. This suggests that pure and empathetic solidarity is a challenge to corporatism and patriarchy, to established power structures that marginalize minorities to reinforce their own positions of power. It also implies that the cluster actualizes a similar hostility to the representation of post-truth narratives that are so often the work of hegemonic patriarchal agendas. Moreover, the representation of Angelica's self-sacrifice reconfigures theoretical positions on selfhood to allow for an altered understanding of collective identity and the reevaluation of what the representation of survival drives can mean. This appraisal of self-sacrifice through Lacan's mirror stage outlines damaging notions of fixed and alienating identities that must give way to the flow of desire as understood by a Deleuzo-Guattarian framework. It is a vital shift that negates the alienation of fixed identity by positioning the identification of the collective in a state of flux that knows pure empathy and weaponizes it against the self-empowering regimes of the dominant class. Thus, the representation of the collective birth at the Reykjavik Opera House reinforces the previously detailed observations that pure empathy can be mobilized as a challenge to established prejudices. Self-sacrifice operates as part of this mechanism but is best understood as the coming together of collective senses of selfhood, while the collective birth of the cluster outlines the coming into being of selfhood as the projection of self-acceptance. Rapturously, the alignment of the cluster's shared dialogue of imagined births interweaves the various arrangements and collisions of the orchestra, promoting selfhood in a structure of reciprocated appreciation. Consequently, this delivers further nuance to the proposition that empathy, as the cluster knows it in its purest form, is not only a challenge to established sociopolitical disorders but also a way of recognizing self-love. Perhaps, therefore, the most effective panacea to the pressures and demands of late capitalism is not a text that elicits an emotional response, but one like *Sense8* that represents empathy in its purest, most radical form.

Works Cited

Dekhakhena, A. (2017), "The Hoax of Democratization in Iraq Since US Invasion: The Legacy of Neoliberalism," *SSRN*. Available online: https://ssrn.com/abstract=3165068.

Deleuze, G., and F. Guattari (1983), *Anti-Oedipus: Capitalism and Schizophrenia*, trans. R. Hurley, M. Seem, and H. R. Lane, Minneapolis: Minnesota University Press.

Greven, T. (2016), "The Rise of Right-Wing Populism in Europe and the United States: A Comparative Perspective," Washington, DC: Friedrich-Ebert-Stiftung. Available online: https://www.fesdc.org/fileadmin/user_upload/publications/RightwingPopulism.pdf.

Kristeva, J. (1980), *Desire in Language: A Semiotic Approach to Literature and Art*, Oxford: Blackwell.

Lacan, J. ([1949] 2006), "The Mirror Stage as Formative in the Function of the *I* Function as Revealed in Psychoanalytic Experience," in *Ecrits*, trans. B. Fink, 75–81, New York: Norton and Company.
Smith, D. (2004), "The Inverse Side of the Structure: Žižek on Deleuze on Lacan," *Criticism*, 46 (4): 635–50.
Verhaeghe, P. (2014), *What About Me? The Struggle for Identity in a Market Based Society*. Victoria, Australia: Scribe.
Verhaeghe, P. (2015), "On the New Discontents of Civilisation," *Journal of the Centre for Freudian Analysis and Research*, 26: 70–89.

10

Dancing in the Streets: The Politics of *Sense8*'s Pleasure Activism

So Mayer

In *Dancing in the Streets: A History of Collective Joy* (2006), American social historian Barbara Ehrenreich traces a subversive and submerged thread of ecstatic practices of collective celebration that has sought to counter Eurowestern Christian colonial capitalism's destruction of collective joy. It is a dyad of destruction and resistance that she dates back to the persecution of followers of Dionysus in classical Rome. That *Sense8* constructs its narrative through the coming together of bodies in dance, sex, and violence, as well as shared feeling, stands it in the lineage of the Dionysian. In this essay, I consider the extent to which this embodied ecstatic becomes an effective resistance. Ehrenreich writes that, "it may seem petty to focus on the obliteration of communal ritual and festivity. But in any assessment of the impact of European imperialism, 'techniques of ecstasy' ... must at least be counted among the losses" (2006: 180). Finding medium-specific forms of "communal ritual and festivity" to revive and practice "techniques of ecstasy" towards social change must be considered a hallmark of the Wachowskis' oeuvre, coming to a climax (all puns intended) in *Sense8*'s radical movement between and through dance, combat, and sex choreographies with camera movement and match cuts. "Art is political," as Hernando says. "Never more so than when insisting it is not. ... It is a language of seeing and being seen."

The series' ecstatic (sometimes literally) "dancing in the streets" is often folded into dancing in the sheets, rendering sexual spaces public in the dual sense of political and communitarian. *Sense8* can be read as enlarging the important assertion that "Pride was a protest" with a reminder that dancing (and fucking) in the streets is itself an action of resistance, a form of what adrienne maree brown names "pleasure activism," unbounded assent-based embodied practices of liberation within the asymmetrically disembodying spaces of colonial capital(s) (2019: 13–15). While corporate Pride may seek to contain such dancing as merely symbolic demonstration of embodied liberation that refuses the limitations of the built environment and of policing, *Sense8* invokes the history Ehrenreich traces to enact a commitment to dancing in the streets as a technique of political change from the cellular to global level.

A Way to Chart Possibilities

In *Sense8*, the stakes of choreographed movement are high. Dancing actively *remaps* streets: not only in the temporary autonomous zone of Pride, or the Foucauldian ritual times—all organized around dancing—of Pride, the wedding, the nightclub, the birthday, and New Year's Festivities that turn streets into interconnected heterotopia, but also through what Bishakh Som calls a "trans cartography" in her graphic novel *Apsara Engine* (2020). Som's story "swandive" opens at a conference on intersectional cartography where the presenter, Onima Mukherjee, speaks in bubbles that unfurl across panels showing enfolded urban geometries. She says:

> Maps can circumscribe and set boundaries but can also lay the groundwork for an infinite number of itineraries, of infinite play within and despite boundaries. ... I imagine trans geographies to be a means of using cartography as a generative tool rather than a descriptive device. A way to chart possibilities, ways of being that have yet to manifest themselves. (2020: 128)

As the story unfolds, Onima invites another conference goer, who is also trans and South Asian-American, to realize such an imagined desire map with her; a map whose suggestive outlines, drawn on a hotel wall with red wine, enfold other stories in the collection.

Sense8 could be considered one of Mukherjee's maps, a "generative tool" whose possibilities for radically egalitarian living are activated by choreographies that invite us, as viewers, to extend their potential beyond the limits of the show's imagination. The show makes a physically and cinematically highly skilled response to the question Judith Butler quotes frequently from Gilles Deleuze quoting Baruch Spinoza, "What can a body do?" through forms of dancing that folds up streets and/into/like sheets. In doing so, it holds out a map, a trans geography that suggestively enmeshes cartography and choreography as a strategy for our reading of the show and toward our larger lived experience of liberation.

That map is most fully dreamed and realized in—as its title suggests—the feature-length pivot episode S02:E01 "Happy Fucking New Year." It is framed by two collective celebrations: of the sensate cluster's shared (re)birthday, and of the globally shared, although temporally staggered experience of the New Year. The episode moves from the individual date of "first breath," as Riley describes it, to the globalized marker of the shift from one year to another as prescribed by the Eurowestern Julian calendar. There is no related episode where we see Sun celebrate Seollal, two lunar months after winter solstice, and nor do we see Kala mark the first day of Chaitra; the show presents a consistent Americanization of "global" culture, as Claire Light identifies in her article for *Nerds of Color* (2015).

Kala and Rajan's Italian beach honeymoon, like the dance Rajan commissioned for their engagement party (by *Slumdog Millionaire* [Danny Boyle, 2008] choreographer Longinus Fernandes), both documents and reinforces their class status, and the Americanization of global elite culture. Like *Bride and Prejudice* (Gurinder Chadha, 2004), their European jaunt pastiches and appropriates the trend of Bollywood films featuring international honeymoon travel. Yet the local specificities and zeitgeist-surfing of the music and choreography for the sensate birthday party does show a shift from the first season in which, as Light describes, "American pop is specific, non American pop is generalized and clichéd, as in the Bollywood dance, or entirely absent" (2015). The main dance, by Lito and Dani, in the birthday sequence was choreographed by world salsa champion Charlene Rose, winning a nomination for a World Choreography Award in the Motion Picture Category (Kilday 2017). Rose posted a video of herself rehearsing with Miguel Ángel Silvestre on Instagram, evidence that the cast performed their own dances (Rose 2019). However, the sequence incorporates other dance and musical styles, including Berlin techno, global beach rave, T'ai chi, and Kenyan house/funk/disco by Just a Band. Known as the first Kenyan band to go viral, their "Huff + Puff" follows the salsa track, and is followed in turn by "Hands Up"—played by Riley, DJ'ing through Kala at the beach party—by Dutch dance music "titans" Hardwell & Afrojack, which became a global festival hit in summer 2017: literally charting possibilities through which music moves transnationally (Rishty 2017).

In a series of cuts that constellates *Sense8*'s construction of liberatory movement as pleasure activism, the episode shifts the group bacchanal from dance to sex via what is simultaneously a confession and a fight scene, as Sun tells Kala, who is nervous about having sex with her husband, about winning a Hapkido tournament during her adolescence and having sex with her opponent, a boy called Woo-ji, in the changing rooms afterwards. Jetta's 2014 cover of Ten Years After's 1971 song "I'd Love to Change the World" cues a sensate sex scene: a reinterpretation of a gold-selling slow grind that had been previously used to soundtrack the trailers for three notably macho, dystopian films: *Dawn of the Planet of the Apes* (Matt Reeves, 2014), *Nightcrawler* (Dan Gilroy, 2014), and *Terminator Genisys* (Alan Taylor, 2015). The sex scene moves between the same-location IRL sexual pairings—Nomi and Amanita, Riley and Will, Lito and Hernando, Wolfgang and a Tinder hook-up—and the cluster's collective experience.

In contrast to the graphic signification of sexual acts between the pairings, the collective sexual experience is predominantly expressed through synchronized, ecstatic, and almost ritualized head and hand movements across the group. These expressive choreographic techniques—including nudity—are reminiscent of Pina Bausch's *Rite of Spring*, originally performed in Wuppertal in 1975, and probably the most influential postwar choreography. Bausch's presentation of "sweat-streaked, filthy and audibly panting" dancers (Jennings 2009) define what has become a transnational élite dance practice marked by muscularity and overt sexuality that both marks and redefines gender norms, not least by making visible the effort of dance. Linking sexual choreography to both salsa and Hapkido, the collective sex scene stresses virtuosity and expertise between skillful bodies as a source of pleasure for both the viewer and the sensates.

Shared and repeated choreographic materialities express the sensates' constellation of embodied knowledge and transformative potential, not least as *the* audiovisual strategy that engages the viewer and instructs them on how to read the show. Gestural unity combined with the solicitation of arousal draws our attention. As Rosalind Galt observes in this volume,

> The unity of gesture [in the post-Pride performance watched by Nomi and Amanita in the opening episode] that transforms the dancers' bodies into a single entity will be repeated throughout the series as a formal mechanism through which the sensates' experiences and embodiment are shown as aligned and in emotional sync ... repeated most clearly in the orgy scenes in which the sensates and their various partners share group sexual encounters. (p. 89)

From these kinesthetics, Galt theorizes the show's mobilization of a romantic and erotic polycentrism; what could be called a poly-tics that evokes, as Alexandre Segade notes in *Artforum*, the ideas of Michael Hardt and Antonio Negri in theorizing the multitude (2017).

The evocation only goes so far. In orgasmic release, the sequence reverts from cluster "visiting" to cut between the same-location pairings, suggesting that sexual "techniques of ecstasy" are not enough to break national, class, and gender boundaries toward a radical politic. Jetta sings that she'd *love* to change the world, not that she can: in fact, the song is downbeat about the possibility of transformation, a reminder that freedom and social justice is not at hand, but only potential. This is particularly true so long as Sun remains in prison. The first half of the episode is overtly structured by the contrast between types of incarceration—of which Sun's is the most extreme and unbreakable—and bodily practices of freedom. In Som's terms, it is a liberation map, imagining forms of movement out of incarceration, and from entrapment to embodied freedom. En route to the birthday "sex-nic" that cues the shared dance party, Nomi and Amanita zoom out of the city on a motorbike, intercut with Capheus driving the brand-new matatu he has received from Mr. Kabaka and his daughter. Movement—the essence of the moving image, in terms of moving bodies and movement from frame to frame—is often configured as the only "safe space" in *Sense8*, and S02:E01 intensifies that concept. Riley and Will have to keep moving between borrowed apartments to evade Whispers; and Lito, Hernando, and Dani leave Lito's apartment (and his metaphorical closet) after their sex tape is leaked. When Sun is placed in solitary confinement, she continues her martial arts training within the small cell; in fact, she continues to practice high kicks striking the wall after a guard cautions her that her stay in solitary will be extended. Nomi and Amanita need a sexcape because they have been living in hiding on the roof of The Women's Building in San Francisco.

Yet, The Women's Building is also literally situated as a "trans geography [that can ...] generate possibilities," because of two real-world qualities: its location, which gives Nomi a commanding view of San Francisco from her rooftop eyrie, and its history. Like City Lights, the bookstore where Amanita works, The Women's Building is a rare, still independent and non-commodified remainder of San Francisco's 1960s counterculture (Robb 2011). Nomi's bird's-eye view is balanced by a tour of the building via Amanita, who meets her friend Lola outside, their connection suggesting the site's history of queer women of color activism. As she leaves Lola and speaks to Nomi via Bluetooth devices, we follow Amanita up the stairs past the famous MaestraPeace Mural, painted by a collective of Bay Area women muralists in 1994, that flows from the exterior facades through the lobby and stairwell. The last shot shows the stairwell wall behind Amanita's head: a web of the names, the last of which appears to be Black speculative fiction writer and poet Jewelle Gomez. The flowing form suggests that women of color feminisms operate as, themselves, a kind of sensate cluster. Meera Desai, a member of the MaestraPeace artist collective, told the *Mission Local* on the occasion of its 2012 restoration: "Ever since we created the original painting, we've been a sort of family. We're all involved in each other's lives and families" (Hoke 2012). Desai's words capture the resonance between creative collaborations and sensate abilities and suggest the significance of dance and music as shared creative practices for *attuning* the sensates to each other.

Nomi's presence is a recognition that The Women's Building has supported trans-inclusive organizations such as LGBTQQ center LYRIC. Nomi also welcomes Lito when he comes "visiting" after the video leaks: an important

FIGURE 10.1 *Nomi and Amanita in the still space of queer/ed femininity, remapping the world as San Francisco.*

connection in which the building expansively recognizes queerness. When Lito and Hernando flee the paparazzi who have gathered, they do so for Dani's apartment, where Lito dons one of Dani's floral robes as they drink margaritas, watch *Legally Blonde* (Robert Luketic, 2001), and paint each other's nails on the couch. Queer/ed femininity, whose aesthetics and creative practices (painting, specifically, as Nomi also paints Amanita's toenails in Figure 10.1) links the very different spaces of The Women's Building and Dani's apartment, is a rare enclosed safe space. Unlike most genre shows, *Sense8* prizes queer/ed femininity, and also connects it to and through mobility, motility, speed, power, and flight: its influence is palpable in, for example, Noelle Stevenson's revisioning of *She-Ra and the Princesses of Power* for Netflix (2018–20). When Nomi and Amanita leave The Women's Building (traveling to stay with Amanita's mother Grace, in another queer femme space), they extend the building's unique presence and practice out into the city and globally through their cluster: what could be called a "San Franciscization," rather than a generic "Americanization." As a temporary haven it has given not only them, but also Lito, a way to be in—and change—the world.

Maps Can Circumscribe

Like Som's *Apsara Engine*, Stevenson's *She-Ra* is one of a number of post-*Sense8* queer- and trans-centric genre texts that take up the show's ideas, or the ideational space it has created within contemporary culture, directly or indirectly, which "cluster" with the show as its sensate partners. N. K. Jemisin's novel *The City We Became* (2020) is another; in it, New York becomes sensate through a "cluster" of five diverse humans, one from each borough, who are telepathically connected to each other; to a sixth human who is the whole city; and to the geological and architectural city itself. While the guiding spirit of New York is a young, Black, queer houseless artist and hustler whose name we are never told, the borough of Staten Island, significantly, awakens as/in Aislyn Houlihan, a young white woman of Irish descent who lives on the Island, and the daughter of a racist cop. Jemisin's scintillating novel is specifically a swipe at H. P. Lovecraft's racist anti-urbanism, but it also reads like an East Coast conversation with *Sense8*'s dancing in the streets, with the centrality of the cosmopolitan megacity to the show's political possibilities—and with the constraints of the show's commitment to genre conventions around heroism and violence. While there are car chases and fights, they are instigated by the Lovecraftian forces that are trying to prevent the city becoming sentient, and the final "battle" takes place through visual art practices and the radical tenderness of a diverse ensemble that acts in concert. These alternate forces have their place in *Sense8* as well, as the queer/ed femininity described above that is strongly identified with a transnationalized San Franciscan culture of openness. Yet in climactic scenes in S02:E12, it is not, as the episode title suggests, that "amor vincit omnia," but rather a spectacular gun battle in La Forcella in Naples that enables the Eiffel Tower wedding to take place.

The series thus ends with a dynamic or doubling that underlines a persistent deep tension in *Sense8*: in its generic compulsions, in terms of the vexed relationship between queer/ed femme spaces, movements, and pleasures, and the ways in which genres replicate structural and systemic violence. This can be seen in S02:E01 when Lito arrives outside his apartment building to find a crowd of paparazzi after the leaking of the sex film. Behind the flashing cameras, he also sees graffiti painted on his garage door, reading FAGGOT (not, note, JOTO, as would be expected in Mexican Spanish). As the flashing cameras and shouting intensify, Lito pulls the cluster to him in his dissociation. Each of them sees a different pejorative word scrawled before them, in English. Most problematic are two of the words, whose pejorative impact differs from the others: one is NAZI, which is not paired through a glance-object cut with a reaction from a specific character but presumably refers to Wolfgang as a German citizen, albeit one specifically of East German and Russian parentage. The other is PIG, which is linked to Will via a reaction shot. It is distinctive not only because it refers to Will's job rather than his identity, but also because police officers hold structural power, and PIG is a term that punches up, rather than down.

This literally flashed-up glance-object match cut constellates the work that *Sense8* does to include Will within the cluster. As an identitarian pejorative, it suggests that PIG is a part of Will's personality; the series suggests that policing is, in a sense, a heritable trait, through Will's primary, albeit complicated, relationship with his father Michael. The difficult father–son relationship exemplifies toxic masculinity, and specifically white settler masculinity, and suggests that policing is an aspect or outgrowth of that toxicity. Yet the sentimental redemption of the relationship in S02:E09 "What Family Actually Means" marks a generic attachment to the police as something other than PIGs. As Cáel M. Keegan argues, the Wachowskis have used the femme "closet" since *Bound* (1996) to queer the thriller and action genres, and to subvert those genres' investments in a white supremacist, cis heteropatriarchal status quo. Yet, Will represents an embedding of the "action hero" that contrasts sharply with the negative portrayal of policing in the *Matrix* trilogy. *Sense8* features its own bad Agent Bendix, whose name suggestively rhymes with *Matrix*, the Wachowskis' most famous, and most anti-policing, work. Will is depicted, from the opening episode, as a "good cop," both in his work and within the cluster. The conflation of policing and white masculinity is palpable in Will's construction as a savior-rebel, from his meeting with Jonas onward. Yet it is undeniable that Will's police training assists the cluster repeatedly, and that in doing so, his presence both further heroizes the idea of the "good (rebel) cop," and deflects attention from real and critical issues with policing in the United States, and particularly in his home city of Chicago.

As the Colors of Change Hollywood report "Normalizing Injustice" points out, the "good cop" who rebels is one of the granular ways in which the entertainment industry delivers "copaganda," a term popularized in Black Lives Matter abolitionist discourse in 2020, and coined by Dave Zirin, in his *Nation* article reconsidering *The Wire* amid the Baltimore Uprising (Zirin 2015). The report's detailed analysis of US network and streaming shows featuring criminal justice professionals shows it is most frequently a "good guy" endorser character who undertakes wrongful actions, for what are presented as noble or necessary reasons (Colors of Change Hollywood 2020: 31). Egregiously, Will is given a sexist, racist partner with a markedly Hispanic name, Diego Morales (played by Ness Bautista, whose parents are Puerto Rican and Dominican), who voices anti-Blackness in order to enunciate the need for violent policing, and is a more rigid follower of the status quo. While S01:E01 offers a minor critique that appears to comment on the Chicago Police Department's (Chicago PD's) reputation for use of excessive force against Black people, the show displaces Clete Tamark, the Black youth who features in the first episode as a clue to Angelica's birthing of the sensate cluster, with a more conventional and sentimentalized trope familiar across US thrillers and action films: a young white girl, Sara Patrell, whose disappearance traumatized Will as a child. The Chicago PD escapes largely unscathed from a critique of policing that is (re)directed through Jonas's arrest, which is undertaken by federal agents. This storyline resonates with the real-life "black site" of Chicago PD's Homan Square, as investigated by the *Guardian* in 2015, which found the site was staffed by former Guantanamo Bay operatives (Ackerman 2015). Yet the series shifts the critique from the city's police force, which has faced a continued public backlash since the shooting of Black teen Laquan McDonald in 2014, to federal operatives such as Bendix (St Hill 2020).

This allows the show to contrast Will, the good beat cop who rescues Jonas, with the malign and secretive federal agents. Will's policing skills enable him to assist Riley and Nomi, to find out what happened to Sara Patrell (and thus repair his father's failed investigation, redeeming his heritage), and to withstand the torture to which he is subjected by Whispers. While the reversals in which Will is immobilized, imprisoned, and interrogated suggest a critique of both policing and the white supremacist cis heteronormativity it upholds, that is undermined by the fact that any critique of Will's situation as a Chicago police officer is deflected, while his training is validated. In fact, it is paralleled with the more countercultural skills given to the other characters, such as Nomi's hacking or Wolfgang's safebreaking. The dyad of Will and Wolfgang, the two straight white males who face off as cop and robber, suggests a kinship between their skills and moral codes; while interesting, this remains latent. Typing its straight white masculinity further, as simultaneously non-confessional, as a given, and as invisible, this pairing is not explored in the same granular and affective detail as, for example, Lito's and Nomi's queer kinship. Brian J. Smith's coming out subsequent to his appearance on the series suggests just how powerful and inclusive the show's vision of queer kinship can be (Dommu 2019). Yet, as exemplified by the graffiti on Lito's garage door, the homogenizing aspect of the sensate cluster, in which wildly divergent experiences are paralleled, is at its most problematic when it comes to Will.

A Generative Tool Rather than a Descriptive Device

Any argument about *Sense8*'s movement language, particularly in terms of reading it as a liberatory force, has to reckon with Will's inclusion in the cluster as similar to the invitation extended to police forces by corporatized Pride parades internationally. As Kitty Stryker writes resonantly for *Teen Vogue*, "when it's party time, law enforcement certainly can't demand they be welcomed by the people they arrested for speaking up against police brutality" (Stryker 2018). In a 2013 article framed by the street-based movements of both Occupy and Black Lives Matter, dance theorist and curator André Lepecki sets up an opposition that appositely describes the liberatory potential signaled (and foreclosed) in *Sense8*. In "Choreopolice and Choreopolitics: or, the Task of the Dancer," Lepecki considers the flows between two forms of contemporary choreography: street-based movements and countermovements during protests; and choreography more formally considered and framed as such, as it takes place within dance and gallery spaces, but using vernacular movement languages. He argues that the police deploy their own choreography to confront protestors and activists: a choreography that is also dependent on increasingly confrontational, privatized, and surveilled urban space. His argument could be applied to moving image media to argue that it is not just representation that is the problem, as the Colors of Change Hollywood report analyses, but the generic spatialities and choreographies—both embodied and technological—that shape them.

Lepecki sets out the framework for a contrasting and transformative choreopolitics through a quotation from Hannah Arendt, which is particularly resonant for reading the liberatory work that *Sense8* does achieve, and/in its movement toward the political:

> In a posthumously published fragment, written in August 1950 as a preliminary draft for would have been the first chapter of her unfinished *Introduction into Politics*, Hannah Arendt makes the following observation: "[…] we have arrived in a situation where we do not know—at least not yet—how to move politically." We know that for Arendt the notion of a true (or rescued) politics has always been bound deeply, even ontologically, to the notion of freedom. As she writes in several of her essays, "Der Sinn von Politik ist Freiheit"—a sentence translated into English as: "The meaning of politics is freedom." However, "Sinn" (sense) is not quite "Bedeutung" (meaning). Indeed "sense," in its old English usage carries with it a double meaning that conveys more exactly the dynamics underlying Arendt's thought, since "sense" simultaneously refers to signification *and* direction. Thus, politics in Arendt can be redefined as *a general orientation towards freedom*. (2013: 13–14, emphasis in the original)

Knowing how to move politically, Lepecki suggests via Arendt's fragment, arises through understanding "sense" as both "signification *and* direction," or as both intellection and embodied movement.

Sense8 reaches toward a political movement that is "at least not yet" fully formed through its generative choreographic energies. The motility and flexibility that unite choreography and cartography are united by Lepecki in his choice of a term that summons Sara Ahmed's work on queer phenomenologies (2006), "*a general* orientation." For Ahmed, the term "orientation," used with reference to sexuality, necessitates a phenomenology, a reading of an embodied and object-oriented world in which the abstracted objects (and subject positions) of philosophical texts are re-realized in a lived world. "Bullet time" could be described as and by Ahmed's queer phenomenology as that which re-orients the space-time of the action genre by changing the object relations in one of its conventional set pieces, the shoot-out. Keegan points out that, by appearing to move slowly in relation to the bullets and the viewer, while simultaneously appearing to move faster than perception to Trinity, "Neo himself becomes a flickering 'sign with more than one signifier' who evokes the stretch across genders that is transition" (Keegan 2018: 44, quoting cárdenas 2015). The cluster's interactions across match-cuts in *Sense8* perform a similar queer re-orientation as they fragment and recohere conventional mise-en-scène, and also as they center choreographic movement as a narrative strategy. This resonates with Lepecki's unpacking of Arendt, in which there is a constellation of sense as meaning-through-movement (sensing something out) that insists on politics—as in political action, rather than state actors—as freedom, which is itself an orientation.

As Katharina Lindner explores in *Film Bodies* through an enmeshment with Ahmed's language, embodied movement is—acts as—"*a general orientation towards freedom*" in cinema that is concerned with feminisms and queerness, quoting Ahmed's observation that "empathy involves switching orientations" (2018: 51, quoting Ahmed 2006: 182). Switch is, of course, also a significant term in the Wachowskis' canon, as the character in *The Matrix* who was originally written to be gender-fluid across the Matrix/IRL divide, as Lilly Wachowski told Netflix Film Club (2020). For Ahmed, it is the granularity of phenomenological experience, the often-difficult or bruising encounters between bodies and objects that defines lived experience in contrast to the smooth surfaces of the Matrix, that allows for the reader, viewer, or listener to "switch" through an understanding of the affect of these encounters. When Lito summons the cluster to confront the word FAGGOT on the garage door, he is eliciting an Ahmedian "switch" as each of the cluster experience being in or beside Lito's traumatic encounter with a violent and violated object.

Sense8 deploys medium-specific strategies of (dis)orientation—canted angles, overhead and drone shots, rapid cutting, diegetic speed, impossible match cuts that connect distant spaces, actions begun by one character and completed by another, reflexive musical choices that draw attention to themselves, highly choreographed dance/fight/sex "numbers" that forward the narrative—to produce what Zoë Shacklock describes as producing a "queer kinesthesia" rooted in Eve Kosofsky Sedgwick's phrasing of queer as "a continuing movement" (2019: 511, quoting Sedgwick 1993: xii). That the sensate choreography is the necessary focus of all the other formal strategies makes the series' form key to its dis/orienting political function, as we switch orientation constantly and through multiple intersections of camera and embodied movement with sound and image editing. The show's choreographyic is an orientation towards liberatory gender and sexual politics, and simultaneously an inscription of gender and sexual liberation as a choreography for broader political movements.

This is echoed in another of *Sense8*'s "cluster" texts: *Steven Universe* and *Steven Universe Future* (created by Rebecca Sugar, 2013–20), a GLAAD-award winning animation whose musical numbers not only convey crucial affective information but also center dance as a transformative technology. Its main alien/mineral Gem characters are able to fuse into larger, stronger, and stranger beings by dancing together, a radically queer and trans potential that is eventually extended to its human characters. Steven, who is half-human and half-Gem, accidentally fuses through social dance with his friend Connie, forming a non-Gem fusion called Stevonnie. Fusion is so threatening that the Homeworld Gems, who oppose it, use it to create an artificial fusion weapon called a Cluster, an aggregation of many broken, angry Gem shards who are both physically and psychically connected, like the sensate cluster in *Sense8*. Steven is able to befriend the Cluster, and to convince its separate parts to bond with each other—in fact, to use their bonded state to heal into a new being. Through both fusion and his Cluster encounter, Steven is also able to learn about and narrate to others, including the Homeworld Gems who fear him, his own hybridity and (as the transformation of his mother, Rose Quartz) his trans embodiment.

In *Pleasure Activism*, brown writes that "almost everything about how we orient toward our bodies is shaped by fearful imaginations. Imaginations that fear Blackness, brownness, fatness, queerness, disability, difference" (2019:10). *Sense8*'s choreopolitics—the ways in which the centering of its choreography is a general orientation toward freedom—enacts a reorientation toward bodies as a precursor and performance of pleasure activism: that is, it is not just that the show's casting or "representation" is diverse, but that the cluster of different embodiments moves, and moves together, ecstatically within itself; although, just as it does not manage to evade being copaganda, *Sense8* does not challenge the limits of televisual objectification by including fat and/or visibly disabled bodies among its diverse cast.

Within its generic and broadcast frameworks, then, *Sense8* offers a movement *toward* what Lepecki calls a "choreopolitics of freedom," which he situates in resistance to Gilles Deleuze's "control-based system" of intensive urban, digital, and border surveillance (2013: 15, quoting Deleuze 1995: 174). Through Nomi, in particular, *Sense8* engages in order to defeat and deface all three forms of surveillance and the ways in which they are mutually reinforcing. As a hacktivist, Nomi—collaborating with her non-sensate, but jacked-in, contact Bug—enables the sensate cluster to perform the adrenaline-charged near-equivalent of their borderless sensate operations within the real of current global surveillance supremacy, as S02's drama centers on characters' need to cross national borders, facilitated by Nomi's hacks. As a trans woman, Nomi embodies a defiant refusal of borders in a way that is a model and a strategy for what the choreographic can accomplish within both the show's formal aesthetics, and what it can hope to accomplish in the geopolitical world that it invokes and seeks to contest.

Lepecki notes that the choreopolitics of freedom is necessary precisely because "[c]horeographically as well as conceptually, the police can thus be defined as that which, through its physical presence and skills, determines the space of circulation for protesters, and ensures that 'everyone is in a permissible place'" (2013: 16, quoting Deleuze 1995: 183). The sensate cluster's dis-placement and re-placement abilities defy the concept of a "permissible place," in terms of all intersecting social hierarchies and axes of exclusion, command, and control. Will and Riley's relationship exemplifies this: when Will is displaced from his "permissible place" of policing, Riley eventually uses her skills as an orchestrator of choreopolitics to effect a dramatic escape. The temporary autonomous zone of the dance club is one of the Wachowskis' favored (and problematically racialized) scenarios for pleasure activism, as seen in Zion in *The Matrix Reloaded* (2003). As in the cluster's birthday party, in the club, "the choreopolitical [is] the formation of collective plans [in Stefan Harney and Fred Moten's sense] emerging at the edges between open creativity, daring initiative, and a persistent—even stubborn—iteration of the desire to live away from policed conformity" (Lepecki 2013: 22).

Infinite Play Within and Despite Boundaries

Against conformity and surveillance, *Sense8* mobilizes the Wachowskis' formidable arsenal of cinematographic and editing language *at the intersection with* the choreographic, so that the show is constantly moving. The relation between cinematography, editing and choreographed performance is best described in Jessica Cariaga's "8 Awesome Things We Learned About the Making of *Sense8*," where she interviews the actors about the specificities of shooting.

> Silvestre explained that the connections [the match-cuts in "visiting" scenes] weren't created through post production editing, but that the actors' movements in each scene were carefully choreographed, using a piece of wall or a shadow to get actors in and out of their shots. "Every time we do it, it's been different," [Brian J.] Smith added. "We've done actual physical swaps, where someone will slide in on a shot. We've done it so many different ways. It's kind of endless." (Cariaga 2015)

Smith's description perhaps deliberately evokes pornography's utopian promise of infinite abundance, wherein the extraordinary capacities of physical bodies are fantastically enhanced by cinematography and editing toward a plurality of pleasures—the promise that the sexual choreography in *Sense8* itself invokes, within the still-censorious limits of streaming media.

This movement creates a dazzling effect, wherein rapid cuts between the ensemble performing complex choreographies in multiple locations make it difficult to read frame by frame, pushing the viewer toward an ecstatic absorption. This can flatten important critiques and obscure where the show's policing—its copaganda and its Americanization—detract from its choreopolitics. Yet its dazzle is compelling and liberating, causing Segade to recognize it as "quantum," in Karen Barad's queer feminist sense relating to the oscillatory properties of matter (2015). This thinking emerges from a material rather than analogical mode that Barad describes as "a political investment in creating new political imaginaries and new understandings of imagining in its materiality" (2015: 388). What is "quantum" in *Sense8* is thus not its high-concept abstractions about entanglement, but how they are physicalized on-screen toward the viewer's body and the body politic.

In this, *Sense8* resonates with Eliza Steinbock's theory of the "ensemble of shimmers," which they summon to read trans cinema, gathering three interconnected modes:

> The *aesthetic* with its gradations and intensities that register the nuance of difference, the swath of *gender* that binds and undoes subjects depending on the angle of the gaze or the angle of the room's atmosphere, and finally the *affects* that pulse within passionate structures and form circuitous loops through subjective perception. (2019: 145)

Reading with and across these three modes of shimmering "can conceptually accomplish a turn to the more-than-visuality, form an analytic lens, and become a critical practice for affirming transitional and non-binary modes" (Steinbock 2019: 145, emphases in the original).

The *Sense8* ensemble shimmers for all the reasons Steinbock describes: its aesthetic, predicated on and around the collaboration of the splice and the choreographic; the "swath" of gender, in which sensate bodies are wrapped in and draped across gendered possibilities, an experience that produces and is produced by fluid diegetic movements; and its mobilization of affects as "circuitous loops through subjective perception" that, in fact, drive the plot. All of these are exemplified by the "shimmering" relation between the splice and the choreography carried by the bodies of the performers in the sensate "shimmer" that moves between "visiting" and inhabiting. Likewise, the "shimmer" of moving across locations (which also metonymize national cinematic genres) is present in and thematized by the shifts between and within dance, fight, and sexual choreography.

That this joyous dance between bodies is affirming is exemplified in the combat in a deserted restaurant between Wolfgang and the sensate cluster who are attempting to take over Berlin, in S02:E08, whose title—"All I Want Now Is One More Bullet" —makes reference to the famed "bullet time" that this sequence repurposes. Unlike the main/protagonized cluster, who, per Steinbock, "register the nuance of difference ... [through] passionate structures" of social dance that highlight both idiosyncrasy and cultural specificity, the antagonist(ic) cluster are rendered (literally/digitally) as not only homogenous but also two-dimensional object-subjects who "stack." Their synchronized movement, similar to Agent Smith's, and totally flat affect give them a military uniformity. They are emplaced as the show's choreopolice allied to Whispers (obscuring the role of actual police departments), because their shimmering potential has been recruited to fascistic dominance. They fight, and use fucking to fight, but they do not dance.

The uncanny synchronicity of the mostly nameless characters (only Lila Facchini, who invites Wolfgang to the restaurant, her ally Maitake, and Josh are named) draws attention to the presence of the performers who synchronize with the main cast in each fight sequence: their stunt doubles. Josh is played by and named for Joshua Grothe, the show's overall fight choreographer, designer, and coordinator on all twenty-three episodes, who began his work with the Wachowskis on *Cloud Atlas* (2012) as a stunt performer. Grothe brought Maik Müller on board as a double for both Smith and Max Riemelt (Clave 2015); Müller's additional role as fight trainer and assistant choreographer demonstrates the centrality of stunt performers to the Wachowskis' work.

Stunting is an under-theorized aspect of screen performance and choreography; beyond Amanda Micheli's documentary *Double Dare* (2004), information is scarce on its lived experience and body politics, and background information on *Sense8* derives from a video interview by the *Trophy* magazine with *Sense8* stunt performer Jade Dregorius (listed as Jade-Eleena on IMDb), hired by Müller (Clave 2015). Via this interview and her Instagram, Dregorius makes available the work of stunting in a way that mirrors the insights extended to the viewer diegetically via the behind-the-scenes scenes of Lito at work on action movies. Dregorius doubles for Sun Bak, the most proficient martial artist in the cluster. It is a demanding role with scenes that include a number of fighting styles as Sun engages in her own martial arts practice with a teacher and fights in underground kickboxing bouts; she also undertakes street and prison fights on her own behalf, is thrown into fights while visiting other members of her cluster, and eventually fights with the detective trying to solve the murder case, Mun, which invert the anerotic qualities of the cluster face-off by being openly flirtatious.

In the interview, Dregorius—who is Berlin-based—emphasizes the mobility of her work on *Sense8*, highlighting the cultural specificities she encountered in Iceland, Nairobi, and Seoul. Similarly, she outlines the specificities of her fight training in kung fu—which she started at 9—followed by Taekwondo, Thai boxing and training at a Shaolin Temple, then a degree in sports ethics along with training in Muay Thai, MMA and boxing at Shimoza—the gym where she is being interviewed. This accords with the mix of fighting styles used by Sun in the ring and on the streets, which contrasts with the nonspecific style that is referred to as "Hollywood-fu."

The specificity of Sun's skills located diegetically in Hapkido training and profilmically in Dregorius's background in multiple disciplines, contrasts with what Paul Bowman wittily identifies "with a respectful bow to queer theory—[as] the 'pugilonormativity' of most [Hollywood] fight choreography" (2015). It is exactly this pugilonormativity—of both choreography and production design—that *Sense8* pastiches in Lito's moves/movies; a macho pastiche whose cutting edge depends on a dual behind-the-scenes play with Lito's profilmic body: an awareness that he is both an actor, and that he is gay. And yet it reverses homophobic associations with both of those embodiments by demonstrating how his proficiency in fight *choreography* can assist other members of the sensate cluster to defer or delay non-choreographed fights. The layering produced by our awareness of the fights as choreography, which has specific relations to lived bodies and their experiences, makes *Sense8*'s choreopolitics operational. In his study of Hong Kong action cinema, Christophe Gans notes that

> The necessary condition for a choreographer is that combats are filled with signification, and that the confrontation does not stop the action but reinforces its emotional aspect. The American cinema problematizes these points. Often, action scenes stop the storyline, while in Hong Kong cinema it is part of the storytelling (Gans 2001: 114, quoted and translated in Morrisette 2002).

Gans suggests that, in pugilonormative Hollywood cinema, fights operate like the close-up of the female star as described by Laura Mulvey: stopping the action, creating an anxiety of containment.

As Keegan notes, all of the Wachowskis' work is noted for its resistance to pugilonormativity; at least since "bullet time," the sisters' audiovisual work is known for its innovation of the relations between camera movement, performer choreography, and digital effects to produce fight choreography that signifies. Writing about the techniques used for filming the sexual choreography, Keegan notes that *Sense8* shares with *Bound* an "electric, riveting feeling … it doesn't cut away. It takes its time and makes you *stay with it*. It's beautiful and organic, and demands something of you. It refuses objectification. You have to be a bodily witness to what's happening" (Keegan 2018: 151). What is significant about this intimate choreography between performers' bodies, camera, and editing is that it solicits the viewer because it signifies; it has meaning to convey.

Ways of Being That Have yet to Manifest Themselves

Choreography matters in *Sense8*. It is irreducibly material and physical; and, relatedly and significantly, an expressive cinesthetics that is both metonymic for the transformative and itself a "choreopolitics," potentially an effective methodology for social justice. Dance, combat, and sex, and the points where they interconnect, are world-making, world-changing, and (in feminist philosopher María Lugones's phrase (1987: 13–20)), "'world'-traveling"(which Lugones uses to mean two or more people traveling between each other's worldviews)—because they are predicated on and performed by material bodies, and it is the materiality of those bodies that drives the narrative. These choreographies resonate with somatics, one of brown's key methodologies for pleasure activism. She defines generative somatics as the following:

> A path, a methodology, a change theory, by which we can embody transformation, individually and collectively. ... It helps us to develop depth and the capacity to feel ourselves, each other and life around us. Somatics is a practice-able theory of change that can move us toward individual, community and collective liberation. (2019: 17)

Sense8's central high concept—the sensate cluster—is a persuasive, attractive vision of generative somatics.

The ecstasies of sensate dance and sex pleasurably and convincingly call attention to how the show's superhuman abilities are produced as spectacle through human bodies. Social dance and sexual pleasure complicate, but they cannot entirely offset, the more virtuosic martial arts choreographies that are expressive of the show's generic codes of superhuman abilities and violent heroism, which are also delivered by elided stunt performers. The dominant generic codes of science fiction—the superhuman ability, the action hero—undermine *Sense8*'s attempt to both narrate and analogize radical collectivity. One of brown's key, frequent assertions is that "all organizing is science fiction" (2019: 10), a phrase deeply suggestive of the cluster, an organizing-as-protagonist, realizing its political potential through its generative, connective somatics. It may seem petty, in Ehrenreich's words, to try and untangle the show's choreopolicing from its choreopolitics, but it is in its sensate "techniques of ecstasy" that its possibility lies.

Works Cited

Ackerman, S. (2015), "The Disappeared: Chicago Police Detain Americans at Abuse-Laden 'Black Site,'" *The Guardian*, February 24. Available online: https://www.theguardian.com/us-news/2015/feb/24/chicago-police-detain-americans-black-site.

Ahmed, S. (2006), *Queer Phenomenology: Orientations, Objects, Others*, Durham, NC: Duke University Press.

Barad, K. (2015), "Transmaterialities: Trans*/Matter/Realities and Queer Political Imaginings," *GLQ*, 21: 2–3.

Bowman, P. (2015), "Film Fight Choreography: From Realism to Realities," *Martial Arts Studies*, February 25. Available online: http://martialartsstudies.blogspot.com/2015/02/film-fight-choreography-from-realisms.html.

brown, a. m. (2019), *Pleasure Activism: The Politics of Feeling Good*, Chico, CA; Edinburgh: AK Press.

cárdenas, m. (2015), "Shifting Futures: Digital Trans of Color Praxis," *Ada: A Journal of Gender, New Media, and Technology*, 6. Available online: https://scalar.usc.edu/works/shifting-futures-micha-cardenas/index.

Cariaga, J. (2015), "8 Awesome Things We Learned About the Making of *Sense8*," *Indiewire*, August 13. Available online: https://www.indiewire.com/2015/08/8-awesome-things-we-learned-about-the-making-of-sense8-59349/.

Clave, A. (2015), "Behind the Scenes at *Sense8*: Interview with Stunt Woman Jade Dregorius," *The Trophy*, June 5. Available online: https://youtu.be/HD5HFWwCBNo.

Color of Change Hollywood (2020), "Normalizing Injustice: The Dangerous Misrepresentations that Define Television's Scripted Crime Genre," January 2020. Available online: https://hollywood.colorofchange.org/wp-content/uploads/2020/02/Normalizing-Injustice_Complete-Report-2.pdf.

Deleuze, G. (1995), *Negotiations, 1972–1990*, trans. M. Joughin, New York: Columbia University Press.

Dommu, R. (2019), "*Sense8* Star Brian J. Smith Comes Out as Gay," *Out*, November 7. Available online: https://www.out.com/celebs/2019/11/07/sense8-star-brian-j-smith-comes-out-gay.

Ehrenreich, B. (2006), *Dancing in the Streets: A History of Collective Joy*, New York: Henry Holt.

Galt, R. (2021), "What's Queer About a Cluster?: *Sense8*'s Polycentric Imaginary," in D. Shaw and R. Stone (eds.), *Sense8: Transcending Television*, 89–104, London, New York: Bloomsbury.

Gans, C. (2001), *Hong Kong, de la presqu'île à la planète, L'Asie à Hollywood*, Locarno: Cahiers du Cinéma.

Hoke, M. (2012), "Painters Scale Women's Building to Restore MaestraPeace Mural," *Mission Local*, September 13. Available online: https://missionlocal.org/2012/09/painters-scale-womens-building-to-restore-the-maestrapeace-mural/.

Jennings, L. (2009), "Obituary: Pina Bausch," *The Guardian*, July 1. Available online: https://www.theguardian.com/stage/2009/jul/01/pina-bausch-obituary-dance.

Keegan, C. M. (2018), *Lana and Lilly Wachowski*, Urbana: University of Illinois Press.
Kilday, G. (2017), "World Choreography Awards Nominees Revealed", *Hollywood Reporter*, September 20. Available online: https://www.hollywoodreporter.com/news/world-choreography-awards-nominees-revealed-1041383.
Kosofsky Sedgwick, E. (1993), *Tendencies*, Durham, NC: Duke University Press.
Lepecki, A. (2013), "Choreopolice and Choreopolitics: or, the Task of the Dancer," *TDR: The Drama Review*, 57 (4): 13–27.
Light, C. (2015), "*Sense8* and the Failure of the Global Imagination," *Nerds of Color*, June 10. Available online: https://thenerdsofcolor.org/2015/06/10/sense8-and-the-failure-of-global-imagination/comment-page-1/.
Lindner, K. (2018), *Film Bodies: Queer Feminist Encounters with Gender and Sexuality in Cinema*, London: I.B Tauris.
Lugones, M. (1987), "Playfulness, 'World'-Travelling, and Loving Perception," *Hypatia*, 2 (2): 3–20.
Morrisette, M. (2002), "Choreography: The Unknown and Ignored," *Offscreen*, 6 (8). Available online: https://offscreen.com/view/choreography.
Rishty, D. (2017), "Hardwell and Afrojack Put 'Hands Up' for Festival Banger," *Billboard*, June 10. Available online: https://www.billboard.com/articles/news/dance/7990083/hardwell-afrojack-hands-up.
Robb, S. (2011), *Mothering the Movement: The Story of the San Francisco Women's Building*, Denver, CO: Outskirts Press.
Rose, C. (2019), "When I Was Training the Talented @miguelangelsilvestre for @sense8 … Sorry for the Low Quality Video!," @charlenerose3, September 18. Available online: https://www.instagram.com/p/B2idW99FdQC/?igshid=1rchk9y7ava4x.
Segade, A. (2017), "We Belong," *Artforum*, August 24. Available online: https://www.artforum.com/slant/alexandro-segade-on-sense8-70597.
Shacklock, Z. (2019), "Queer Kinaesthesia on Television," *Screen*, 60 (4): 509–26.
Som, B. (2020), *Apsara Engine*, New York: Feminist Press.
St Hill, T. (2020), "I Saw My Friends Beaten by Police. This Is What Happens When Cities Prioritize Property Over Black Lives," *The Intercept*, June 14. Available online: https://theintercept.com/2020/06/14/chicago-police-black-lives-matter-protesters/.
Steinbock, E. (2019), *Shimmering Images: Trans Cinema, Embodiment, and the Aesthetics of Change*, Durham, NC: Duke University Press.
Stryker, K. (2018), "Why Police Aren't Welcome at Pride," *Teen Vogue*, June 22. Available online: https://www.teenvogue.com/story/why-police-arent-welcome-at-pride.
Wachowski, L. (2020), "Why the Matrix Is a Trans Story According to Lilly Wachowski," *Netflix Film Club*, August 4. Available online: https://youtu.be/adXm2sDzGkQ.
Zirin, D. (2015), "'The Game Done Changed': Reconsidering *The Wire* Amidst the Baltimore Uprising," *The Nation*, May 4. Available online: https://www.thenation.com/article/archive/game-done-changed-reconsidering-wire-amidst-baltimore-uprising/.

11

#WeAreTheGlobalCluster: Affectivity, Resistance, and *Sense8* Fandom

Rox Samer and Laura Horak

On February 26, 2020, @Global_Cluster, a *Sense8* fan account, tweeted: "I'm trying to picture a #CoronavirusOutbreak in a world populated by sensates … how do you think it would have gone?" (@Global_Cluster 2020). The tweet articulated new stakes for the utopian longing of *Sense8* fans (the implication of the tweet being it would not have spread as it has). This chapter contends that the desire for global connectivity undergirding the series' narrative and motivating the enthusiasm of its fans is not naive. Rather, the utopianism driving fan activities, including the postcancelation online organizing of "sensies" (as *Sense8* fans refer to themselves) into a "global cluster" is a politicized utopianism, a deliberate articulation of an alternative to the more ambivalent and nefarious forms of global connectivity in our relentlessly dystopian present. We therefore analyze how the affective connections between sensates in the series, as well as those between the series and its fans, have developed and expanded. While the series challenged the digital utopianism of S01 by narrativizing the material inequalities between the core sensate cluster and expanding the sensate world to include compromised sensates, sensate fascists, and apathetic sensates in S02, we study how sensies nonetheless chose to take up the affective language of the series to describe their experiences and longings as fans. In mapping their locations and forming clusters on various scales, they imagined themselves as part of not only a global cluster of *Sense8* fans but also global citizens of sorts. Consequently, we then consider how Netflix took up this same language in its promotion of the series in line with its own global streaming ambitions, before delving into the collision between the corporation and the fandom upon the announcement of the series' cancelation. As we shall see, the global cluster did not mean the same thing to each of these parties, for while the circulation of sensate affect provided the global cluster with hope for a better future, it meant little to Netflix if it did not result in adequate numbers of new subscribers. In issuing the Change.org petition signed by over 500,000 fans that contributed to the making of S02:E12 "Amor Vincit Omnia," sensies registered their affectivity on Netflix's terms, showing the corporation what its algorithms could not predict: that the series had a following that could mobilize and resist, a fan base that would refuse to passively accept whatever the streaming giant Netflix decided.

In a millennial "feels culture," where processes of shared emotional authorship bind publics and counterpublics through social and other online media (Stein 2015: 156), the study of the production and circulation of affect and the attendant fan labor of affectivity means no less than the study of the permeable boundaries of globalized social reality. Thus, Covid-19 shows what we often forget, namely how intimately bound the seemingly far-flung human species is. Indeed, while sickness and mortality as well as fear, hate, and apathy circulate alongside the virus, illustrating the dystopian aspects of this connectivity, we contend that a world populated by the science-fictional sensates and sensies also prompt us to think about the utopian possibilities of the commitments and values of our everyday online connections.

Affect, Affectivity, and *Sense8*

From its start *Sense8* was a series that made its investments in affect apparent. The narrative premise links its eight protagonists such that each has the potential to feel what the others feel, both physically and emotionally. We have argued elsewhere that *Sense8* models and invites an embodied, haptic, intersubjective form of spectatorship (Bailey et al. 2017: 83–5). In the S02:E01 "Happy Fucking New Year" sensate orgy, cut to Jetta's cover of Ten Years After's 1971 hit "I'd Love to Change the World," the viewer does not identify with a given figure but forms a bodily relationship to the many interlaced bodies on-screen. In extravagant scenes such as this orgy and also with the series' entire premise, *Sense8* renders existing technologies science-fictional and in turn increasingly sensual and spectacular. The cluster's form of connection and our invitation to participate in it recalls video conferencing applications, which in recent years have made long-distance communication, including long-distance sex and romance, more perceptual and therefore more visceral than ever before (Bailey et al. 2017: 84).

The series' science-fictional, sensual connections address viewers in a highly affective manner through cinematography, editing, and sound design traditions borrowed from long-standing fan traditions. Where fans often "ship" two or more characters, imagining them in a romantic or sexual relationship via fan fiction or a fanvid, in Sense8 such a remix is the mix—shipping and slash is canon. In the sex scenes shared between the sensates and other scenes where they share a sensual experience, highly charged popular musical tracks guide the edited movement between locations and characters, cultivating our feeling of connection between them, be that romantic, sexual, friendly, or some combination therein. We see this in the iconic S01:E04 "What's Going On?" scene where the sensates sing together as Wolfgang performs karaoke to the 4 Non Blondes' "What's Up?" as his romantic relationship with Kala develops. A fanvid might use the looser editing structure that allows musically guided montage to crosscut between two such characters, isolated in single-person shots (or "singles") to suggest a budding romantic relationship. The sensates' ability to "visit" transforms this editing structure to over-the-shoulder two-shots where, no longer isolated in either singles or locations, Wolfgang and Kala are pictured together in Wolfgang's Berlin karaoke bar and on Kala's Mumbai roof (as well as inside her apartment the next morning, as the two reprise through shared memory the intimacy and singing from the night before). Likewise, S02:E01 begins with Kala swimming in the ocean on her honeymoon in Positano to an Aviici cover of Nina Simone's "Feeling Good," where she is joined by the other members of the cluster. The scene pictures the cluster diving into the water together before cutting between this swim "visit" and what the seven others are up to in their various locations, thereby reversing the ship fanvid structure. While fans have often turned to fandom to rewrite cultural texts and find community, connection, and acceptance through a shared passion, Sense8 thematizes and narrativizes such an intimate, if geographically disparate, connection and builds upon the aesthetic traditions of media fandom when doing so.

However, affect is more than the work of a text itself. Affectivity describes a form of spectatorial labor through which, following Kara Keeling, film and television viewers contribute to but also negotiate hegemonic or official common senses. In *The Witch's Flight*, Keeling writes: "Technological cinematic machines function to make common their spectators' sense(s) 'producing value and reproducing social relations along the way'" (Keeling 2007: 96). The affectivity or labor of viewers is biopolitical, as it contributes to the ordering of life itself. Importantly for Keeling, however, official common sense is not unilateral but multivalent. Affectivity is thus capable of undermining the logics supporting categories and institutions that enable the reproduction of capitalism, such as race, family, religion, heterosexuality, and the law (Keeling 2007: 98). Keeling acknowledges that "it might be tempting to condemn mass cultural productions, seeing them only as forces colonizing the sensorium from above" (Keeling 2007: 24). Doing as much, however, denies the affectivity or labor of the sensorium from below, that is, on the part of the spectator, including queer spectators, trans spectators, and spectators of color. In a chapter on Pam Grier's Blaxploitation films of the 1970s, Keeling argues that despite the attempts of films like *Foxy Brown* (1974) and *Coffy* (1973) to conform the formal excesses they unleash to normative understandings of gender and sexuality, affectivity inevitably shakes loose racialized queer forms of surplus value that exceed strategies of containment. For this reason, Keeling sees these films as participating in two projects, one that would seek to contain the Black butch and femme and another that corresponds to a different organization of social reality. Such queer figures coexist in an antagonistic relationship with the reality upheld by official common sense.

We make a similar argument for *Sense8*, sensing in it too "kernels of perception that might be capable of supporting alternate forms of sociality" (Keeling 2007: 5). Thus, while critiques of the series that point to its use of racialized stereotypes, naive multiculturalism, and various hetero- and homonormativities ring true, just as critiques of Blaxploitation's use of racialized stereotypes of violence and hypersexualization did as well, we argue these analyses do not account for affectivity's potential for developing multiple projects simultaneously in the sensorium of spectators. To the hundreds of thousands of fans who authored, circulated, and signed the Change.org petition, many of whom are queer, trans, and/or of color, the cancelation of the series was accompanied by feelings of loss, not solely for the series as a text itself but for global queer kinship found and felt through its fandom. Put in Keeling's terms, sensies' affectivity pried from the series' normative representations a surplus value, which briefly made an alternate organization of social reality perceptible. The first academic critiques of *Sense8* were published in the nearly two-year gap between S01 and S02 (e.g., Bailey et al. 2017; Lothian 2016). What appeared to many as naïve white digital utopianism in which it is imagined that technology—or in this case science fictional metaphors for technology—can easily enable the transcendence of gender, racial, linguistic, and socioeconomic difference in S01 transformed in S02 to a more nuanced negotiation of the challenges of connectivity and its many—including dystopian—usages. While a number of fans were emotionally invested in the series by the end of S01, the fact that a global petition for the series' renewal after S02 circulated so widely invites a consideration of what geographically and otherwise diverse fans found there.

As our own attention to series' group sex scenes as well as otherwise sensual scenes of "visiting" and "sharing" have pointed to, one utopian pursuit the series undertakes is the "dream[ing] and enact[ing] new and better pleasures" (Muñoz 2009: 1). Alexis Lothian was quick to address the fact that the series' first orgy leaves out Black and Asian characters, "highlighting the racial limitations of dominant queer representation" (Lothian 2016: 95), but the Wachowskis and J. Michael Straczynski took such critiques into consideration for the second and third orgies, which include all eight of the original sensates. Furthermore, in S02, Sun and Capheus each received romantic and sexual storylines. *Sense8*'s fannish montages could be considered examples of a queer aesthetic, allowing the potentiality of a queer future to be sensed by spectators invited to revel in what José Esteban Muñoz calls ecstatic time, stepping out of straight time for a few languid minutes to feel ecstasy (Muñoz 2009: 32). For both Muñoz and the sensates, however, such moments are not ends in themselves. Queer utopia is not solely about new and better pleasures. Instead, pleasure in connection is a tool for undermining the reproductive logics of capitalism. This is seen as early as S01:E04, which ends with Nomi and Amanita's reprise of 4 Non Blondes' "What's Up?" as they escape from the hospital where Nomi's mother had colluded with the medical institution to lobotomize her trans daughter. Nomi begins speaking the lyrics and tells Amanita she's "had this song stuck in [her] head all day," and the scene cuts to Nomi and Riley singing it together from the latter's contemplative hill in London, whereby the song takes on a more melancholic connotation than before as the stakes of the previously perceived queer utopia become knowable in the transphobic present. Subsequently, with S02's expansion of such montages, utopian moments of ecstatic connection are frequently disrupted, as violence breaks out between the cluster and those they are resisting.

Sense8 explores the lived experiences of its sensates and the oppressions they face in the world as a result of who they are independently of being sensates, but it also folds these experiences into the science-fictional premise of human-sensate oppression. This becomes the focus of S02, which unfurls the world of sensates from a single cluster and a single evil sensate villain to a vast network of clusters who cannot agree on how to best live a sensate life. Sensate nationalism or "sensorium pride" emerges as a motivation among those sensates least interested in social justice. Sensates like Lila Facchini are perfectly willing to collaborate with Biological Preservation Organization (BPO) as long as they are able to carve out a city for their own cluster, eradicating the humans living there, who, knowingly or not, have caused them to live in hiding for millennia. S02 thus asks whether sensate allegiance ought to be to other sensates alone or to freedom for sensates and non-sensates alike. In determining they would be stronger in their resistance through connections with other sensates, the original cluster organizes a meeting through Riley's rave remix of "What's Up?" and duly encounter a range of models of resistance as well as various forms of sensate ambivalence. One new sensate warns Riley that "trying to change the world leads to suffering; all we can change is ourselves," while Puck explains his enthusiasm for networked orgies but wants no part in political conflicts between clusters. While S01 idealized sensate connections, seemingly oblivious to any need for negotiation of difference that might come from meeting another in one's mind, S02 takes some of these criticisms into account. The sensate mode of connection that was first idealized for its difference from the oppressive societal conditions is revealed to not be better in any essentialist way. If we think of sensate connection as an intensified science-fictional version of global digital connectivity, S02 teaches viewers that digital technologies offer forms of organizing that can be used for a variety of causes, including a range of radical politics from fascist to anti-fascist. Digital technologies offer tools capable of supporting multiple organizations of social reality, and the second season of *Sense8* encourages viewers, through the metaphors of its genre and appeals to affectivity, to disentangle these possibilities.

I Am Also a We

Since S01:E01 "Limbic Resonance," *Sense8* fans have celebrated the show's vision of diverse marginalized people (especially queer and trans people) finding new forms of connectivity, its narratives of bravery and authenticity in the face of adversity, and the value it sets on heart. Blog posts, articles, and fan-authored statements about *Sense8* fans highlight how queer and trans viewers flocked to the show, taking up one of the show's taglines—"I am also a we"—as a crystallization of what the show meant to them. Nomi speaks this phrase while recording a vlog in S01:E02 "I Am Also a We" before riding with Amanita in the Dykes on Bikes contingent of the San Francisco Pride parade. As a montage of her cluster plays, Nomi states:

> For a long time, I was afraid to be who I am because I was taught by my parents that there's something wrong with someone like me. Something offensive, something you would avoid, maybe even pity. Something that you could never love. My mom, she's a fan of St. Thomas Aquinas. She calls pride a sin. ... I was afraid of this parade because I wanted so badly to be a part of it. So today, I'm marching for that part of me that was once too afraid to march. And for all the people who can't march, the people living lives like I did. ... Today I march to remember that I'm not just a me, I'm also a we. And we march with pride. So go fuck yourself Aquinas.

The montage of Nomi's primary cluster of sensates then expands to include hundreds of people marching, dancing, and riding on motorcycles in the Pride parade. Thus, "I am also a we" names a form of queer and trans kinship that exceeds domestic familial and localized community boundaries.

In a 2018 blog post, *Sense8* fans Margaret Hernández (United States) and Siddy Nickhead (Sri Lanka) reflect on a photo montage of "I am also a we" *Sense8* tattoos (Figure 11.1):

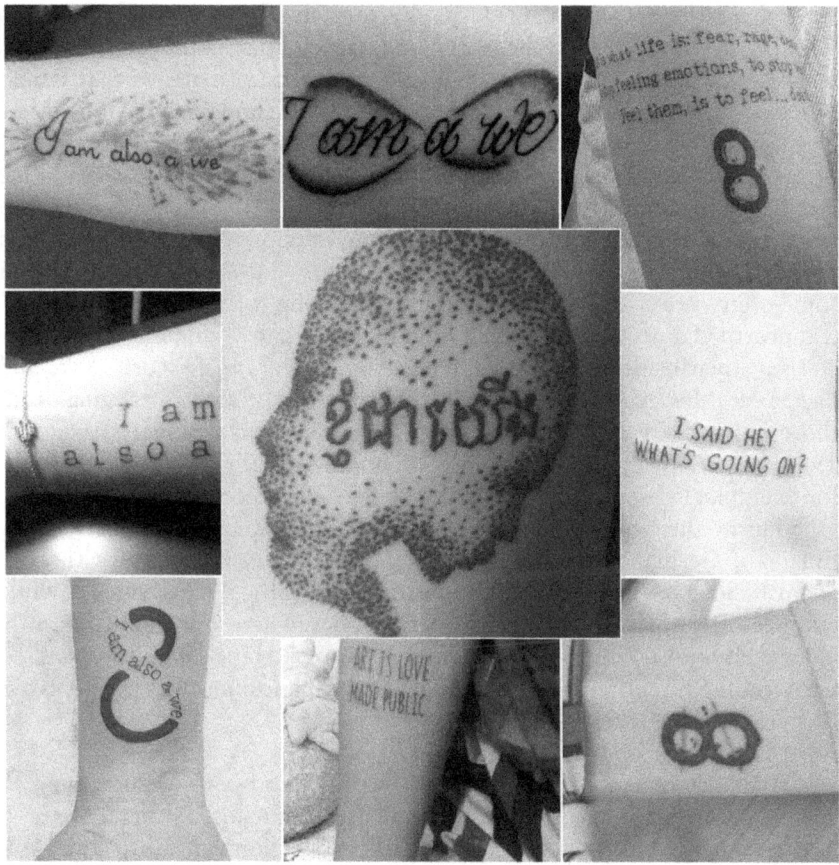

FIGURE 11.1 *"I am also a we"* photo collage of Sense8 tattoos. Source: https://medearants.wordpress.com/2018/04/29/welcome-to-the-cluster/.

> We are the volunteers, the bullied, the dreamers and the believers who had little conviction of our place in the world before *Sense8*'s empowering message that kindness, empathy and heart were super powers after all. From the Middle East to the USA to Europe and beyond, fans reside in every part of the world and have made lasting friendships with people who, like ourselves, have heart. (Hernandez and Nickhead 2018)

Hernández and Nickhead summarize several key aspects of *Sense8* fandom. First, many fans state that they came to the show from a place of loneliness, depression, disconnection, or victimization. Second, they say the show made them braver, more authentic, and more connected through the example set by the characters and by connecting with the cast and other *Sense8* fans who share these values. Third, *Sense8* fans, like the show's eight main sensates, hail from around the world, and participating in the series' fandom helps break down geographic, linguistic, and cultural barriers that would otherwise separate people. In addition, fans report fundamental shifts in the way they perceive and relate to the world after being "birthed" into a cluster of fandom: "*Sense8* changed my brain"; "I think the show has made me lean harder into my bisexuality and into polyamory"; "I had always tried to ignore my gender identity before [but] after watching *Sense8* I knew I had to take the plunge and finally start living as my authentic self"; "I was in some pretty heavy depression going into watching it [but] watching *Sense8* … unearthed a new lease for life I didn't know I had" (HunterSG1 2020).

Using platforms like Reddit, WhatsApp, Telegram, Discord, Kik, and Facebook Messenger, sensies formed their own "clusters" ranging from those based on a common birthdate (the series' sensates share August 8, 1988, i.e., 8/8/88) to regional, national, and eventually global clusters (see, for example, lightnofox 2019; sayonara_d 2020; objectivechestpain 2020). One fansite dubbed itself "Global Cluster" and hosted African, Australian, Brazilian, German, French, Indian, Italian, Nordic, Philippines, Russian, Spanish, South American, and UK clusters (The Global Cluster n.d.), while another offered a "Find Your Cluster" service where one could instantly video chat with fellow fans using tlk.io or Google Hangout (Cluster United Chat n.d.). One cluster making webpage featuring testimonials by successful clusters, explains:

> This is where *Sense8* stops being a TV show and become something so much more. … It inspires us to become better humans and to take care of each other. A cluster is a special real life connection with people that can become life long friends and they become a window to different part of the world. (Sense8 Cluster Maker n.d.)

While some fans struggled to get their cluster off the ground, those that did form were genuinely international, with one including people from "Argentina, Thailand, Japan, Germany, Spain, and 3 Americans" and another with "2 in Australia, 2 in the US, 1 each in Guatemala, Italy, Bahrain and the Philippines" (Trescadi 2019). Perhaps most elaborate in its ambition was the Sensorium website, mobile app, and game, which promised that users would be able to form various kinds of clusters, share media, play music directly to clustermate's phones, and play video games inspired by the series' narrative—but also experience sensate "sharing" and "visiting" via an app "that will mimic what life as a Sensate can encompass in every single way" (Gupta and Gutiérrez n.d.). At its height, the Sensorium webapp claimed to have more than 1,500 members and 80 active clusters, but it did not last long enough to deliver on most of its overly ambitious promises (R/Sense8 2018). While existing platforms often fail to live up to these

FIGURE 11.2 *Map of sensies worldwide by an anonymous fan. Source: https:// www.zeemaps.com/map?group=2569939.*

utopian longings, *Sense8* fandom did attempt to align the social media universe to *Sense8* values of family, inclusion, and love. Indeed, all these attempts at interconnectedness illustrate a common desire among sensies to create and see themselves as a specifically *global* kinship, which also materialized in fan mapping practices. Through maps, sensies represented themselves *to* themselves as a specifically global collectivity in a way that may not be unique to *Sense8* (cf. Creampuff World Domination n.d.) but is particularly suited to the show's rhetoric of global connectivity (see Boni 2018). One fan made a map of the show's filming locations (uuin 2019), another mapped the countries in which the hashtag #Sense8 trended after the final episode (@Sense8fighter 2018), and another mapped sensies who identified their locations using a Google form (Sense8 Worldwide Cluster n.d.). While the highest concentration of pins in Figure 11.2 is in North America and Europe, there are also many in Latin America, India, East and Southeast Asia, and along the coast of Australia, while Africa has the fewest pins, thereby also highlighting issues of development and social and economic inequality in relation to access to the internet and Netflix, as well as the company's global ambitions.

#netflixeverywhere?

Netflix itself was quick to use *Sense8*'s vocabulary of global connectivity when promoting the show, harnessing its affective resonance for marketing purposes. Tweets and other social media posts authored by official Netflix accounts as well as the series' actors regularly hailed "our cluster" and "the global cluster." Between May 28 and June 4, 2015, the official *Sense8* Instagram account shared photos of the series' key locations, each with the caption "Home. #Sense8" in the language of the location pictured. Then on June 5 the S01 release date was shared with a photo of the abandoned Church from the opening scene with the caption: "You are one of us. You're coming home with me. #Sense8 is Now Streaming." Following this, the series' Twitter, Facebook, and Instagram handles regularly interpellated its "cluster family" as "global." Five months after the release of S01 in October 2015, the Twitter account mounted a campaign to visualize the geographical breadth of *Sense8* fandom by declaring it "Sense8 o'clock" everywhere in the *Sense8* universe (Nairobi, Seoul, etc.) and asking fans to share a photo of their location in celebration. In anticipation of S02 and later the finale (S02:E12), Netflix's messages to the series' fandom grew increasingly emotional. Promotions for S02:E01 in December 2016 and the rest of S02 in May 2017 led with "Survive Together" and "Stronger Together," thereby uniting *Sense8* characters and their fans. The cast referred to each other on Instagram as "#sense8 family!" too. On August 8, 2016, the official *Sense8* Instagram handle released a montage of the eight lead actors singing "Happy Birthday" (Le 2017). Cut together in rapid and looping montage, the video is another example of officially authored content made for fans that takes on the aesthetics of fan-made content. A year later, the Netflix US handle tweeted a gif of the sensates blowing out their birthday cake from S02:E01 with the caption: "Tell your cluster it's time to celebrate! #HappyBirthdaySense8." On June 2, 2018, the official *Sense8* Twitter handle tweeted, "I am also a we. Happy Pride Month, cluster fam." Each of these tweets and many like them included the pointed use of emojis of hearts, rainbows, and party hats in imitation of affective fan vernacular.

However, affects do not belong to individuals or corporations but "circulate between bodies and signs" (Ahmed 2004: 117). While affects work like capital in that "affect does not reside positively in the sign or commodity, but is produced only as an effect of its circulation," some signs increase in affective value as a result of movement, such that "the more they circulate, the more affective they become, and the more they appear to 'contain' affect" (Ahmed 2004: 120). This fast and wide circulation of affect can be beneficial to capital when it gets more people to watch more, thus Netflix encouraged the circulation of *Sense8* affect hoping that it might generate greater financial capital in the form of more subscribers. The speed of affect's circulation is key as it minimizes affective labor time. Today, especially, when all our favorite shows are at our fingertips via Netflix or Pirate Bay and binge-viewing has become the norm, this has become more obvious. Across streaming's brief history, media studies scholars have noted a dilution of fan passions and a shift in fan dynamics (Click et al. 2017). Lost is the time of synchronous screening "cooler talk" as only the most avid or engaged fans slow down to puzzle out elaborate storylines and coordinate synchronized rewatches. The average viewer is instead on to the next series. But, as Keeling argues, those images that confront what official common senses hide, such as the possibility of an entirely different social organization, "circulate more slowly because their production as images of value requires more affective labor time" (Keeling 2007: 99).

While Ted Sarandos, chief content officer for Netflix, claimed Netflix "doesn't care when consumers watch their shows, whether it's the day they're released or two years later" (Nocera 2016), Netflix nevertheless canceled *Sense8* three weeks after S02 was released, supposedly because viewership did not grow sufficiently to recoup the show's production costs. The series and the affective labor time it asked of viewers tested the confines of its distribution platform with its emphasis on viewership within four weeks of a show's release and completion rates for full seasons during that same four-week window. In this light, the cancelation of *Sense8* after two seasons was the beginning of a trend that now defines Netflix's original content strategy (Adalian 2018; Andreeva 2019; Mitovich 2019; Roettgers 2019).

At the 2016 Consumer Electronics Show in Las Vegas, Netflix CEO and cofounder Reed Hastings used the language of connectivity and "sharing" familiar from *Sense8* to reflect that "when we started the company 20 years ago, we dreamed of the day when the Internet would have enabled us to deliver TV shows and movies to the billions of people with whom we share the planet" (Van Grove 2016). In his statement, now available on YouTube (CES 2016), a mosaic of hundreds of flags appears behind Hastings as he declares: "Today I am delighted to announce that *while* we have been here on stage at CES, we switched Netflix on in Azerbaijan. In Vietnam. In India. In Nigeria. In Poland. In Russia. In Saudi Arabia. In Singapore. In South Korea. In Turkey. In Indonesia. And in a hundred and thirty new countries" (CES 2016). The flags behind Hastings disappear in favor of gray screens sliding by, which arrange themselves into a map of the world. As the screens flick from gray to red an enormous text appears: "#netflixeverywhere." Standing in front of this display, speaking increasingly emphatically, Hastings declares:

> While you have been listening to *me* talk the Netflix service has gone *live* in nearly every country of the world but China, where we hope to also be in the future. Today—*right now!*—you are witnessing the birth of a global TV network. Whether you are in Sydney or St. Petersburg, Singapore or Seoul, Santiago or Saskatoon, you now can be part of the internet TV revolution.

Indeed, during Hastings's speech, Netflix was "turned on" in 130 new countries (all except 4: China, Crimea, North Korea, and Syria). The rhetoric clearly echoes that of the *Sense8* credits and its fandom, announcing a revolutionary new form of connectivity. Hastings claims his announcement is not only about his company's international reach but also about inviting international viewers ("you") to join this collective "revolution."

Like *Sense8* fans, Hastings represents Netflix's new global viewer base to itself *as global* through the map made up of screens. But when S01 of *Sense8* was released in June 2015, of the show's nine main shooting locations, only viewers in the United States, Mexico, Germany, and the UK could legally watch it. Indeed, at the same time as Hastings was heralding Netflix's global community, the corporation was also ramping up its VPN-detection technology and geoblocking response to illegal audiences that *Variety* called its "black market diaspora" (Wallenstein 2014). Never mind that in countries with low GDPs and weak currencies compared to the US dollar (such as India and Nigeria) only wealthy elites could afford Netflix's monthly price geared to Western markets and high-speed internet without data caps (Lobato 2019: 79, 118, 124). And, while Netflix has innovated new "Open Connect" technology to deliver high-resolution content to their global subscribers, placing servers full of Netflix content in local ISPs and IXPs that get refreshed nightly, a map of these servers' locations reveals Netflix's global priorities, with the highest density in North America, followed by Europe and then Latin America, while Asia has relatively few servers and Africa hardly any. Thus, while Hastings implied that all parts of the world would be equally invited to the Netflix "revolution," many of Netflix's decisions, from pricing to server locations, reveal that this invitation to potential audiences of *Sense8* was much less global than it seemed.

Fans Respond to *Sense8*'s Cancelation

On May 5, 2017, two years after releasing S01 (and eighteen months after turning on "everywhere"), Netflix released S02, only to announce on 1 June—well within the infamous four-week window—that they were canceling *Sense8*. Heartfelt official Twitter posts about being part of the #GlobalCluster notwithstanding, the company decided *Sense8* was not performing well enough to justify its production expense (Kilday 2017). Within a few days, however, fans from around the globe, using the hashtags #IAmAWe and #WeAreTheGlobalCluster, had mounted a campaign to bring the series back that included a Change.org petition with over 500,000 signatures (THE GANG Sense8FANS 2017). While this was far from the first time fans of a particular television series had united to protest its cancelation (see Chin et al. 2013; Jenkins 1991), the geographical scope of the *Sense8* campaign was unprecedented. Much of the fan activism was spearheaded by fans in Argentina and Brazil, and the Change.org petition was authored in sixteen languages, making clear that, despite the show's textual Anglophone and American/European biases and the lack of equal access to Netflix's streaming services around the globe, the series had nonetheless resonated deeply with fans of many cultural and linguistic backgrounds. In their petition letter these global fans stressed the need for shows and movies that "provide the world with a message of love, diversity and respect" such as *Sense8*, which "has given the world a new way of seeing others: with acceptance, love and understanding." Many fans mailed single flip-flops to Netflix with the message "*Sense8* needs closure like Lito needs his flip-flop," referencing a scene in which a despairing Lito fills his partner Hernando's phone with lovelorn messages that degenerate in coherence to the point of lamenting his missing footwear. Crucially, moreover, fans sent flip-flops not only to Netflix headquarters but also to their nearest Netflix corporate offices in the United States, the Netherlands, Brazil, India, Japan, and South Korea. In this way, a global fandom took on a global company. On June 8 Netflix responded to fan activism by reaffirming their decision on Twitter and Tumblr, once again appropriating the language of the show:

> To our *Sense8* family ... We've seen the petitions. We've read the messages.
> We know you want to #RenewSense8, and we wish we could #BringBackSense8 for you.
> The reason we've taken so long to get back to you is because we've thought long and hard here at Netflix to try to make it work but unfortunately we can't.
> Thank you for watching and hope you'll stay close with your cluster around the world.
> #SensatesForever (Sense8 n.d.)

Rather than mollify the situation, however, the message revealed the tensions between the kind of fandom Netflix had hoped to cultivate (i.e., enthusiastic viewers from all over the world who would drive new subscribers to the platform) and the kind of fandom they got (i.e., enthusiastic viewers from all over the world who banded together to pressure Netflix to reverse their decision). The fact that fan actions exceeded the boundaries imagined by the company is in some ways typical of the operation of fandom, from Rudolph Valentino's famously "hysterical" fans in the 1920s (Hansen 1991: 243–96) to the moral panic around "entitled fans" bullying the media industry in the summer of 2016 (Stanfill 2019: 184–9). Netflix's message was rather cynical in that it maintained the rhetoric of family, pretended that the decision was out of its hands, and encouraged fans to continue imagining sensates "forever" despite their grief over *Sense8*'s cancelation. As one fan exclaimed on Twitter, "How dare @netflix say 'To OUR Sense8 family' ... U didn't back this show from day 1 so NO u have NO place in OUR Family! #Bringbacksense8" (@hajek_ciara 2017).

Sensies responded to this confirmation of cancelation by redoubling their efforts. One warned: "#BringbackSense8 @netflix we're gonna keep fighting. This isn't over yet" (@Tessa_102 2017). They formed further clusters to make the breadth of their geographical reach ever the clearer. As the AfricaCluster, managed by fans in South Africa, Namibia, Tanzania, Somalia, and Kenya, recounts,

> Despite all our heart and raw energy Netflix issued a statement around a week later claiming that it would not be possible to create a continuation to the *Sense8* story. … We needed to get organized and show them that, just like the show's characters, if enough people from around the world come together and combine their skills, we can take down any corporation, no matter how powerful they appear to be. Suddenly groups and clusters began forming all over the world, linking the most unlikely of people together, all with the goal of saving a show that represents love, unity and acceptance for everyone. Ours was one of those groups, born of the desire to unite African *Sense8* fans and to amplify our collective voice in order to bring *Sense8* back. (Africa Cluster n.d.).

In sum, *Sense8* fans marshalled their affective investment in the series and repurposed the series' and fandom's highly affective discourse to make their demands legible to corporate Netflix, which, despite claims to love their "cluster fam," had pulled the plug on "their" series. Indeed, the insufficient growth of new subscribers may have been at least partly because Netflix had not provided *Sense8* with inter- and intra-seasonal windows for relatively synchronized fan engagement that enables the affective engagement and interactivity that complex science fiction and fantasy series demand. Whereas HBO maintained a weekly release schedule for *Game of Thrones* and had standard gaps between seasons even while expanding its distribution from cable to its streaming service HBO GO, the haphazard release schedule of *Sense8* meant that the series could not generate or sustain the sort of discourse necessary to grow its audience (Elrod 2019: 189). Consequently, in this era of digital streaming TV, *Sense8* arguably "provides an especially suggestive example of how the affective engagement and interactivity of fans can operate in opposition to industry agendas" (Elrod 2019: 185). Whereas Netflix organizes its subscribers into "taste communities," fans, with their affectively laden discourse, "can essentially sell what data or algorithms cannot" (Elrod 2019: 187). That being said, while *Sense8* fans' clustering and the like may not build the platform's subscriber base sufficiently, in their campaign for the series renewal sensies used hashtags as algorithms to harness their fannish affectivity and sell themselves back to the company.

On June 29, 2017, three weeks after reaffirming their decision to cancel *Sense8*, the official *Sense8* Twitter account announced: "Death doesn't let you say goodbye. 2 hour finale episode in the works. Tell your cluster" (@sense8 2017) and appended a page-long single-spaced letter from creator Lana Wachowski. She described her grief at *Sense8*'s cancelation and stated:

By myself, there was nothing I could do.

But just as the characters in our show discover that they are not alone, I too have learned that I am not just a me. I am also a we.

The passionate letters, the petitions, the collective voice that rose up like the fist of Sun to fight for this show was beyond what anyone was expecting.

In this world it is easy to believe that you cannot make a difference; that when a government or an institution or corporation makes a decision, there is something irrevocable about the decision; that love is always less important than the bottom line.

But here is a gift from the fans of this show that I will carry forever in my heart: while it is often true that those decisions are irreversible, it is not *always* true.

Improbably, unforeseeably, your love has brought Sense8 back to life ...

It is my great pleasure as well as Netflix's (believe me, they love the show as much as we do but the numbers have always been challenging) to announce that there will be another two hour special released next year. After that... if this experience has taught me anything, you NEVER know.

Thank you all. Now let's go find out what happens to Wolfgang. (@ sense8 2017)

Wachowski again uses the language of the show to describe the actions of the show's fans, contending that they have actualized the show's promise in their fight to bring it back. They have proved to her, the principal creator, that her utopian dreams are (at least in part) realizable in the real world. However, there is a strange switcheroo in which Netflix is at once the evil corporation that must be fought by the fans and also, in the end, the savior of the show that is part of the "global cluster" the show has brought into being. But on the whole fans were thrilled that Netflix responded to their pressure and that they could look forward to a two-hour special that would tie up at least some of the show's loose ends. Like Lana Wachowski, fans were exhilarated to know that their collective efforts could make a difference and many continued to agitate for three more seasons, holding that the Wachowskis had originally conceptualized the show in a five-season narrative arc. The fans behind the Twitter feeds @IAmWeCampaign, @Global_Cluster, and @sense8united posted a new Change.org petition calling for a full-fledged season three (Sense8 Fandom n.d.). It includes a trailer for *Sense8 Revolution*, a documentary-in-progress by Buenos Aires sensie Martin Erhardt, who invited fans from around the world to send him video clips explaining how *Sense8* impacted their life (Erhardt 2018). At the time of writing, the petition has 86,922 signatures (out of a goal of 150,000). Fans continue to think with the show through a variety of fan works, including a series of vids by Ine (@Sen_se8) on Twitter that dubbed character dialogue from English into each character's native language, thus reconceiving the show's oft-critiqued Anglocentrism (@Sen_se8 2020). But the momentum of fan activism diminished after the release of S02:E12, which wrapped up many of the hanging narrative threads and gave fans one last utopian, sensual montage as the original cluster and their human partners, altogether in person after attending Nomi and Amanita's wedding atop the Eiffel Tower *and* through the medium of their empathetic sensate connections, "share" in the happy couple's wedding night.

Conclusion

One central question that has circulated among *Sense8* fans is whether their devotion to each other, the show, and its values could result in broader social change. One sensie asked on Reddit: "Can we seriously as a cluster, band together to make a genuine change in the world?" (justplainoldMEhere 2019). In their accounts of participating in the fandom, first through forming clusters and then in the global #RenewSense8 campaign, sensies state that they found these activities transformative on a personal level, in terms of feeling connected to others and having the courage to live authentically. Hernandez and Nickhead write: "This is one thing that sets us apart from many other fan bases. ... *Sense8* made us better people within, thanks to the many teachings it instilled in us, thanks to the hope it gave us for a better world, thanks to the lessons, the cast camaraderie, and the pure love it gifted us all" (Hernandez and Nickhead 2018). These kinds of personal transformations contribute to the survival of marginalized people. They build on the New Age movements of the 1970s that similarly preached love, connection, and expanded consciousness. This connection is especially apparent in *Sense8* fan Sheila Applegate's call for a Global Peace Meditation devoted to renewing *Sense8* (Applegate 2018).

While *Sense8* fandom activity faded after the finale aired, suggesting that advocating for the series' continuance was the end of #TheGlobalCluster writ large, in March 2020, sensie activity picked up as the global spread of Covid-19 led to widespread public health calls to "socially distance" by staying home and avoiding physical contact. Sensate connectivity, which permits psychically and physically experiencing various locations and, perhaps most importantly, many forms of touch, from the friendly to the sexual, without leaving home, became a particularly powerful longing. As one sensie tweeted, "Once again wish I was a #Sense8 & could have sex and hugs and personal talks while obeying all physical isolation rules" (@miss_confuse13 2020). A blogger explained, "Why Netflix's *Sense8* Is the Perfect Binge While Social Distancing," reasoning that it "goes out of its way to prove that we are never alone, even if the people we love aren't nearby" (Stacey 2020). *Sense8* actors Jamie Clayton and Tuppence Middleton suggested a global viewing party in the shadow of Covid-19 (@MsJamieClayton 2020; @Tuppence 2020), a call quickly taken up by Nickhead and other fans (Nickhead 2020). A few days later, Netflix again joined the fray, releasing first a video called "#Sense8DayRewatch March 28th 2020 | Netflix Worldwide Quarantine' "(yet another montage, this time of poignant moments from S02:E01 accompanied by that episode's cover of Leonard Cohen's "Hallelujah") and then a video entitled "'What's Going On?' March 28th 2020 #Sense8DayRewatch" featuring a montage of *Sense8* fans from around the world, joined by Kenyan actor Paul Ogola (Jela), singing along to "What's Up?"

In fact, much of the collective response to the Covid-19 pandemic on social media exemplifies the sort of empathy and connectivity at a distance that sensies have long called for. At the time of writing, we see this in everything from grassroots efforts to make up for equipment shortages (e.g., creating ventilator valves with 3D printers, sewing face masks, and sending them to hospitals), to city-wide and community Mutual Aid projects to provide money, food, and protective equipment to the most vulnerable people. We also see it in the thousands of different efforts to create a sense of togetherness through online technologies, from Zoom happy hours and birthday parties to Facebook Live musical performances; Instagram dance classes; and orchestras, choirs, and dance troupes performing together at a distance through montage. The way people have used music to create a sense of togetherness in spite of required physical distancing is especially reminiscent of *Sense8*'s musical montage sequences. In short, the global connectivity *Sense8* modeled for its fans has become an example for us all. Covid-19 has only made clearer capitalism's devastation of human life and the unevenness of this devastation on various geographic, economic, and racial scales as well as the untenability of relying on discrete family units to nurture all and the ease with which so many would rather turn to bigotry and racism rather than face strident critiques of capitalist cisheteropatriarchy. As each of us recalibrates for a post-Covid world (or a post-pandemic world, should Covid-19, like AIDS, now play a regular part), *Sense8* and sensies would encourage us to remember "I am also a we" and that "we" is global.

Works Cited

Adalian, J. (2018), "Inside the Binge Factory," *New York Magazine*, June 11. Available online: https://www.vulture.com/2018/06/how-netflix-swallowed-tv-industry.html.

AfricaCluster8 (n.d.) "Africa Cluster." Available online: www.africacluster8.com.

Ahmed, S. (2004), "Affective Economies", *Social Text* 22 (2): 117–39. Available online: https://doi.org/10.1215/01642472-22-2_79-117.

Andreeva, N. (2019), "Feeling the Churn: Why Netflix Cancels Shows After a Couple of Seasons & Why They Can't Move to New Homes," *Deadline*, March 18. Available online: https://deadline.com/2019/03/netflix-tv-series-cancellations-strategy-one-day-at-a-time-1202576297/.

Applegate, S. (2018), "#GiveSense8Season3 Global Meditation by Sheila Applegate," *Live Sense 8 Podcast with Sheila Applegate & Zac Hansen*, February 2. Available online: https://www.livesense8.com/givesense8season3-global-mediation-by-sheila-applegate/.

Bailey, M., m. cárdenas, L. Horak, L. Kaimana, C. M. Keegan, G. Newman, R. Samer, and R. Sarkissian (2017), "*Sense8* Roundtable," *Spectator*, 37 (2): 77–88.

Boni, M. (2018), "Digital Maps and Fan Discourse: Moving between Heuristics and Interpretation," *NECSUS: European Journal of Media Studies*, 7 (2): 141–60.

CES (2016), "Reed Hastings, Netflix—Keynote 2016," YouTube, January 6. Available online: https://www.youtube.com/watch?v=l5R3E6jsICA.

Chin, B., B. Jones, M. McNutt, and L. Pebler (2013), "*Veronica Mars* Kickstarter and Crowd Funding," *Transformative Works and Cultures*, 15. Available online: https://doi.org/10.3983/twc.2014.0519.

Click, M. A., J. Gray, J. Mittell, and S. Scott (2017), "Futures of Fan Studies: A Conversation," in M. A. Click and S. Scott (eds.), *The Routledge Companion to Media Fandom*, 437–50, New York: Routledge.

Cluster United Chat (n.d.), "Find Your Cluster," Cluster United Chat. Available online: http://clusterunitedchat.weebly.com/.

Creampuff World Domination (n.d.), "Creampuff World Domination," Google Maps. Available online: https://www.google.com/maps/d/drive?state=%7B%22ids%22:%5B%221s0xOs7Cwzme DwucEANoFEAMUHLA%22%5D,%22action%22:%22open%22,%22userId%22:%22114945768239083840789%22%7D.

Elrod, J. M. (2019), "Navigating the Nebula: Audience Affect, Interactivity, and Genre in the Age of Streaming TV," *Participations: Journal of Audience & Reception Studies,* 16 (2): 167–95.

Erhardt, M. (2018), "*Sense8* Revolution Teaser 2019," YouTube, September 30. Available online: https://www.youtube.com/watch?time_continue=203&v=T8f-qyqgwZQ&feature=emb_logo.

THE GANG Sense8FANS (2017), "Sense 8 Season 3 Renewal," *Change*, June 1. Available online: https://www.change.org/p/netflixlat-netflix-sense8-sense-8-season-3-renewal.

The Global Cluster (n.d.), "The Global Cluster," *Global Cluster*. Available online: https://globalcluster8.wordpress.com/.

@Global_Cluster (2020), "I'm Trying to Picture a #Coronavirus Outbreak in a World Populated by Sensates ... How Do You Think It Would Have Gone?," Twitter, February 26. [post deleted] (accessed March 5, 2020).

Gupta, P., and L. Gutierrez (n.d.), "Sensorium". Available online: https://web.archive.org/web/20180903050439/http://sensorium.online/.

@hajek_ciara (2017), "How Dare @netflix Say 'To OUR Sense8 Family' .. U Didn't Back This Show from Day 1 so NO u Have NO Place in OUR Family!

#Bringbacksense8," Twitter, June 9. Available online: https://twitter.com/hajek_ciara/status/873076028754624514.
Hansen, M. (1991), *Babel and Babylon: Spectatorship in American Silent Film*, Cambridge, MA: Harvard University Press.
Hernandez, M., and S. Nickhead (2018), "Welcome to the Cluster!," *Medea Rants*, April 29. Available online: https://medearants.wordpress.com/2018/04/29/welcome-to-the-cluster/.
HunterSG1 (2020), "R/Sense8—Sense8 Changed My Brain," Reddit, February 18. Available online: https://www.reddit.com/r/Sense8/comments/f63bdy/sense8_changed_my_brain/.
Jenkins, H. (1991), " 'It's Not a Fairy Tale Anymore': Gender, Genre, Beauty and the Beast," *Journal of Film and Video*, 43 (1/2): 90–110.
justplainoldMEhere (2019), "R/Sense8—Our Cluster," Reddit, August 3. Available online: https://www.reddit.com/r/Sense8/comments/clf2ly/our_cluster/.
Keeling, K. (2007), *The Witch's Flight: The Cinematic, the Black Femme, and the Image of Common Sense*, Durham, NC: Duke University Press.
Kilday, G. (2017), "Netflix's Ted Sarandos Talks 'Sense8' Cancellation, Cannes Film Debate: 'I'm Not Anti-Theater,' " *Hollywood Reporter*, June 10. Available online: https://www.hollywoodreporter.com/news/netflixs-ted-sarandos-talks-sense8-cancellation-cannes-film-debate-im-not-anti-theater-1012224.
Le, H. B. (2017), "Sense8 Saying Happy Birthday," YouTube, August 8. Available online: https://www.youtube.com/watch?v=gC5HPMp0vV0.
lightnofox (2019), "R/Sense8—Anybody Here Wanna Create a Cluster of between 5 and 11 ?," Reddit, December 10. Available online: https://www.reddit.com/r/Sense8/comments/e8r17w/anybody_here_wanna_create_a_cluster_of_between_5/.
Lobato, R. (2019), *Netflix Nations: The Geography of Digital Distribution*, New York: New York University Press.
Lothian, A. (2016), "*Sense8* and Utopian Connectivity," *Science Fiction Film and Television*, 9 (1): 93–5.
@miss_confuse13 (2020), "Once Again Wish I Was a #Sense8 & Could Have Sex and Hugs and Personal Talks While Obeying All Physical Isolation Rules," Twitter, March 24. Available online: https://twitter.com/miss_confuse13/status/1242310648782114817.
Mitovich, M. W. (2019), "Is Netflix Cancelling Shows Before People Have a Reasonable Amount of Time to Watch Them?," *TVLine*, June 25. Available online: https://tvline.com/2019/06/24/is-netflix-cancelling-shows-too-quickly/.
Muñoz, J. E. (2009), *Cruising Utopia: The Then and There of Queer Futurity*, New York: New York University Press.
Netflix (n.d.), "Where Is Netflix Available?," Help Center. Available online: https://help.netflix.com/en/node/14164.
Nickhead, S. (2020), "Attention Sensies and Everyone Who's Feeling Overwhelmed and Stressed Due to the Current #lockdown Situation, Let's Reconnect with Our Shared Humanity with a #Sense8DayRewatch on March 28th! Join in and Leave the Blues behind! #IAmAlsoAWe," Twitter, March 24. Available online: https://twitter.com/SiddyNickhead/status/1242317058089590784.

nickmaran (2018), "R/Sense8—A Truely Global Cluster???," Reddit, February 2. Available online: https://www.reddit.com/r/Sense8/comments/7ur6np/a_truely_global_cluster/.

Nocera, J. (2016), "Can Netflix Survive in the New World It Created?," *New York Times*, June 15. Available online: https://www.nytimes.com/2016/06/19/magazine/can-netflix-survive-in-the-new-world-it-created.html.

objectivechestpain (2020), "R/Sense8—Just Finished Re-Watching Sense8 Again and Now I'm Left Feeling So Desperate for a Cluster of My Own!," Reddit, January 5. Available online: https://www.reddit.com/r/Sense8/comments/ekkorx/just_finished_rewatching_sense8_again_and_now_im/.

Roettgers, J. (2019), "Why Netflix Will Keep Breaking Hearts and Canceling Shows," *Variety*, March 20. Available online: https://variety.com/2019/digital/news/netflix-show-cancellations-metrics-business-1203167540/.

R/Sense8 (2018), "R/Sense8—Update from Sensorium: A Real Life Sensate Experience!," Reddit, June 10. Available online: https://www.reddit.com/r/Sense8/comments/8xu8gf/update_from_sensorium_a_real_life_sensate/.

sayonara_d (2020), "R/Sense8—Does Someone Want to Create a Cluster?," Reddit, January 13. Available online: https://www.reddit.com/r/Sense8/comments/eobpjk/does_someone_want_to_create_a_cluster/.

@sense8 (2017), "Death Doesn't Let You Say Goodbye. 2 Hour Finale Episode in the Works. Tell Your Cluster," Twitter, June 29. Available online: https://twitter.com/sense8/status/880495946370568194.

@Sen_se8 (2020), "What If We Had a Different Type of #Sense8 Where All Characters Spoke Their Native Language? Discover the Sensorium Version Here: Https://T.Co/GE0AqEArYJ," Twitter, February 9. Available online: https://twitter.com/Sen_se8/status/1226531177504309252.

Sense8 (n.d.), "To Our Sense8 Family ….," Tumblr. Available online: https://sense8.tumblr.com/post/161601416234/to-our-sense8-family.

Sense8 Cluster Maker (n.d.), "Sense8 Cluster Maker," *Sense8 United*. Available online: https://web.archive.org/web/20190523061920/http://sense8united.com/clustermaker/.

Sense8 Fandom (n.d.), "Sense8 Season 3 Is Written. NETFLIX Renew It Already!," *Change*. Available online: https://www.change.org/p/netflix-sense8-season-3-is-written-netflix-renew-it-already#:~:text=Lana%20Wachowski%20announced%20that%20she,hour%20special%2C%20following%20the%20cancellation.

@Sense8fighter (2018), "Since the Release of 'Amor Vincit Omnia' on June 8, #Sense8 Has Trended and/or Is (Still) Trending on @netflix in All the Red Countries!!!," Twitter, June 17. Available online: https://twitter.com/sense8fighter/status/1008245322785619969.

Sense8 Worldwide Cluster (n.d.), "Sense8 Worldwide Cluster," *ZeeMaps*. Available online: https://www.zeemaps.com/map?group=2569939#.

Stacey, S. (2020), "Why Netflix's *Sense8* Is the Perfect Binge While Social Distancing," *Cultures*, March 20. Available online: https://culturess.com/2020/03/20/why-netflixs-sense8-is-the-perfect-binge-while-social-distancing/.

Stanfill, M. (2019), *Exploiting Fandom: How the Media Industry Seeks to Manipulate Fans*, Iowa City: University of Iowa Press.

Stein, L. E. (2015), *Millennial Fandom: Television Audiences in the Transmedia Age*, Iowa City: University of Iowa Press.
@Tessa_102 (2017), "#BringbackSense8 @netflix We're Gonna Keep Fighting. This Isn't Over Yet," Twitter, June 8. Available online: https://twitter.com/Tessa_102/status/872982380327424001.
Trescadi (2019), "R/Sense8—Did Any of the 'Find Your Cluster!' Initiatives Work for You?," Reddit, October 15. Available online: https://www.reddit.com/r/Sense8/comments/dibkxq/did_any_of_the_find_your_cluster_initiatives_work/.
uuin (2019), "R/Sense8—Sense8 Filming Location World Map Is Open for View, Contribution and Edit. It's a World Class Production, Cost Was Too High. Which Scene and Which Place Is Your Favorite?," Reddit, March 19. Available online: https://www.reddit.com/r/Sense8/comments/b31esx/sense8_filming_location_world_map_is_open_for/.
Van Grove, J. (2016), "Netflix Strives for World Domination with Global Launch," *San Diego Union-Tribune*, January 6. Available online: https://www.sandiegouniontribune.com/business/technology/sdut-netflix-global-launch-ces-2016-2016jan06-story.html.
Wallenstein, A. (2014), "Australia's Fevered Streaming Market Isn't Waiting for Netflix," *Variety*, March 19. Available online: https://variety.com/2014/digital/news/australia-flooded-with-streaming-content-providers-and-netflix-isnt-even-there-yet-1201138144/.

12

Revisiting the Cluster

Cáel M. Keegan

An enthrallingly realized dramatic series that marks Lana and Lilly Wachowskis' first foray into television, *Sense8* is perhaps too unusual and too romantic for a "peak TV" environment saturated with forebodingly dystopic rebooted properties (Keegan 2018). As much a critique of popular science fiction (Rothman 2015) as it is a speculative explosion of televisual form, *Sense8* defies categorization, "skipping gleefully" (Li 2017) across the narrative styles that organize the streaming television market. Despite its recognition for Outstanding Drama Series at the 2016 GLAAD awards, Netflix abruptly canceled the series shortly after the release of its second season. Citing a lack of funds, the streaming service-turned-studio announced the termination on June 1—the opening day of LGBTQ Pride month in the United States and only eleven days before the anniversary of the Orlando Pulse massacre. Because *Sense8* was one of few contemporary Netflix Originals to feature lead transgender and queer characters, including multiple queer characters of color, the timing of the cancelation was received as especially insensitive. Fan response was swift and global: campaigns erupted on Twitter and Facebook, calls and emails flooded into Netflix customer service and to Netflix CEO Reed Hastings, while a Change.org petition authored by THE GANG Sense8FANS, posted from Buenos Aires, demanded a renewal in sixteen separate languages (Krishna). Internet journalism covering the cancelation pointed to a "troubling trend" at Netflix, which seemed to be axing its most diverse shows (Jones 2017; Ryan 2017). Yet by June 29, 2017, Netflix executives had acquiesced—at least partially, granting *Sense8* a feature film-length finale episode. Revisiting *Sense8*, I conclude this anthology with reflections on a show that transcended television as a medium, achieving a historically unprecedented connection with its streaming audience.

Sense8 is groundbreakingly transnational, shot in at least sixteen cities in eleven different countries around the world, meaning that the Wachowskis and cocreator J. Michael Straczynski effectively engineered an intercontinental audience that demanded Netflix recognize its legitimacy. That is to say, the speculative "cluster" formation shared between telepathic characters on *Sense8* became a powerful metaphor for the desiring, geographically diffuse body of its viewership. The series created a symbolic structure for the emergence of its own fandoms and social media affinity cultures: Facebook groups for viewers of *Sense8* reference the cluster as a new kind of social formation and consumer model and users on platforms as diverse as Facebook, Friendesque, Reddit, and WhatsApp match birthdates to sort themselves into fan clusters. Much as they accomplished with *The Matrix* (1999) nearly twenty years previously, with *Sense8* the Wachowskis appear to have again found the point where new technologies and speculative narrativity converge. In this networked era of "spreadable" media (Jenkins 2013) and online cultures sewn together through the sharing of likes and emojis, *Sense8*'s affectively enmeshed characters reflect how social media shapes our sense of the world. The telepathically entwined, orgiastically sensational encounters within the show's fictional cluster subjunctively point toward the interconnected global era it feels like we *might* achieve—if only we could move beyond our differences and "come together."

While the Wachowskis' earlier works examine time in anachronic (*V for Vendetta*, 2005) and diachronic (*Cloud Atlas*, 2012) modes, *Sense8* is an exploration of global simultaneity through a uniquely synchronic approach to temporality. *Sense8*'s storyline is constellated through the senses of eight characters spread over the globe, who come to realize that they are not human, but a separate hominid species of sensates living secretly among humans in psychically linked groups. When a cluster is born, its sensates begin to mutate into merged consciousness, their brains morphologically shifting and the borders of their bodies falling away.

The eighth "sense" referenced in the series' title is the enhanced capacity for empathetic contact that the sensates experience within their cluster. Cluster members can share sensations, memories, affects, skills, and communicate directly across time and space through a telepathic/telekinetic link that the show achieves through an editing process that transposes the sensates' bodies across its globally disparate settings. Gradually, the eight main characters form a unified symbiosis—an eight-fold composite character—to evade and defeat the Biologic Preservation Organization (BPO), a eugenicist entity that lobotomizes sensates and uses them as remotely operated weapons. The premise, ethos, and realization of *Sense8* were always ripe for descriptive, diagnostic, predictive, and prescriptive analysis.

Although *Sense8* is notable for the strength of its queerness, *trans* is the necessary keyword in any attempt to understand the series (Shaw 2017). The Wachowskis' recent comings-out as transgender women provide an unavoidably "reorienting paratext" (Mittell 2015: 294) for reading *Sense8* as possessing a distinctly trans sensibility. As a text that "provokes a new understanding of the Wachowskis as transgender auteurs" (Bailey et al. 2017: 76), *Sense8* contains clear analogies to the oppressive role of medicine in transgender people's lives and the desire for alternative forms of queer and trans kinship, but also explores trans as an intra/intersubjective experience of entangled sensories—a constant navigation between what is internally sensed and what is externally perceived. While to become sensate is quite literally to gain additional bodies, *Sense8*'s characters must also learn to feel across and through the lived forms—race, ethnicity, gender, sexuality, nationality—represented by their various embodiments and situated lifeworlds. *Sense8* thus presents an "astonishing exploration of trans phenomenology" (Bailey et al. 2017: 79), achieving a unique televisual language that aestheticizes transgender subjectivity as both a narrative and pedagogic form.

Sense8 also displays the Wachowskis' "insatiable appetite for genre" (Li 2017) while staging a confrontation with the obstacles of formalized space and time—how they order the senses, producing divisions, categories, provisional forms, lines of demarcation we cannot feel across. Like the digital sharing technologies echoed by its affective network, *Sense8* aims to "annihilate time and space" (Bailey et al. 2017: 83) as they are generically arranged. The series' global shooting schedule—one of the most ambitious in television history—necessitates a direct engagement with both pace and place as obstacles to its own production. *Sense8*'s textual composition is arrayed against these same barriers: formally in its mashups of genre and style, narratively in the speed of its thriller plot, geographically in its denial of national borders, and politically in its flouting of sex and gender normativities. Dislodging its characters from linear time and space, *Sense8* scrambles how gender and race are plotted. For example, Nomi's transgender identity is communicated outside of the medico-juridical narrative of "sex change" and its hopeless entrapment in the "wrong body" (Carter 2013: 133), while Sun/Capheus often form a combinatory character that collapses the developmental hierarchy established between East Asia and East Africa. Although it suspends racial and linguistic differences to establish the immediate intimacy of its psychic connections, it narratively transposes the species logic of race into the new kinship formation of the psychic cluster, breaking with the structure of race as it is predetermined under modernity. *Sense8*'s slow motion action sequences and cluster orgies suspend colonial temporality, inducting us into an "ecstatic time" (Muñoz 2009: 32) in which race cannot limit the body's position in or access to the world, to sensations, to other bodies. A utopian response to modernity's concretized orders of experience, *Sense8* widens our proprioceptive positions, giving us the sensations of a thickened "now" and a multiplied "here." Resisting realism's totalizing account of the present, *Sense8* also helps us feel a "then and there" (Muñoz 2009: 1) with subjunctive immediacy—as if they were already happening.

The title of S01:E01, "Limbic Resonance," refers to the speculative limbic system that, when activated, gives the sensates their enhanced awareness in illustration of a psychiatric theory that the human limbic system is not self-contained, but extends beyond the edges of the body through affect and is impacted by other bodies in proximity (Lewis et al. 2002). As the sensate cluster activates, racialized and gendered geographies fold together as the sensates' previously separate worlds compress, pulling them and us into the "centripetal complexity" (Mittell 2013: 52) of new and inescapable sensations. Space and time contract rapidly as the sensates' enhanced sensories gather into a collective point of immediacy. In the case of the show's characterization, that point is its central transgender figure, Nomi. The opening credits both begin and end in San Francisco, an overtly queer/trans space (the Gay Beach section of Dolores Park and San Francisco Pride are both depicted) where Nomi is physically located. Nomi thus occupies the nucleus of the sensate cluster as a point of attachment for the growth of its matrix, which extends outward in multiple facets as the sensates in her cluster are born. In ancient Greek, the name "Nomi" is phonologically equivalent to γνώμη (gnome), meaning "to know." The name indicates "a means of knowing, a mark [and] an organ by which one knows, the mind" (Liddle 2002: 166).

The name "Nomi" can be translated as "one who is marked by knowledge" by possessing an organ of special insight. For Nomi, this organ is her sensate awareness, which is represented as a speculative extension of her transsubjectivity—a feeling that *something is there* that others cannot perceive. Nomi's central presence in the series is an initiatory lesson for how *Sense8* will require both its characters and audiences to sense differently. In becoming sensate, Nomi and her cluster will become a "we"—in other words, a "no me." A sensate is therefore "one who knows they are not one."

S01 of *Sense8* spends the bulk of its time emphasizing the provisionality of perception, showing viewers how to engage with its unique aesthetic language. Intuitive parallel editing and traveling sounds de-center our notions of spatiality, causality, and discrete embodiment. New surfaces condense across time, space, and genre, multiplying our proprioceptive lenses. We learn to understand when a body in the frame is physically or psychically present (or both), to deduce who is visible/audible to whom, and to notice details in the surround (setting, time of day/night, lighting, auditory cues) to remember where each character is materially located. As the cluster event catalyzes, sensations begin to mix among the characters' various locations: Will, in Chicago, hears Riley's DJ set in London; Kala, in Mumbai, feels the rain in Berlin—where Wolfgang is drinking coffee;

a chicken flies from Capheus's bus in Nairobi and lands on Sun's desk in her office in Seoul. These sensationally pedagogic moments combine with *Sense8*'s many dialogic meditations on art to incite a different common sense: rather than positing a utopian world in which race, gender, and the body are merely transcended into a purely post-racial humanism, *Sense8* preserves race as a sense of shared speciation, offering us an "empathetic diversity" (Lothian 2016: 94) of interwoven, interdependent sensations within its sensate collectivity.

Most negative criticism of *Sense8* has focused on the manner in which it embeds its sensate characters in culturally-specific narratives. Claire Light writes that "*Sense8*'s depiction of life in non-western countries is built out of stereotypes ... suffused with tourist-board clichés" (2015). The series does indeed portray its characters of color in recognizably "ethnic" narratives: a Kenyan man struggles to acquire AIDS drugs for his dying mother; an Indian woman weighs a love marriage that feels unfulfilling; a Korean woman sacrifices herself to save her father's honor; a gay Mexican actor is closeted by the Latin culture of machismo. *Sense8* mobilizes these stereotypes through its larger assertion of "racial nationalism" (Bailey et al. 2017: 81), a conceit the series uses as shorthand to build quickly toward the global shape of its cluster formation.

These racialized scripts make the series' attempt at a global address more cognizable to white and Western viewers, but they also pose a larger analytical value to the text, which questions how genre attributes fixed values to race, gender, and location. Much like Violet in the Wachowskis' first film, *Bound* (1996), or like Neo in *The Matrix* (1999), the sensates are embedded in generic worlds that operate as constructs for theirs and the audience's perceptions: Nomi inhabits a hacker thriller, Lito a telenovela, Capheus an action movie, Wolfgang a heist film, Will a cop show, Sun a martial arts film, Kala a Bollywood romance, and Riley a maternal melodrama. These stock narratives and their highly identifiable, ethnically specific geographies are necessary to *Sense8*'s central conceit—an exploration of how static forms limit which stories can be told and which modes of life can thus become cognizable to others. However, this cannot be accomplished without citing the very genres and scripts it hopes to complicate, resulting in a scenario in which the sensates are "trapped in the exact social circumstances stereotypically assigned to their races" (Kessler 2017). *Sense8* thus mobilizes race, gender, and nationality as stereotypic forms of personhood even as it metanarratively comments on them as constructs—a bimodal strategy the series forces both its characters and audience to straddle. *Sense8* therefore becomes increasingly dynamic to the extent that it intersectionally punctures its generic settings, transferring the sensates across their artificially bounded experiences as they sensorially interface.

Although it does engage with the medical history of eugenics directed at both transgender and of color bodies, *Sense8* is ultimately more interested in displacing or transposing race into other forms than directly confronting it. This is readable even in its linguistic design, which relies heavily on a monolingual deployment of English dialogue between characters. Transcultural interaction between the sensates is often softened by the prosthetic use of English, a strategy ostensibly intended to make Anglophone viewers more comfortable and to bring down the costs of translation in the production schedule. By suggesting that the sensates share English as a sort of psychic "tongue" (Keegan 2016) that transcends their ethnically specific cultures, *Sense8* inadvertently reifies the lingual effects of global colonization. Linguistic friction—the way language difference sticks in the engine of secular humanism—is largely evacuated through the use of English as a universal language. There *are* scenes in which sensate characters notice that they can use and/or understand each others' native speech. This most notably takes place between Sun and Capheus (Sun seems surprised to meet a Black man who speaks Korean, to which Capheus replies, "You speak Swahili?") and is humorously referenced in S02 when Nomi points out that she can speak "seven languages ... and some shitty French from high school!" However, these moments cannot be structurally sustained and consistently collapse into accented English, maintaining Anglophone viewers' sense that some of the sensates are "foreign." *Sense8* would likely have been impossible to make or consume without some standardization of linguistic format. However, were it to accurately reflect the global population, over half of its characters would be Asian and the cluster would speak Mandarin, rather than English. The series' language design thus illustrates how media attempting to represent the "virtual community" (Shaw 2017) of a new globalism can remain structurally tethered to Western presumptions.

Despite these limitations, *Sense8* is undoubtedly a televisual triumph, presenting viewers with a cinematic grandeur, global diversity, and technical sophistication that have expanded, even transcended, the grammar of the medium itself. In addition, although it represents a break with Hollywood, the series is nonetheless a decidedly Wachowskian text. There is the same colossal thematic ambition, the same concern with closed worlds and their ethical consequences, the same pressure against dictated form, the same interest in speculating an after to our gendered and racial constructs. By industry standards, the series is simply the most recent in the Wachowskis' long history of aesthetically daring, challenging-to-market works. Yet, what makes the show so compelling—and so reflective of its time—is its immersive, hopeful immediacy: *Sense8*'s speculative stretch is ultimately an inner one. Rather than pushing its vision into a distant future, the series turns subjunctivity inward, asking how we might arrive at our senses, and thus the lives of others, differently. In all its incompleteness, *Sense8*'s utopianism is nonetheless the speculative sensation that things could already be moving toward that empathetic field it asks us to touch within and between ourselves. To feel beyond the "prison house" (Muñoz 2009: 1) of

FIGURE 12.1 *Our shared moment in* Sense8, *occupied so fully together that we burst the present world's seams.*

the here and now is not to turn toward some far-off place, but to occupy our shared moment so fully together that we burst the present world's seams (Figure 12.1).

Works Cited

Bailey, M., m. cárdenas, L. Horak, L. Kaimana, C. M. Keegan, G. Newman, R. Samer, and R. Sarkissian (2017), "Sense8 Roundtable", *Spectator*, 37 (2): 77–88.

Carter, J. (2013), "Embracing Transition, or Dancing in the Folds of Time," in A. Aizura and S. Stryker (eds.), *The Transgender Studies Reader* 2, 130–43, London: Routledge.

Jenkins, H. (2013), *Spreadable Media: Creating Value and Meaning in a Networked Culture*, New York: New York University Press.

Jones, K. (2017), "Netflix Cancels Two Beautifully Diverse Shows, and We're Not Happy About It," *Vox*, June 7. Available online: http://www.voxmagazine.com/arts/tv/netflix-cancels-two-beautifully-diverse-shows-and-we-re-not/article_c9316eee-4bb9-11e7-9ec1-73c316fc45b9.html.

Keegan, C. M. (2016), "Tongues without Bodies: The Wachowskis' *Sense8*," *TSQ: Transgender Studies Quarterly*, 3 (3–4): 605–10.

Keegan, C. M. (2018), *Lana and Lilly Wachowski: Sensing Transgender*, Urbana: University of Illinois Press.

Kessler, S. (2017), "Eleven TV Shows Professors Are Watching This Summer," *Public Books*, June 19. Available online: http://www.publicbooks.org/11-tv-shows-colleagues-watching-summer/.

Krishna, R. (2017), "Inside the Totally Insane and Sort of Effective Fan Campaign to Bring Back *Sense8*," *BuzzFeed*, June 29. Available online: https://www.buzzfeed.com/krishrach/how-fans-brought-sense-8-back.

Lewis, T., F. Amini, and R. Lannon ([2000] 2017), *A General Theory of Love*, New York: Random House.

Li, S. (2017), "Netflix by Netflix: 'On Sense8,'" *Los Angeles Review of Books*, May 16. Available online: https://lareviewofbooks.org/article/netflix-by-netflix-on-sense8/.

Liddle, H. G., and R. Scott (2002), *An Intermediate Greek-English Lexicon*, Oxford: Oxford University Press.

Light, C. (2015), "Sensate and the Failure of Global Imagination," *Nerds of Color*, June 10. Available online: http://thenerdsofcolor.org/2015/06/10/sense8-and-the-failure-of-global-imagination/.

Lothian, A. (2016), "*Sense8* and Utopian Connectivity," *Utopia Anniversary Symposium, Science Fiction Film and Television*, 9 (1): 93–5.

Mittell, J. (2015), *Complex TV: The Poetics of Contemporary Television Storytelling*, New York: New York University Press.

Mittell, J. (2013), "The Qualities of Complexity: Vast Versus Dense Seriality in Contemporary Television," in J. Jacobs and S. Peacock (eds.), *Television Aesthetics and Style*, 45–56, New York: Bloomsbury Academic.

Muñoz, J. E. (2009), *Cruising Utopia: The Then and There of Queer Futurity*, New York: New York University Press.

Rothman, J. (2015), "Sympathetic Sci-Fi," *The New Yorker*, July 14. Available online: http://www.newyorker.com/culture/cultural-comment/sympathetic-sci-fi.

Ryan, M. (2017), "A Troubling Trend in Cancellations: Are Inclusive Shows in Danger?," *Variety*, June 1. Available online: http://variety.com/2017/tv/opinion/canceled-shows-2017- sense8-get-down-underground-sweet-vicious-1202450885/.

Shaw, D. (2017), "*Sense8* and Sensibility: How a TV Series Is Transcending Geographical and Gender Borders," *The Conversation*, May 25. Available online: http://theconversa-tion.com/sense8-and-sensibility-how-a-tv-series-is-transcending-geographical-and-gen-der-borders-77377.

CONTRIBUTORS

Luis Freijo is a doctoral researcher in the Department of Film and Creative Writing at the University of Birmingham and holds an AHRC-funded Midlands4Cities Doctoral Scholarship. His research expertise is in the dynamics of World Cinema as it relates to genre studies and, in particular, the global Western. He has published widely in English and Spanish on classic Hollywood cinema, European filmmakers and stars, and American television series. He has recently coauthored books on *Grupo salvaje* (2019), *Alien* (2019), *Los siete magníficos* (2020), and *El apartamento* (2020) and contributed chapters on the relation between genre filmmaking and politics to *The Routledge Companion to European Cinema* (2021) and *Screening the Crisis: U.S. Cinema and Social Change in the 21st Century* (2021).

Rosalind Galt is professor of Film Studies at King's College London. She is the coauthor with Karl Schoonover of *Queer Cinema in the World* (2016), author of *Pretty: Film and the Decorative Image* (2011) and *The New European Cinema: Redrawing the Map* (2006), and coeditor of *Global Art Cinema: New Theories and Histories* (2010). Her research addresses the relationships among history, cinematic style, gender, and sexuality, and she has published widely on international art cinemas, avant-garde histories, and feminist and queer film theory. She is currently completing a book on decolonization and the Malay vampire film.

Laura Horak is associate professor of Film Studies at Carleton University and director of the Transgender Media Portal (transgendermediaportal.org). She is author of *Girls Will Be Boys: Cross-Dressing Women, Lesbians, and American Cinema, 1908–1934* (2016) and coeditor of *Silent Cinema and the Politics of Space* (2014), *Unwatchable* (2019), and a special issue of *Somatechnics* on trans/cinematic/bodies.

Cáel M. Keegan is associate professor of Women, Gender, and Sexuality Studies at Grand Valley State University. He is author of *Lana and Lilly Wachowski: Sensing Transgender* (2018) and has published multiple journal articles on queer/transgender theory and the politics of media aesthetics in *Genders*, *Queer Studies in Media and Popular Culture*, *MedieKultur*, *Transgender Studies Quarterly*, *Social Alternatives*, and the *Journal of*

Homosexuality. He is special editor for Arts and Culture at *Transgender Studies Quarterly* and senior cochair of the Queer and Trans Caucus of the Society for Cinema and Media Studies.

John Lessard is associate professor of English and Film Studies at the University of the Pacific. His publications include work on East German cinema, phenomenology, and queer culture. Forthcoming publications include essays on East German amateur film, on transnational slash in *Queer/Adaptation*, and a monograph on the maternal body entitled *Intimacy and Alienation: Gender and Sexuality in East German Film* (2018). He is currently researching a monograph on amateur film culture in the former GDR.

Amanda D. Lotz is a professor and leader of the Transforming Media Industries research project in the Digital Media Research Centre at Queensland University of Technology. She is the author, coauthor, or editor of nine books that explore television and media industries including *We Now Disrupt This Broadcast: How Cable Transformed Television and the Internet Revolutionized It All* (2018), *The Television Will Be Revolutionized* (2007), and *Portals: A Treatise on Internet-Distributed Television* (2017).

So Mayer is the author of *A Nazi Word for a Nazi Thing* (2020), an essay on queer visual cultures against fascisms, as well as three books and three edited collections on film feminisms. They have written for *Film Quarterly*, the Criterion Collection, the *Observer*, and for magazines such as *Sight & Sound*, the *White Review*, and *Literal*, among others. They work with queer feminist film curation collective Club des Femmes, and program for Queer Lisboa (2021–). So is a cofounder of industry campaigners Raising Films, a bookseller at Burley Fisher Books, and a poet.

Will McKeown is a researcher at the University of Birmingham. His research is focused on the theory and practice of self-sacrifice, particularly in the context of neoliberalism and his thesis is concerned with the prevalence of the sequel in contemporary screen media. He has published articles on Korean cinema in *New Cinemas* and on Catalan cinema in *Horror Studies*.

Rox Samer is assistant professor of Screen Studies in Clark University's Department of Visual and Performing Arts. They are the author of *Lesbian Potentiality and Feminist Media in the 1970s* (forthcoming) as well as the editor of a special issue of *Spectator* dedicated to the study of transgender media (Fall 2017), which included an early scholarly roundtable on *Sense8*. They are currently working on a documentary film, *Tip/Alli*, on the work, life, and influence of feminist science fiction author James Tiptree Jr. (aka Alice B. Sheldon, 1915–1987).

Zoë Shacklock is a lecturer in Film Studies at the University of St Andrews. Her research explores the aesthetics and affects of contemporary narrative television, with a focus on questions of medium specificity, the body and embodied spectatorship, gender and sexuality, and structures of empathy. She has published on the series *Game of Thrones*, *Orphan Black*, and *Outlander*. Her forthcoming monograph explores the centrality of the body within contemporary "quality television," using the framework of kinesthesia to suggest that bodily spectacle within these prestige programs remains grounded within quintessentially televisual features, such as intimacy, community, empathy, and the structures of serial narration.

Deborah Shaw is professor in Film and Screen Studies at the University of Portsmouth, UK. Her research interests include transnational film theory and Latin American cinema, and she has published widely in these areas. She is the founding coeditor of the Routledge journal *Transnational Cinemas* (*Transnational Screens* from 2019), and her books include *Contemporary Latin American Cinema: Ten Key Films* (2003), *The Three Amigos: The Transnational Filmmaking of Guillermo del Toro, Alejandro González Iñárritu, and Alfonso Cuarón* (2013), *The Transnational Fantasies of Guillermo del Toro* (coedited with Ann Davies and Dolores Tierney, 2014), and *Latin American Women Filmmakers: Production, Politics, Poetics* (coedited with Deborah Martin, 2017).

Rob Stone is professor of Film Studies at the University of Birmingham, UK, where he codirects B-Film: The Birmingham Centre for Film Studies. He has published on Spanish, Basque, Cuban, European, independent American, and World Cinema and is the author of *Spanish Cinema* (2001), *The Wounded Throat: Flamenco in the Works of Federico Garcia Lorca and Carlos Saura* (2004), *Julio Medem* (2007), and *Walk, Don't Run: The Cinema of Richard Linklater* (2013; 2nd edn, 2018). He also coauthored *Basque Cinema: A Cultural and Political History* and *Cine Vasco* (with María Pilar Rodríguez, 2016), and coedited *The Unsilvered Screen: Surrealism on Film* (2007), *Screening Songs in Hispanic and Lusophone Cinema* (2013), *A Companion to Luis Buñuel* (2013), *Screening European Heritage* (2016), and *The Routledge Companion to World Cinema* (2018).

James Walters is Reader in Film and Television at the University of Birmingham. His books include *Alternative Worlds in Hollywood Cinema* (2008), *Film Moments* (with Tom Brown, 2010), *Fantasy Film* (2011), the BFI TV Classic on *The Thick of It* (2016), and *Television Performance* (with Lucy Fife Donaldson, 2019).

INDEX

activism 2, 5, 26, 85, 90, 172
   choreography as activism 27, 186–8
   fan activism 208, 209, 212
   hacktivism 8, 160, 163, 188
   online activism 26
   pleasure activism 177–94
   queer activism 90, 103, 147
   queer women of color activism 181
Agyeman, Freema. *See* Amanita
Ahmanson-Lovelace Brain Mapping Center 137
AIDS 8, 65, 89, 145, 213, 223
al Mansour, Haifaa 5
Altered Carbon 37
Amanita 8, 12, 13, 14, 19, 23, 46, 47, 66–8, 77–9, 82–4, 89, 96, 99, 102, 103, 112, 116, 127, 130, 136, 147, 156, 164, 180–2, 201, 202, 212
   as a Black lesbian 67
Ameen, Aml. *See* Capheus
Amsterdam 3, 82, 111, 124, 132
Anarchos Productions 33
Andrews, Naveen. *See* Jonas
Angelica 9, 71, 84, 89, 105, 110, 132, 142, 166–8, 170–1, 174
   and birth of the cluster 73–6, 84, 107, 184
   as a cluster-mother 160
   and religion 75, 110
Anglocentrism 9, 23, 125, 212
Annihilation 37
Aoki, Steve 45, 136
Apsara Engine 178, 182
Archipelago 9, 71, 75, 76, 135
art-house cinema 9
audience
   Anglophone viewers 53, 224
   binge viewing 34, 45, 47, 60–1, 208

camera as audience 16
community of viewers 49
digital viewers 79
international viewers 43, 208
modern audience 126
multinational audience 36, 37, 207
queer audiences 90
streaming audiences 48
viewer's gaze 61
viewership 35, 39, 208, 220
viewing 46–7
Western audiences 9, 54
See also Netflix
auteurism 2, 9, 43
   transgender auteurs 221
authenticity 13, 52, 57, 68, 142, 143, 202, 203, 212

"Back Where I Belong" 80
Bae Doona. *See* Sun
Baumbach, Noah 5
Bausch, Pina 180
Bautista, Ness. *See* Diego
Bello, Valeria. *See* Lila
Berlin 2, 7, 11, 15, 62, 85, 97, 125–8, 130, 131, 135, 141–4, 148, 150, 159, 161, 179, 191, 199, 223
Best Exotic Marigold Hotel, The 10
binary 18, 67, 77, 95, 159
   non-binary 190
   self-other binary 160
Biological Preservation Organization. *See* BPO
birth 6, 15, 75, 110, 160, 166–8, 172–4
   birth of the cluster 9
   church and birth 72
   Christian evangelical analogy 73

INDEX

sensate's birth 137, 184
  See also Angelica
Black Lives Matter 184, 185
  copaganda 184, 188, 190
Black Mirror 37
Black Mirror: Bandersnatch 43
Blaxploitation 200
Bloodline 36
body
  body politic 190, 191
  body-swapping 1, 10, 14, 15, 17
  fragmented image of the body 166
  male bodies 147
  propre (body proper) 106
  suffering body 73
  viewer's body 190
Boksuneun naui geot (Sympathy for Mr. Vengeance) 9
Bollywood 10, 12, 68, 179, 223
Bound 184, 192, 223
BPO 1, 7, 8, 35, 76–7, 95, 102, 109, 111–13, 115, 118, 148, 149, 151–4, 156–7, 162–5, 201, 220
Bride and Prejudice 179
Bright 37
Brooklyn Nine-Nine 3. *See also* fanbase
Bug 8, 12, 82, 83, 102, 124, 133, 164, 188

cantaores 134
  poet-*cantaor* 134
cante jondo (flamenco deep song) 123
cante universal (universal song) 123
Capheus 8, 12, 17, 19, 20, 23, 24, 50, 51, 82, 96, 100, 103, 125, 127–30, 133, 137, 144–5, 147, 150, 154–6, 161, 164, 170–3, 181, 201, 221, 223–4
  and politics 8, 145, 155, 156
cartography 21, 154, 178–9, 186
  trans cartography 178
Chazelle, Damien 5
Chicago 2, 8, 9, 24, 62, 96, 125, 127, 141, 150, 161, 184, 223
  as a policed space 147, 148, 150, 151, 184–5

choreography 15, 27, 45, 89, 177–80, 186–93
  choreography as activist techniques 127, 86
  fight choreography 187, 192, 193
  martial arts choreography 193
  sexual choreography 177, 180, 187, 188, 190–3
  See also editing; montage
choreopolitics 186, 188–90, 192, 193
Chuck 3. *See also* fanbase
cis
  capitalist cisheteropatriarchy 214
  cis lesbian 5
  cis-washing 78
  supremacist cis heteronormativity 185
cityspace 141–50, 156
  global city 151–7
City We Became, The 183
Clayton, Jamie 5, 8, 10, 13, 19, 213
  See Nomi
Cloud Atlas 9, 107, 191, 220
Cloverfield Paradox, The 37
Club de Cuervos 36
cluster
  birth-cluster 74
  erotopolitics of the cluster 115, 119
  as an intimate community 27
  queerness of the cluster 103
  See also connectivity; synchronicity
Coffy 200
Colors of Change Hollywood 184, 186
Community 3. *See also* fanbase
community
  and connectedness 15
  empathetic community 159
  evolution of community 52
  political community 106, 117
  vision of community 47
  See also cluster
community of citizens 130
community of sentiment 21, 124, 129, 130, 138
connectivity 9, 22, 159, 160, 197, 198, 200, 207, 212, 213
  global connectivity 53, 197, 202, 205, 213, 215

interconnectivity 2
language of 207
cosmopolitanism
  cosmopolitan politics 154
  cultural cosmopolitanism 152, 153
  frontier cosmopolitanism 141–2, 152, 153, 156–7
  moral cosmopolitanism 152, 153, 155
  multinational cosmopolitanism 37
  political-legal cosmopolitanism 152, 153
  unethical cosmopolitanism 155
  See also cityspace
COVID-19 198, 212, 213
Cox, Laverne 13
credits. *See* title sequence
Cuarón, Alfonso 5

Daniela 8, 20, 24, 90, 101, 102, 103, 125, 133, 142, 143, 151, 163, 164
Dark 54
Dawn of the Planet of the Apes 180
Deadwood 3. *See also* fanbase
Dee Rees 5
"Demons" 136
Desai, Tina. *See* Kala
Designated Survivor 5
Dickensian 12
diegetic
  diegetic and extra-diegetic songs 135
  diegetic and non-diegetic sources 136
  diegetic polycule 101
  extra-diegetic soundtrack 128
Diego 8, 147, 148, 184
Disclosure 19
Double Dare 191
Downton Abbey 12
Dregorius, Jade Eleena 191
Duck Soup 16
DuVernay, Ava 5
dystopia 1, 180, 197, 198, 200

Eddy, The 5
editing 4, 15–17, 65, 96–9, 114, 136, 148, 154, 155, 161, 187, 189, 190, 193, 198, 199, 220, 222

  See also choreography; montage
empathy
  radical empathy 1, 4–6, 14, 15, 26, 75, 84, 123, 124, 130, 131, 135–7, 161, 165, 168, 169, 173
  in relation to spectatorship 4, 124
  See also cluster
ethnicity 80, 91, 93, 153, 221, 223, 224
  See also race
"Experience" 23
Extinction 37

Facchini, Lila. *See* Lila
fanbase
  fan activism 209, 212
  fan campaigns 3
  fan communities 37, 47
  fandom 28, 131, 197–8, 199, 200, 203–13
  fanvid 199
  See also Netflix
"Feeling Good" 97, 137, 199
Felix 8, 78, 82, 83, 84, 114, 143, 144, 164
feminism 73, 92, 95, 131, 146, 181, 187, 190, 193
Fincher, David 5, 34
Flandersui gae (Barking Dogs Never Bite) 9
flashbacks 9, 105, 128, 166
4 Non Blondes 75, 125, 199, 201
Foxy Brown 200
frontier
  cities as a frontier spaces 27, 150, 151, 156
  frontier cosmopolitanism 141, 142, 152, 153, 156–7
  global frontier space 149, 152
  urban frontier 149, 151
  See also cityspaces
Fukunaga, Cary 5

García Lorca, Federico 123–4, 130, 134–5, 138
gay
  gay action film star 4, 8, 12, 25, 223
  gay cinema 95

gay marriage 92, 94
  See also Lito
gaze
  female gaze 11, 97
  male gaze 11, 97, 148, 149
  sexual gaze 148
  tourist gaze 143, 148, 149
  viewer's gaze 61
gender
  gender construction 16
  gender discrimination 145
  gender identities 4
  gender oppression 150
  gender performativity 147
  gender reassignment 8, 137
  heteronormative gender binary 77
  liberatory gender 188
Gisaengchung (Parasite) 9
GLAAD 2, 188, 219
Glass, Dan 6
globalisation
  global connection 52
  global distribution 1, 52, 152
  global imagination 25, 52, 91
  global simultaneity 52, 220
  global village 54
Gurry, Christopher. *See* Puck
Gwoemul (The Host) 9

Hail Satan? 85, 86
"Hallelujah" 83, 84, 102, 136, 213
"Hands Up" 179
Hannah, Daryl. *See* Angelica
Harding, Matthew 128, 129
Hastings, Reed 32, 34, 41–2, 54, 207–8, 219
HBO 3, 35, 58, 210
Hemlock Grove 34, 35
Hemon, Aleksandar 6
heteronormativity 12, 19, 20, 27, 67, 92, 99, 142
  heteronormative gender binary 77
  heteronormative identities 16, 92
  heteronormative models 77
  white supremacist cis heteronormativity 185

Hernando 8, 14, 20, 22, 23, 79, 83, 90, 100, 101, 103, 125, 133, 142, 164, 177, 180–2, 209
Herrera, Alfonso. *See* Hernando
heterotopia 178
"Hollywood-fu" 192
"Home We'll Go (Take My Hand)" 136
homophobia 1, 12, 22, 66, 78, 103, 130, 143, 151, 157, 163, 192
Homo sapiens 42, 47, 111, 164
Homo sensorium 9, 19, 42, 47, 111, 116, 164
  post-racial humanism 223
  See also sensate
homosexuality 20, 78, 82, 123, 130, 134, 142, 151
  See gay; queer
House of Cards 5, 32–5, 38, 46, 69, 70
"Huff + Puff" 136, 179
Hung 13

Ibarra, Eréndira. *See* Daniela
identity
  cis- and/or hetero-normative identities 16
  collective identity 16, 134, 162, 185
  multiplicitous identity 170
  self-identity 161
  representations of identity 161
"I'd Love to Change the World" 136, 179, 198
"I Feel You" 132, 133
Imitation Game, The 12
Irishman, The 5
It's a Wonderful Life 82, 103

Jela 9, 164, 213
Jetée, La 108
Jonas 6, 9, 25, 45, 74, 80, 89, 90, 107, 113, 135, 162, 165, 184, 185
jouissance 105–6, 109, 113, 118
  See also sexuality
"Juego y teoría del duende" (Play and Theory of *duende*) 123
Jupiter Ascending 9

Kala 7–12, 20, 23–5, 45, 50, 51, 68, 71, 82–4, 90, 97, 98, 101, 109, 114, 125–30, 135–7, 144, 150, 151, 154–6, 160, 171–3, 179, 199, 223
  and religion 11, 45, 71, 97, 151
kineticism 53
Klimek, Johnny 128
Kohli, Purab. *See* Rajan
Kûki ningyô (Air Doll) 9

language
  English as default language 65
  monolingualism 53
  multilingualism 52, 54
  native language 65, 212
  and virtual community 130, 224
LasTesis 131
Lee, Spike 5
LGBTQ 2, 4, 21, 23, 71–2, 76–8, 80, 86, 147, 181, 219
  See also Pride
Lila 9, 113, 114, 148, 153, 191, 201
Lionheart 50
Lito 4–16, 20, 22–5, 45, 46, 49, 50, 65, 72, 79, 80–4, 90, 97, 99, 100–3, 125, 127, 130, 132–4, 136, 137, 142, 143, 145, 147, 148, 151, 154, 160, 163, 169, 179–83, 185, 187, 191, 192, 209, 223
  and Pride 4–6, 72, 79–80
London 2, 8, 62, 96, 125–8, 131, 141, 148, 150, 159, 170, 201, 223
L Word, The 5
L Word: Generation Q, The 5
LYRIC 181

Mad Men 37
MaestraPeace Mural 181
Magnolia 126
Maina, Mumbi. *See* Zakia
Man at the Crossroads 50
Maniac 5
Mann, Terrence. *See* Whispers
Marco Polo 35, 36
Marriage Story 5
masculinity
  Mexican masculinity 80
  toxic masculinity 20, 184
  traditional male power 147
  white male hero 43, 149
  white masculinity, 184, 185
matriarchy 75
Matrix, The 18, 184, 187, 220, 223
Matrix Reloaded, The 189
Mauff, Max. *See* Felix
McCoy, Sylvester. *See* Old Man of Hoy
McTeigue, James 6
Mexico City 2, 4, 5, 8, 14, 49, 62, 75, 79, 103, 130, 125, 127, 131, 136, 141–6, 151, 208
  Diego Rivera museum 14, 49, 50, 97
Middleton, Tuppence. *See* Riley
Mindhunter 5
mirror stage 16, 166, 168–72, 174
Mission Local 181
Mitchell, David 6, 107
monogamy 23, 82, 92, 95–6, 100–2, 144
  nonmonogamy 90, 92, 93, 94
  See also polyamory
montage 15, 52, 54, 64, 83, 99, 101, 116, 124, 135, 199, 201, 202, 206, 212–13
  birth montage 15, 160
  credits montage 53–4, 62
  montage in S02:E01 15, 45, 83–4, 97, 101, 102, 135, 137, 141
  musical montage 45, 82, 84, 124, 135, 137, 199, 213
  queer aesthetic montage 201
  of the sensates' birthday celebrations 45, 206
  See also editing
Mounsey, Gabriel 132
Mudbound 5
multiculturalism 52, 76–7, 84
  colonial concept of multiculturalism 91
  naive multiculturalism 200
multiplicity 27, 53, 124, 128, 129, 130, 134, 136–8, 150, 151, 161, 169–71
Mumbai 3, 7, 11, 15, 50, 62, 97, 126, 127, 128, 141, 144, 145, 150, 151, 199, 222

Mun 8, 20, 23, 25, 133, 165, 191
music 45, 62, 71, 74, 82, 83, 96, 123–38
  diegetic songs 124, 128
  Emmy nomination 2
  English-language music 153
  extra-diegetic songs 135
  music as religion 75–6, 86
  universal song 123–5, 135–6
  See also montage; synchronicity
musicality 123–4, 130, 134, 136, 138
  See also synchronicity
mythology 27, 49, 71–3, 124
  birth myths 72, 75
  myth of gentrification 143
  myth of the urban space 143
  See also religion

Nairobi 3, 8, 15, 50, 62, 125, 127, 141, 144–6, 150, 154, 156, 159, 161, 192, 206, 223
Naples 132, 133, 148, 149, 156, 183
Nappily Ever After 5
Narcos 36, 60
Nashville 3. *See also* fanbase
Nerds of Color 53, 179
Netflix
  autocue 45
  budgets of 34–8
  cancellation of *Sense8* 2, 4, 9, 14, 219
  evolutionary discourse 27, 42, 44, 47
  global medium 43, 54
  global rights 32–4
  global viewer 1, 32, 36–7, 208
  internet-distribution 31, 32, 36, 38
  linear television 38, 39, 42, 55
  Netflix Film Club 187
  Netflix library 32–3, 35–6, 38–9
  subscriber-funded 31, 32, 38
  taste communities 36, 37, 211
  See also audiences; fanbase; television
Nightcrawler 180
Night Watch, The 111

Nomi 5, 7–9, 12, 13, 17, 19, 20, 23–5, 45–51, 66–8, 71, 77–80, 82–4, 89, 90, 96, 97, 99, 100, 102, 103, 112, 116, 125–30, 132–7, 147, 156, 160, 162–5, 170, 179–82, 185, 188, 189, 201, 202, 212, 213, 221, 222–4
  and activism 5, 77, 147, 163, 188
  as a transgender female 5, 8, 13, 25, 77, 147, 181, 185, 189, 221, 222
"Nothing Matters When We're Dancing" 103, 130
nudity 10, 11, 148, 180

OA, The 37
Occupy 154, 185
Ogola, Paul. *See* Jela
Old Man of Hoy 9, 76, 132
Onwumere, Toby. *See* Capheus
Orange Is the New Black 13, 25, 32, 60, 61, 69, 70
orgy
  clusterfuck 27, 105, 108, 109, 115–18
  ecstasy 27, 94, 101, 106, 177, 180, 193, 201
  final orgy 23, 101, 141, 156
  first orgy 200
  orgiastic imagery 109
  polysexual orgy 99, 100
  telepathicorgy 14, 21, 27, 108, 110, 171
  See also sexuality
Orlando Pulse massacre 219
other
  apparitional other 110
  death of the other 111–13
  encountering the other 154
  nonconforming others 73
  othered 162
  self-other binary 160
  sense of otherness 67
  songs of oppressed others 123
  touch of the other 112
  understanding of the other 165
Our Virgin of Guadalupe 75
overworld 150–3
Ozark 61

pansexual 8, 20, 114
Paris 23, 103, 130, 131, 141, 148, 149, 156
  Eiffel Tower 13, 149, 157, 183, 212
Paris Is Burning 81
pastiche 10–14, 179, 192
patriarchy 73, 164, 165, 172, 173
  cisheteropatriarchy 213
Pew Research Centre (The Global Divide on Homosexuality) 78
physicality 16, 17, 49, 169
Playing For Change 129, 130
"Poema doble del Lago Edén" (Double Poem of Lake Eden) 123
"poeta cuenta la verdad, El" (The Poet Tells The Truth) 123
"poeta en Nueva York, Un" (Poet in New York) 123
poly
  polycentrism 102, 180
  poly imaginary 90, 93, 99
  polyqueer 93
  poly sexualities 92
  as a televisual form 90
  See also cluster
polyamory 22, 82, 90, 92, 93, 103, 116, 204
polyglotism 23, 29
polynormativity 93
Pose 81
postmodernism 12, 14
post-truth 159, 164, 165, 172
post-truth narratives 165, 172, 174
Pride
  LGBTQ Pride 77–80, 219
  political history 78
  Pride flag 147
  Pride as a protest 178
  as a religious celebration 72, 77–9
  San Francisco 78, 84, 89, 202, 222
  São Paulo 4, 6, 8, 72, 79–80
  Vancouver 81
Puck 9, 84, 132, 201
pugilonormativity 192

quantum 23, 190
quantum entanglement 105

queer
  global queer 79, 200
  as an ideality 22
  notion of the chosen family 81
  queer aesthetic 19, 201
  queer congregation 72, 79
  queer/ed femininity 182, 183
  queer eroticism 27
  queer identities 62, 71, 99
  queer kinesthesia 187
  queer phenomenology 187
  queer polyamory 82
  queer polycule 90
  queer spectators 200
  queer subjectivity 14–15
  queer throuple 82
  queer utopia 17, 18–19, 21, 22, 200–1
  promiscuous queer 93
  social solidarity 89
  See also activism
queerness 18, 19, 22, 23, 50, 90, 91, 93, 94, 97, 103, 154, 182, 187–8, 221
'Quiero llorar porque me da la gana' (I want to cry because I feel like it) 123

race
  pastiche of race 11
  race/ethnicity 93
  racial nationalism 223
  representations of race 25, 91
  as a stereotype 200, 223
  structure of race 221
  See also ethnicity
racism
  racist anti-urbanism 1, 90, 109, 183, 213
  toxicity of racism 109
Rajan 8, 11, 23, 82, 83, 90, 97, 98, 101, 114, 133, 144, 154, 155, 160, 164, 179
"Rapist in Your Path!, A". *See* "Violador en Tu Camino, Un"
religion
  conservative Christian ethos 72, 78, 85, 86

Hinduism 82
Judeo-Christian religions 27, 71–3, 82, 86
as a negation of sexuality 73
religious fanaticism 151
See also mythology
'Réplica' (Rejoinder) 138
Reykjavik 2, 8, 62, 137, 141, 148, 159, 161
Opera House 172, 174
Riemelt, Max. *See* Wolfgang
Riley 8, 9, 12, 15–16, 19, 20, 23, 24, 71, 74–6, 79, 82, 83, 96, 99–101, 103, 109, 124–8, 130, 132–3, 135–7, 141, 148, 150, 160, 161, 163, 168, 170, 172–3, 179–81, 185, 189, 201, 223
as a cluster-mother 75, 127, 137, 223
and music 8, 74–6, 79, 96, 128, 130–3, 136, 148, 172, 179, 201, 223
Rite of Spring 180
Roma 5
Rose, Charlene 179
Run Lola Run 107
Russian Doll 43

S01:E01 "Limbic Resonance" 1, 14, 19, 23, 26, 74, 89, 96, 110, 128, 141, 144, 154, 170, 184, 202, 222
S01:E02 "I Am Also A We" 16, 77, 80, 90, 97, 143, 202
S01:E03 "Smart Money's on the Skinny Bitch" 7, 96, 143, 154, 161
S01:E04 "What's Going On?" 6, 45, 96, 125, 132, 144, 199, 201
S01:E05 "Art is Like Religion" 16, 23, 26, 45, 97, 143, 145, 147, 161, 169
S01:E06 "Demons" 11, 14, 15, 45, 98, 116, 137
S01:E07 "WWN Double D?" 17, 45, 46
S01:E08 "We Will All Be Judged by the Courage of Our Hearts" 66, 79
S01:E09 "Death Doesn't Let You Say Goodbye" 14, 46, 49, 86, 96
S01:E10 "What Is Human?" 6, 15, 89, 110, 137, 160, 163, 172
S01:E11 "Just Turn the Wheel and the Future Changes" 97, 163
S01:E12 "I Can't Leave Her" 11, 132, 137, 168
S02:E01 "Happy Fucking New Year" 5, 15, 22, 45, 72, 81, 82, 97–100, 102, 116, 135–6, 179, 181, 183, 198–9, 206, 213
S02:E02 "Who Am I?" 47, 79, 81, 116, 124
S02:E03 "Obligate Mutualisms" 102, 105, 107, 112–13, 116
S02:E04 "Polyphony" 6, 45
S02:E05 "Fear Never Fixed Anything" 12, 75, 102, 132, 163
S02:E06 "Isolated Above, Connected Below" 6, 79, 98
S02:E07 "I Have No Room in My Heart for Hate" 155
S02:E08 "All I Want Now Is One More Bullet" 191
S02:E09 "What Family Actually Means" 184
S02:E10 "If All the World's a Stage, Identity Is Nothing But a Costume" 154
S02:E11 "You Want a War?" 3, 5, 9, 102, 127
S02:E12 "Amor Vincit Omnia" 3, 5, 15, 23, 24, 26, 77, 82, 98, 101, 103, 111, 116, 127, 132, 148, 153, 157, 183, 198, 206, 212
San Francisco 2, 8, 9, 12, 14, 17, 50, 62, 66, 84, 89, 100, 103, 125, 127, 136, 141, 147, 151, 181, 202, 222
opening sequence 63
queer/trans space 78, 222
See also Pride; The Women's Building
San Francisco Gay Men's Choir 84, 103, 136
Sara 8, 112, 148, 184, 185
"*Save Me*" 126
science-fiction 1, 2, 6, 14, 19, 20, 21, 25, 26, 35, 37, 92, 193, 198, 200–2, 210, 219
science-fictional imaginary 91
science-fictional sensates 198

INDEX

Scorsese, Martin 5
self-sacrifice 159–74
   fetishization of survival 167–8
   See also Angelica
sensate
   global digital connectivity 200, 202
   human-sensate oppression 201
   sensorium pride 201
   See also homo sensorium
Sense8: Creating the World 15, 78
sensies. *See* fanbase
sensorium 89, 96, 97, 116, 117, 199–200, 204, 220, 223
Seoul 3, 7, 9, 15, 41, 62, 125, 127, 141, 145–7, 156, 170, 192, 206, 207, 223
Sex Education 25, 43
sexuality
   bisexuality 92, 104, 204
   collective sex 180, 200
   cyber-sex 21
   fullness of sex 116
   Heidegger's notion of ecstasy 106
   heterosexuality 10, 80, 82, 92, 99, 199, 200
   hypersexualization 200
   male sexuality 11, 92
   negation of sexuality 73
   nonsexual 19, 94, 102, 103
   promiscuity 93–5, 103, 107
   psycho-sexual drama 6
   same-sex marriage 26, 91
   sex change 221
   sex choreographies 177, 180, 190–2
   sexism 90, 130, 184
   sex-nic 181
   sexual conservatism 22
   sexual freedom 86, 124
   sexual gaze 148
   sexual hierarchies 92
   sexual identities 4, 92, 99, 142
   sexual imaginary 98, 99
   sexualization of white characters 23
   sexual politics 21, 188
   techniques of ecstasy 177, 180, 193
   See also orgy
She-Ra and the Princesses of Power 182

She's Gotta Have It 5
Silvestre, Miguel Ángel. *See* Lito
simultaneity 42, 45, 47–9, 97, 128
   global simultaneity 52, 220
Sin tetas no hay paraíso (There's No Paradise without Tits) 10
Slumdog Millionaire 179
Smith, Brian J. 10–11
   See Will
Sommers, Michael X. *See* Bug
Sonetos del amor oscuro (Sonnets of Dark Love) 123
Sopranos, The 58, 59
special effects 15, 35
Spectral 37
Star Trek 26
Star Trek: Discovery 26, 37
stereotype
   cultural stereotypes 25, 223
   of femme fatale 148
   gender stereotypes 146
   nationality as stereotype 223
   non-western countries 53, 223
   racial stereotypes 65, 200, 223
   of violence 143, 144
Steven Universe 188
Steven Universe Future 188
Stonewall 78
Stonewall riots 78
Straczynski, J. Michael 1, 6, 43, 200, 220
subtitles 36, 37, 54
Sukku Son. *See* Mun
Sun 6–9, 16, 17, 20, 23–5, 83, 84, 96, 97, 102, 103, 116, 125, 127, 130, 132, 134, 136, 137, 145–6, 154, 156, 160–5, 169, 170, 172, 179–81, 191, 192, 201, 211, 221, 223, 224
   and martial arts 7, 25, 65, 72, 145, 161, 181, 191, 193, 223
survivalism 166, 167
synchronicity 124, 126, 128–30, 134, 136, 138, 191, 206
   See also music; musicality

telepathy
   telepathic abilities 110, 112, 114, 125, 161, 163, 168, 169, 171, 172, 183, 220

telepathic English 24, 130
telepathic orgies 14, 21, 27, 108, 171, 220
telepathic soundtrack 135
telepathic/telekinetic link 220
See also cluster
television
  global television 54
  history of television 41, 42, 54–5
  international television 36, 43, 54, 66
  linear television 38, 39, 55
  online television 42, 44, 48, 49, 55, 60, 67
  queer television 103, 154
  streaming television 1–5, 10, 21, 26, 32, 39, 42, 44, 47, 48, 52, 54, 55, 60, 128, 184, 190, 198, 206, 207, 208, 211, 219–20
  television narratives 66
  televisual liveness 48, 51, 52
  transcendence of television 2, 5, 26, 43, 71, 160, 219, 220
  See also Netflix
Terminator Genisys 180
3% 54
Time to Thrive 5
title sequence 52, 57–70
  opening credits 52–3, 74, 222
Todd 76, 77
togetherness 17, 54, 97, 159, 169, 173, 213
trans* 18, 19, 27, 71, 72, 81, 90, 97, 109, 115
  trans*/queer 109, 115
TRANSform Me 13
transgender
  and aesthetics 147, 221
  Black trans woman 78
  exploration of trans phenomenology 97, 221
  sex change 221
  trans cartography 178
  trans-centric genre 182
  transgender auteurs 221
  transgender lesbian 67
  transgender woman 8, 13, 25, 26, 221

trans geography 178, 181
trans grammar of filmmaking 15, 16
trans identities 18
transness 19, 91
transphobia 1, 13, 22, 91, 97, 109, 157
trans subjectivity 221–2
transnationalism
  active transnationalism 130
  geographical and transnational jumps 170
  transitional space 19
  transnational connections 2, 22, 52, 161
  transnational empathy 163, 166, 172
  transnational phenomenality 107
Tykwer, Tom 6, 107, 125, 128

utopianism
  digital utopianism 197, 200
  in the orgy sequences 101
  politicized utopianism 197
  queer utopia 17–19, 21–3, 92, 201
  utopian dream 53, 212
  utopian ethos 115
  utopian sense of inclusivity 24
  white digital utopianism 200
  See also cluster

Velvet 10
Veronica Mars 3. *See also* fanbase
victimization 203
"Violador en Tu Camino, Un" (A Rapist in Your Path) 131
violence
  big-budget violence 149
  BPO violence 148, 152
  colonial violence 113, 152
  fake violence 143
  global/local violence 150, 151
  heroism and violence 183
  isolation and violence 90
  legitimate physical violence 147–51
  male violence 146
  sex and violence 16, 27, 177
  as subject to performativity 148
  violence-ridden poverty 130

violence of the sensates 152, 156
violent frontiers 141, 156, 157, 191
V for Vendetta 220

Wachowski, Lana 1, 3, 6, 9, 18, 38, 43, 57, 75, 81, 116, 211–12
Wachowski, Lilly 1, 6, 9, 17, 19, 43, 75, 187
Walk Off the Earth 45
"What's Up?" 75, 76, 125, 127, 128, 131, 132, 199, 210, 213
When They See Us 5
"Where the Hell Is Matt?" 128
Whispers 7, 8, 20–1, 45, 47, 73, 76, 77, 84, 111, 113, 115, 118, 124, 136, 143, 147–8, 161, 168, 170, 181, 185, 191
Will 6, 7–11, 15–17, 19–20, 23–5, 74, 76, 78, 82–5, 90, 96–7, 99, 101, 107, 109, 111, 112, 116, 124–8, 132–7, 147–8, 150, 156, 160, 168, 170–2, 180, 181–5, 189, 223

and police 112, 137, 147, 151, 154, 163, 183–5, 189
Winslow Wachowski, Karin 52, 57
Wire, The 184
Wolfgang 7–9, 11, 20, 23, 24, 78, 82–5, 90, 97, 98, 101, 109, 113, 114, 125–8, 130, 133, 135, 137, 143, 144, 148–50, 160, 164, 171, 180, 183, 185, 191, 199, 223
and violence 7, 86, 143, 148, 149, 150
Women's Building, The 181–2
worlding 114, 116, 154, 156–7

xHamster 4

"You've Got Time" 61

Zakia 8, 20

www.ingramcontent.com/pod-product-compliance
Lightning Source LLC
Chambersburg PA
CBHW072145290426
44111CB00012B/1980